Dual Career Couples: New Perspectives In Counseling

By Marian Stoltz-Loike, Ph.D.

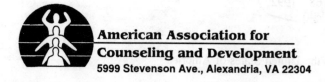

American Association for Counseling and Development
5999 Stevenson Ave., Alexandria, VA 22304

Copyright © 1992 by the American Association for Counseling and Development

American Association for Counseling and Development
5999 Stevenson Avenue
Alexandria, VA 22304

Cover design by Sarah Jane Valdez

Library of Congress Cataloging-in-Publication Data

Stoltz-Loike, Marian.
Dual career couples : new perspectives in counseling / by Marian Stoltz-Loike.
   p. cm.
  Includes bibliographical references.
  ISBN 1-55620-093-5
  1. Dual-career families—United States—Psychological aspects
  2. Problem families—Counseling of—United States.   I. Title.
HQ536.S768   1992
306.87—dc20
                                          91-47674
                                          CIP

To John

Contents

Part II

List of Tables

Preface

Who is the dual career couple? Are they a pair of young professionals with much money to spend and little desire to be restricted by responsibility? Or are they a pair of haggard, overworked partners who have no time for themselves or one another?

Two decades of research have described the parameters of dual career couples. The findings indicate that couples are often stressed by the demands placed on them by their dual career lifestyle. However, when they are committed to their own careers and the careers of their partners, there is a high degree of satisfaction in the relationship. Moreover, because of a higher standard of living, greater self-esteem, and collegiality between the partners, these couples have high-quality couple relationships.

Most male and female college graduates anticipate being involved in a relationship, raising a family, and pursuing careers. Currently, over 3 million dual career couples are employed, which represents about 20% of employed couples. It is anticipated that the number of dual career couples will increase substantially over the next decade. This book represents a novel approach to counseling dual career couples that includes (1) the theoretical perspectives necessary for counselors to develop a sophisticated approach to working with dual career couples, and (2) an action agenda consisting of questionnaires and assessment instruments that counselors can use with their dual career couple clients.

Counselors from all specialties will benefit from reading *Dual Career Couples: New Perspectives in Counseling*. The book outlines the stresses and challenges dual career couples face, as well as plans for helping dual career couples learn negotiation, communication, and conflict resolution skills. Additionally, the book provides a comprehensive review of the corporate response to dual career couples that explains what corporations have done and still need to do to address dual career concerns.

This book was written for counselors and other mental health professionals. Special sections on career counseling and family systems provide counselors with strategies for addressing the needs of dual career couples. Hundreds of studies and scores of books were reviewed for this book. It is expected that the integrated approach presented here will encourage the development of creative methods for counseling dual career couples and spur further research on career development among women, nontraditional role development among men, and the relationship between the dual career couple lifestyle and its effects on children, family, and careers.

Acknowledgments

Many people took the time to provide ideas, perspectives, and information critical to the development of this book. Many are also members of dual career couples or single parent families, so that their professional perspectives were further bolstered by their personal experiences. I would like to acknowledge some of these individuals here.

A number of people shared their comprehensive knowledge of the corporate response to dual career couples, including Bruce Donatuti, Elaine Hicks, Diane Leeds, Marcy Swerdlin, Amy Segal, and Sue Wilkie. Libby Keating offered valuable perspectives on relocation. Arlene Johnson was kind enough to share her wealth of knowledge concerning corporate relocation and other dual career couple issues, giving me a new perspective on future directions of corporate change about family issues. Nancy Arnosti offered an insightful, integrated perspective on the relationship between the corporate culture and the family friendliness of a company. I would also like to thank Sue Wilkie and Lucia Gilbert for directing me to important information on the corporate response to dual career couples.

I would like to thank Mark Savickas for his helpful, constructive comments on an earlier draft of this book, and Vicki Rachlin and Nancy Garfield for helpful reviews of the same. Ellen Piel Cook read earlier drafts of parts of this book and provided incisive comments. All of their insightful critiques were well appreciated. I would also like to thank Sue Zimmerman Mandelstam for providing feedback critical to the development of various questionnaires and assessment instruments.

Elaine Pirrone, the Acquisitions and Development Editor at AACD, has been a pleasure to work with. She offered helpful comments on writing, style, and on functioning as a partner in a dual career couple.

I grew up in a dual career couple household, which made it easier to anticipate the realities of this lifestyle for parents and children in the family. I would like to thank my parents, Morris and Sylvia Stoltz, for providing me with my first model of a successful dual career couple. They gave me the confidence to believe that despite all of its strains and demands, I could pursue a dual career couple relationship, have children, and find each of my roles meaningful. I would also like to thank my mother-in-law, Paula Loike Schulman, for believing that I could write an important book in the time allotted even before I had written my first word.

I have spent the past 15 years as a partner in a dual career couple. Over that time I have given birth to four children, Chaim, Gila, Devora, and Ashira, and together with my husband, John, have faced many challenges and rewards typical of other dual career couples. Now that all of my children are in grade school or high school, the conflicts have been reduced and the rewards are manifold. The pride that they have in my work has been a great reward for me. My children have provided me with insight and understanding about dual career couples and human interactions critical to the integrated approach I present in this book.

It is impossible for me to acknowledge sufficiently the support I received from my husband, John. He was always available to discuss a new idea or approach to presenting a topic, and was always willing to read another draft of a chapter. In many ways, John demonstrated that my career was as important to him as is his own career, which is the touchstone of success within the dual career couple.

Biography

Marian Stoltz-Loike, PhD, received her BA from Harvard University in 1976 and her PhD from New York University in 1984. She is a corporate consultant specializing in family and career issues. Dr. Stoltz-Loike has been invited to speak across the country on issues related to dual career couple balance and family and career concerns to audiences ranging from physicians and mental health professionals to academicians and attorneys.

Dr. Stoltz-Loike has published a variety of articles concerning family and career issues. She is on the editorial board of *The Career Development Quarterly* and will be guest editor for a special section on family and work linkages soon to be published. She is an active member of AACD and NCDA and chairs the NCDA special interest group on work and family linkages.

Dr. Stoltz-Loike is part of a dual career couple. She lives in Queens, NY, with her husband, John, a scientist at Columbia University, and her son and three daughters.

Introduction

Over the past 30 years, the prevalent pattern of family life has shifted from the single earner couple (breadwinner father/homemaker mother) to the dual earner couple (Barnett & Baruch, 1987; Pleck & Staines, 1985). Today, both partners in dual career couples value their work and want success and upward mobility on the job, and are willing to cope with long work hours, inflexible schedules, and time away from families (e.g., Bird & Bird, 1986; Chester, 1990). *Dual career* couples are couples where both partners are highly career-committed, and view employment as an essential part of their self-definitions. In *dual earner* couples, however, partners work for other motives such as material rewards, are less achievement-oriented, and may derive self-definition and self-worth from other sources. Couples also may be earner-career couples, where one partner is highly career-committed and the other is working for other reasons.

In some dual career couples, both partners pursue careers that require a significantly high and continuous level of career commitment; in other dual career couples, one partner's career takes priority, although both partners are career-committed. Their dedication to work presents special challenges in balancing family and career concerns. In response to the special challenges of dual career couples, a growing number of counselors are seeking targeted strategies to help these couples balance their positions as members of a "working family" (Stoltz-Loike, 1990, 1991, 1992a, 1992b). Currently, new tools are emerging for mental health practitioners to assist dual career couples to function in their roles as parents, partners, and employees.

As these roles become less stratified, balancing dual career responsibilities becomes even more critical for both men and women. Today, however, dual career issues largely remain women's issues. The vast majority of literature on dual career couples concerns the impact of the wife's employment on children's cognitive (Easterbrooks & Goldberg, 1985; Hoffman, 1984, 1989; Zambara, Hurst, & Hite, 1979), social (Belsky & Rovine, 1988; Hock, 1980; Rabinovich, Suwalsky, & Pedersen, 1984) and emotional (Barglow, Vaughn, & Molitor, 1987; Benn, 1986; Chase-Lansdale & Owen, 1987; Hoffman, 1984) development. Furthermore, within a counseling setting, employed women are more likely than employed men to discuss how working affects their children (Braverman,

1989; McGoldrick, 1989). Women are also more likely to base career decisions on considerations related to both family and career, whereas men focus more exclusively on career concerns (Betz & Fitzgerald, 1987; Williams, 1990). Because of changing attitudes, however, dual career issues of the future will be the concern of both men and women (e.g., Baber & Monaghan, 1988; Bridges, 1987; Covin & Brush, 1991).

New research protocols that evaluate the impact of dual career factors should be developed. For example, relationship satisfaction or children's success in school could be viewed as a function of either the traditional or the role-sharing characteristics of a dual career couple. Alternatively, each partner's concept of marital equity might serve as an independent variable in studies of couple relationships or parent-child interactions. As a final example, an individual's career success could be a function of reported equity in a couple's relationship. These new perspectives on dual career couples would herald a more gender-sensitive way to look at their conjoint impact on family and career issues. Moreover, it would identify career, child, or interpersonal areas that would benefit most directly by counseling interventions.

Both men and women can be encouraged to bring their partners into the counseling process as an essential way to reach a more equitable balance of their many concerns. During counseling sessions, discussions can focus on what career means to each partner, and on establishing a new balance between work, family, and household responsibilities. These conjoint sessions might allow each partner to flourish more completely within multidimensional environments.

FOCUS OF THE BOOK

A primary purpose of this book is to develop an integrated perspective for counseling dual career couples. This perspective incorporates approaches from career counseling, developmental psychology, couple and marriage counseling, and gender psychology. *Gender psychology* underscores the distinct ways that men and women perceive and interact with the world both at work and at home. *Couple/marriage and family counseling* defines couples as functioning within a system, and analyzes the impact of one partner's choices on the other partner and family members. *Career counseling* theory underscores the need for assessing and planning for effective career choices. *Developmental psychology* offers the perspective that changes in career roles may reflect the evolution of family and individual needs.

Early experiences within their families of origin affect individuals' beliefs and expectations about couples, families, and careers. Because the views each partner holds may change with time, reequilibration of the relationship balances is often required.

Moreover, couples' attempts to renegotiate their idiosyncratic balances will be influenced by other gender issues, the developmental stages of their family, and each partner's career. By using the integrated counseling approach described in this book, counselors can help dual career couples to equilibrate their various roles more effectively.

The integrated approach is derived from research and theory in three related areas: (1) personality and gender psychology, (2) the family system, and (3) career counseling and human development.

Personality and Gender Psychology

Determinants of human personality have intrigued psychologists. Physical development (Adler, 1964) and physiological differences, like temperament (Thomas, Chess, & Birch, 1970), can affect personality development and social interactions. Additionally, early childhood experiences (Freud, 1931, 1940) and other interactions with the environment (Perls, 1969) affect human personality. Differences in genetic endowments and environmental experiences account for the rich variety in human personality and the many adaptive and maladaptive ways that people interact with their environments. A person's gender reflects psychological and physical characteristics that affect how the individual views the world and how others respond to the individual. A central observation in dual career couples is that family, career, and other interpersonal issues affect men and women differently. For example, men and women vary with regard to affect expression (Cook, 1990), interpersonal relations (Cook; Holder & Anderson, 1989; McGoldrick, 1989), satisfaction with mate (Walsh, 1989), children's need for them (Braverman, 1989), and attitudes toward work (Walsh). These differences translate into how men and women face different crises, resources, expectations, and opportunities throughout their lives (Cook).

Men and women in dual career couples often have different perspectives with regard to work and family conflicts. For example, the sharing of dual career husbands in housework is critical for both partners' continued participation in the labor force. Men may find it difficult to become equitable participants in housework because this poses a challenge to their gender identities (Sekaran, 1986). Women also may constrain men's ability to participate fully at home because of their traditional gender role socialization (Yogev & Brett, 1985). Because few male role models for sharing work and home responsibilities exist (Gilbert,1985), counselors can intervene in the role expansions of both men and women as they strive for more equitable sharing at home.

Men and women work in a gender-based context in a work force that is typically stratified by sex (e.g., Erez, 1988; Walsh & Egdahl, 1980) and functions by using outdated models of family structures. Employers often develop company rules as if workers lived in the context of the traditional family, someone else were taking primary responsibility for the household, and the worker's main (and perhaps only) concern were with his or her job (Berardo, Shehan, & Leslie, 1987). Moreover, many women are uncomfortable with the corporate culture, its "old boy network," and its aggressive and risk-taking orientation (Catalyst, 1983). These issues can pose particular problems and conflicts for partners in dual career couples as they pursue their various roles.

Understanding gender differences can help counselors to develop specific interventions for the problems that dual career couples face and to address the couples' unresolved and unresolvable conflicts and choices. For example, parents may experience strong doubts about the impact of nonparental caretakers on their children (see, for example, Hock, Gnezda, & McBride, 1984, with respect to mothers). Other prime issues for counseling might be helping couples with (a) the unresolvable conflicts of employment, (b) societal expectations of women or (c) both men's and women's personal expectations about children's need for them. Another appropriate issue for counseling might be to develop strategies for women and men to maximize time with children to achieve a sense of involvement in their children's lives.

The Family System: Becoming a Family

Becoming a couple involves successfully separating and individuating from one's parents and forging a new interdependent bond with another adult (Ables & Brandsma, 1984; Ulrich & Dunne, 1986). The intimacy of a long-term relationship provides the catalyst for partners to achieve greater autonomy, self-identification, and personal awareness. Marriage and commitment to a long-term relationship begin with an intense, romantic honeymoon stage, where fantasy predominates and the beloved becomes overidealized (Ables & Brandsma). Later in the relationship, couples must possess or develop substantial maturity to satisfy both their personal and their partner's needs. Communication, negotiation, problem-solving skills, conflict management, and values clarification become essential skills for the well-functioning couple. Using these skills effectively establishes *couple equity*, defined as the perceived balance over time between the partners in their various roles (Berardo et al., 1987; Rapoport & Rapoport, 1971, 1975, 1976; Spitze, 1988) and the sense among partners that the relationship is fair.

For dual career couples, there may be a particularly pronounced effect when partners recognize the meaning of their significant other's commitment to work. Few couples negotiate details of dual career lifestyles prior to marriage (Ulrich & Dunne, 1986), and married men and women may still hold different long-term expectations about the dimensions of the relationship (Sekaran, 1986). Women may expect their partners to take on substantial household responsibilities and provide psychological support for their careers, and men may never have thought that marriage to their dual career spouses would be any different than their parents' single earner or dual worker marriages (Sekaran). When children are born, dual career couples also experience conflict over the meaning of the maternal role (Gilbert, 1985; 1988). As couples' career and family demands change, verbalizing their many assumptions about the contributions and expectations for each partner is critical. Counselors can assist couples to communicate effectively about individual needs and to deal with unrealistic assumptions. Important concerns may center on achieving reciprocity as part of the balance of power within a relationship, developing communication skills to negotiate for change in the relationship, and redefining relationship expectations and achieving realistic, limited goals within the relationship and between the couple and the external world.

Dual career couples may also experience relationship stresses because women and men lack familial role models for balancing family and career. A man may remember how his mother always kept dinner warm until his father returned from work. His employed partner may expect him to participate in dinner preparation, leading him to wonder about her devotion to him. A wife may wonder if she is fulfilling her roles as wife and mother when her husband participates equitably in parenting and housekeeping roles. However, participation of both partners in household chores and child care is necessary if dual career women are to continue to advance in their careers (Berardo et al., 1987). Many dual career men are not willing to be equal participants (Gilbert, 1985), which can create marital tension and dissatisfaction (Hochschild, 1989).

Dual career couples have little free time. The responsibilities of their multiple roles make unplanned free time nonexistent, placing a severe strain on the flourishing of their relationship. In couples with children stress can be more acute because there is even less time for the parents to be alone, especially as financial demands become more intense. Career counselors can assist dual career couples to develop effective time-management skills, to set priorities, and to plan attainable goals. Moreover, couples can be encouraged to pursue "time-outs" and private vacations, when possible, to maintain their connectedness to one another.

Counselors also can assist couples to verbalize plans for their dual career future. Dating couples, couples in early stages of a relationship, and couples with children may need to discuss their different expectations and assumptions about future career and family responsibilities. Together with a counselor, couples can plan for equity in their current couple relationship as well as plan for future work- and family-related changes.

Some employment-related issues that couples may want to discuss include perspectives of each partner on work relocation, relative balance of occupational status between the two partners, and attitudes toward a "commuter relationship." By discussing these issues couples can prepare for future events and crises, with full knowledge and understanding of possible consequences. Moreover, open communication about career concerns can enhance the couple's relationship.

Career Counseling and Human Development

People, both as individuals and as couples, experience a variety of changes related to experience and maturation. Within a dual career couple, developmental changes are evident in three areas: (1) individual psychological development, (2) individual career development and maturation, and (3) family development. A variety of theories of psychological development exist (Kohlberg, 1976; Piaget, 1950, 1954, 1962, 1969, 1970; Super, 1951, 1953, 1964, 1980, 1983, 1986). Erikson, for example, identified eight stages in human psychosocial development and their developmental challenges from infancy to old age, which are basic to psychological well-functioning (Erikson, 1950, 1968a, 1968b). Individual psychological growth and development have significant implications for adult functioning because how successfully individuals resolve their developmental challenges can affect the couple's relationship and their career aspirations, decisions, and choices. Moreover, the salience of an individual's success and achievement will vary with his or her psychological stage of development. Thus, information about psychological growth and development can provide couples with important insights into career, personal, and relationship issues.

Career theorists have been concerned also with the interrelationship of psychological development, maturational factors, and career choice. Super has been a major proponent of a life-span approach to career development, exemplified by his Career Development Assessment and Counseling Model (Nevill & Super, 1986). A critical aspect of his model is the relationship of career development to a knowledge of stage-related developmental tasks, coping strategies, changes in life career roles, and effects of transitions (Super, 1986). Other important psychological characteristics of career development include values, career maturity, self-concepts, and the relative salience of the different roles individuals are involved in over time (Nevill & Super, 1986, 1989; Super, 1983).

Other multifactor approaches to career development have been proposed to explain career choice. In Gysbers and Moore's (1987) life career development theory, career choice is dependent on the integration of roles, settings, and events. Career choice may also be based on personality variables, choice dimensions, and environmental conditions interacting within a broad system. At different points in time and personal development, each of these factors may have a distinct effect, predicting various career decisions (Osipow, 1983).

An individual's stage within an institutional hierarchy can also affect dual career couple functioning. Hazard and Koslow (1986), for example, described the worker's advancement within an organization as occurring through a four-stage progression (not all workers advance through all four career stages): (1) an early apprenticeship stage involving learning about company structure, (2) an independence/specialization stage involving the person's responsibility for significant company projects, (3) an interdependence/management stage involving responsibility for teaching and supervising subordinates, and (4) a stage involving directing the path of an organization as an upper-level manager or CEO. The demands of work, on-the-job stress, and personal autonomy vary with each stage of organizational structure. Analogous career progress may occur for professionals in other fields. For example, academicians can progress from the postdoctoral stage to junior faculty, to department chair, and to other positions in university administration such as dean or president.

Each partner's career stage is related to particular demands within a dual career couple. When partners are in different career fields, communication about each partner's current and anticipated future career path is critical. This information can assist couples to balance their individual career needs with their development as a couple and a family.

Families face distinct challenges at different stages of development. In early stages couples are most concerned with their relationship and their work. If they decide to have children, the stresses and strains couples experience may lead them to reevaluate their roles, priorities, and time allocation. Parents' career progress may also be related to the number of children and the age of the youngest child at home (Geerken & Gove, 1983; Voydanoff, 1988). As children grow and eventually leave home, parents have greater opportunities to pursue their personal and career goals.

For dual career couples, balancing evolving family needs with individual needs and career developmental stages is a difficult and challenging task. Successful negotiation of this challenge leads to the goal of family/career equity. Moreover, by adopting a life-span perspective of career and family development, dual career couples may be able to cope more effectively with the stresses of a particular stage.

STRUCTURE OF THE BOOK

This book is divided into three parts. Part I—chapters 1 to 4—reviews the literature relevant to dual career couples and the integrated approach to counseling dual career couples. Chapter 1 contains a general overview of the literature on dual career couples, chapter 2 focuses on gender issues and individual differences, chapter 3 reviews the family systems approaches to couple/marriage and family counseling, and chapter 4 discusses career, developmental, and couple issues. Part II—chapters 5 to 9—focuses on intervention strategies for career counselors working with dual career couples and offers step-by-step programs for counseling dual career couples. Chapter 5 presents an overview of the integrated approach to counseling dual career couples. Chapter 6 discusses methods for assessing each partner's career and family status. Chapter 7 focuses on strategies for developing effective negotiation and communication within a gender-sensitive context. Chapter 8 discusses counseling techniques to assist couples to live with conflict as part of establishing new role definitions. Chapter 9 focuses on defining success within a life-span career developmental framework. Chapter 10 in Part III reviews the corporate response to the special needs of dual career couples. In preparing this chapter, I spoke with family and work experts at Catalyst, the Conference Board, and other groups as well as the family and work program coordinators at a wide variety of Fortune 500 corporations. Examples are used to discuss dual career issues like flexible benefits, on-site day care, spousal relocation, flextime, and job sharing. Chapter 11 offers conclusions and future directions for dual career couple counseling.

This book is directed to counselors who work with members of dual career couples. These counselors may be trained in marriage and family techniques, career counseling skills, or various other counseling disciplines. Each of these mental health professionals can benefit from the issues related to dual career couples presented in this book. To make this book accessible to a wide variety of counselors, the first four chapters review theoretical information from four different perspectives, each of which relates to dual career couple concerns. Those counselors already familiar with this material can feel free to skip to Part II, chapter 5, which details the author's applied, integrated perspective to counseling dual career couples.

The reader is also cautioned that this book is not meant to be a comprehensive course in effective marriage and family counseling or career counseling. Rather, practitioners in both these disciplines require extensive training and coursework. The theoretical information provided is intended to offer an expansive perspective to all mental health practitioners.

This book focuses on the dual career couple needs of heterosexual couples. It is difficult to extrapolate conclusively from heterosexual couples to homosexual couples because the female and male sex roles related to aspects of couple functioning do not apply in a parallel way (Eldridge

& Gilbert, 1990). Many of the issues related to equity, growth and development, and family functioning may apply to homosexual couples as well.

This book summarizes a great deal of research on dual career issues and other relevant topics. The literature on these various topics has addressed the White middle class. There is a need to expand research and theoretical perspectives to people of color and to other ethnic groups and to identify areas where different groups overlap or differ. If a specific study used this enriched perspective, it has been highlighted in the text.

Part I

Part 1

1 Perspectives on Dual Career Couples

COUPLES WHERE BOTH PARTNERS are employed represent the largest segments of workers at all major corporations. Estimates show that these couples represent 60% to 70% of current employees and it is expected that this percentage will rise to 80% within the next decade (Johnson, 1990). Their needs and lifestyles will affect future corporate development and the concerns of counselor clients. Members of dual career couples are highly committed to their careers and are productive members of their institutions; however, their achievements are associated with individual and couple stresses, role conflicts, and challenges. Researchers have studied and documented the parameters of the dual career relationship over the past two-plus decades and found that couples now require more action-based approaches to address their lifestyle challenges effectively.

This chapter surveys findings on family, career, and couple aspects among dual career couples as a prelude to proposing an action agenda for counselors who work with them. Counselors can use this information to address the normative concerns of both dual career couples and individuals considering pursuing a dual career couple lifestyle. Later chapters will use this information as the basis for life-span strategies for functioning as part of a dual career couple.

DEFINITION OF DUAL CAREER COUPLE

Dual career couples form a unique subset of dual employed couples. Both members of dual career couples are highly committed to their careers and view work as essential to their psychological sense of self and as

3

integral to their personal identities. They see employment as part of a career path involving progressively more responsibility, power, and financial remuneration. Dual earner couples and other couples where both partners are employed may define their employment as relating to rewards such as money for paying bills, an opportunity to keep busy, or an additional resource to "help out" rather than as an integral element of their self-definitions.

Currently, about 20% of all working couples are part of dual career couples, making them a substantial group characterized by distinctive psychological and career profiles. Moreover, within particular professions and among young professionals, dual career couples may represent significantly more than 20% of working couples. Partners in dual career couples benefit through their higher couple earnings, as compared to single earner couples, participation in intellectually stimulating jobs, and increased self-esteem. Couples can also experience significant career-related problems, such as competitive feelings between spouses, or conflicts between family and career needs. Recognizing how career achievement is interdependent, and understanding the interplay of family and career success within the dual career couple, are two significant challenges to the mental health professional who works with dual career couples. Another concern for counselors is that dual career couples develop couple skills like negotiation and communication to function more effectively within their multiple roles.

Successful dual career couples have redefined the roles of partners within the couple. For example, in traditional couples, role definitions account for the functions of each partner—he's the breadwinner, she's the caretaker, and they are bound together by their dependence on complementary provision of services. In dual career couples, both partners have greater financial independence and may also both participate more actively in caretaker roles and other home roles, reflecting their distinct expectations and overlapping, noncomplementary roles. Counselors can help couples redefine their roles and recognize contradictions between their behaviors and beliefs. For example, women may criticize how their male partners perform household tasks, although they expect their partners to participate equally in household chores. Men may support their partners' careers but still expect home-cooked, hot meals every evening. In both cases, couples are overtly supportive of dual career couple lifestyles as they covertly advocate traditional roles.

A variety of critical questions are relevant to counselors who work with dual career couples: How do the needs of dual career couples differ from those of other workers? How do their needs as individuals, workers, and couples interact? In what ways do individuals' beliefs, expectations, and goals affect their partners' ability to function within the career world? How does the interrelationship of the supportiveness of the work and home environments affect the ability of dual career couples to function within their multiple roles? What impact do children have on dual career couples' work and family life? This chapter reviews factors that facilitate or block dual career couples' individual and couple success.

IMPACT OF DUAL CAREER COUPLE LIFESTYLE

Dual career couples have a greater family income than they would have if only one partner were employed, increasing their purchasing ability and elevating their standard of living. Additionally, partners experience increased self-worth and self-perception of competence (Sekaran, 1986). Women, in particular, experience greater power within the family (Grossman & Stewart, 1990), and husbands who do not feel threatened by their wives' career roles value their enhanced lifestyles and their wives' personal satisfaction (Sekaran, 1986). Couples also enjoy the collegiality of having a partner with whom they can share intellectual career and noncareer concerns and who may provide new perspectives on their work.

Impact on Relationship

For dual career couples, family choices can affect career mobility, and career commitment can affect family choices. Assessment of factors that affect plans to marry or have children and the continuity of the couple's relationship routinely focus on the parameters of women's careers (e.g., Bronfenbrenner & Crouter, 1982; Cotton, Antill, & Cunningham, 1990; Greenberger, Goldberg, Crawford, & Granger, 1988; Hiller & Dyehouse, 1987; Hiller & Philliber, 1978, 1980, 1986; Hoffman & Nye, 1974; Philliber & Hiller, 1978, 1979, 1983). As dual career couples become the norm, it is critical to evaluate career and family factors that affect the future plans of men. For example, men or women may choose to forego marriage or childbirth because of career issues. The studies cited in this section reflect those in the literature. Readers are encouraged to broaden their perspectives and consider the role responsibilities that both partners in dual career couples have for family and career concerns, and how both men and women can make career or family decisions to address anticipated work-family conflicts.

Women who are highly career-committed are more likely to be employed in higher-status occupations and are more likely to postpone marriage (Gilbert, Dancer, Rossman, & Thorn, 1991; Schoen & Urton, 1979; Spitze, 1988) and childbirth (Gilbert et al.; Wilk, 1986). They may have less motivation to marry because their employment provides important sources of intellectual fulfillment and financial security (Spitze). Moreover, having a personal income increases women's independence within a relationship and their willingness to dissolve an unsatisfying relationship (Betz & Fitzgerald, 1987).

Male and female college students anticipate being part of dual career couples in the future (Baber & Monaghan, 1988; Bridges, 1987; Covin & Brush, 1991; Spade & Reese, 1991), yet they cannot clearly articulate what this means. When questioned, young men involved with career-oriented women expected that their career would take priority over the women's (Sekaran, 1986; Yogev, 1981), whereas women expected a somewhat greater balance of career priorities and anticipated some of the realistic conflicts that dual career couples must address (Sekaran, 1982; Spade & Reese, 1991). Data related to dual career couple expectations are unavailable, but it makes sense to expect that, among older couples, both knowledge and experience would affect their relationship expectations. Not only do both career-committed women and men tend to marry later, but approximately 35% (e.g., Gilbert, 1985) of partners in dual career couple relationships have been previously married. When they remarry, both career-committed women and men who were formerly part of a dual career couple are well-versed in the demands of a dual career couple lifestyle and can engage in concrete discussions with their partners about the potential for balance within an anticipated remarriage.

Marital Satisfaction

Early research reflected the view that maternal employment was stressful for the family and was similar to a husband's unemployment. However, interpreting the results of such research has limited value because factors involving the type of work women performed, their satisfaction with their work, or the hours they worked were not included, and the impact of men's employment or the parameters of their work were never assessed (e.g., Hoffman, 1960; Stake, 1979; Wallston, 1973). Other comprehensive studies showed that women found employment preferable to housework (Feree, 1976; Gove & Tudor, 1973), and even when their jobs involved menial tasks, they were more satisfied with their work than being home full-time (Wright & Hamilton, 1978) and experienced lower levels of depression than housewives (Gove & Geerken, 1977; Kessler & McRae, 1982; Wright, 1978). This reflected the positive value that women derived from work and suggested that employment was associated with positive growth among women, much as it was viewed positively for men. Marital satisfaction was found to be highest among employed wives who work by choice, have higher levels of education, work part-time, or receive their husband's support (Voydanoff, 1987). Analogously, husbands experience the greatest martial satisfaction when they support their wives' choice to work or when their wives work part-time (Voydanoff, 1987). Subsequent research substantiated the positive relationship between employment and marital satisfaction among men and women (Gilbert, 1985; Voydanoff, 1987; Yogev, 1982). Negative effects of women's employment are related to specific aspects of their work, such as hours employed or satisfaction with the job (Spitze, 1988). For example, women who work longer hours report greater role conflict and role strain (Guelzow, Bird, & Koball, 1991). Other factors such as high job involvement (Greenhaus, Parasuraman, Granrose, Rabinowitz, & Beutell, 1989) can also affect marital satisfaction directly or through spillover effects.

From a theoretical perspective, employment of both partners in a couple can lead either to mutually interdependent positive benefits, such as an enhancement of family status (Oppenheimer, 1977), or to status competition between partners (Parsons, 1942). Research related to such theoretical perspectives has viewed the employment of both partners in terms of the woman's career attainment, occupational status, or earnings because it was assumed that men were employed and it was the woman's employment that was the unexpected, novel event (e.g, D'Amico, 1983; Safilios-Rothschild, 1975; Velsor & O'Rand, 1984). The results have been somewhat ambiguous. Couples generally reported greater satisfaction when the wife was either working or at home by preference (Benin & Nienstedt, 1985).

Two decades of studies of couple relationships have found no negative impact of the wife's employment on marital satisfaction (Booth, 1979; Glenn & Weaver, 1978; Hoffman, 1989; Hoffman & Nye, 1974; Houseknecht & Macke, 1981; Ladewig & White, 1984; Locksley, 1980; Moorehouse, 1991; Richardson, 1979; Spitze, 1988; Thompson, 1988; Wright, 1978). Moreover, current research indicates that a woman's income has a positive impact on her power in the family and is associated with her husband's increased participation in household roles (Vannoy-Hiller & Philliber, 1989; Voydanoff, 1987). Other studies have found that marital satisfaction of the husband or wife is related to the wife's career attainment, the type of occupation she pursues, the significance attributed to her achievement, and the impact of her achievement on household work (Gilbert, 1985; Philliber & Hiller, 1983; Simpson & England, 1981). Consistent with these findings, several studies reported that when family income increases, there is greater marital satisfaction; however, when the wife's income increases, there is lower marital satisfaction (Garland, 1972; Hardesty & Betz, 1980), and a wife's high earnings affect marital satisfaction negatively (Gilbert, 1985). Several conflicting studies have explored career and marital satisfaction. Philliber and Hiller (1983) found that when the husband held a negative attitude toward women's employment, his wife was more likely to change her employment status to a job with less occupational prestige, leave the work force, or divorce.

Career involvement differentially affects men's and women's marital satisfaction and success. Women's career commitment is negatively associated with marital success (Ladewig & McGee, 1986; Greenhaus et al., 1989). Thus, when the woman is highly career-committed, both the woman and her husband experience greater work-family conflict; when the husband is highly career-committed, neither partner experiences greater work-family stress (Greenhaus et al., 1989). More educated women who presumably have greater employment options divorce more frequently than comparably aged, less educated women (Houseknecht & Spanier, 1980). Similarly, there is a greater likelihood of divorce and lower marital satisfaction among career-committed women (Betz & Fitzgerald, 1987), which may relate to the greater ability of financially independent women to leave an unsatisfying relationship or express their negative attitudes. Also, career-committed women are more likely to engage their husbands in discussions of role sharing when children are young (Guelzow et al., 1991), which may be worthwhile for the couple but may also be associated with stress or marital disruptions. Dual career couples' pursuits of nontraditional roles can create strain as both partners confront their personal gender stereotypes regarding male and female roles (see chapter 2). Particular sources of stress within dual career couples may derive from a lack of flexibility in the couple or in the work environment. Couples characterized by a supportive family environment and gender-free attitudes experience the greatest degree of marital satisfaction (Ladewig & McGee, 1986).

What conclusions can counselors draw from these diverse findings regarding the relationship of marital satisfaction and employment? First, satisfaction among wives seems to be related to whether or not they are implementing their preferred lifestyles, whether it is to be home or to be employed. In today's recessionary economy, however, preferred employment choices may not be easily implemented. Second, there is no reason to expect a negative impact of the wife's employment on the marital satisfaction of either the husband or the wife. It is only when couples subscribed to traditional gender expectations of the woman's role at home that the wife's employment was associated with a negative impact on their relationship. Circumventing and unlearning traditional gender expectations is difficult for most couples and may be opposed by other family members, friends, and society (see chapter 2).

Impact of Children

The presence of children within the family complicates but does not necessarily derail dual career pursuits. The demands of children can be formidable, but they vary with children's ages. The effect of preschoolers on career continuity has been of great interest because of their dependence on parents and the lack of adequate day care facilities for children, making employment and the care of young children prime areas of conflict. As parents adjust to the presence of young children at home, there may be excessive pressure on the adult couple relationship, largely because of children's constant demands and the lack of time available for parents to nurture their own relationships. At various ages, children's needs compete with career needs as parents strive to address both physical and psychological dimensions of the parent-child relationship. Blended families and visits by noncustodial children are associated with distinct family demands and may also represent sources of family stress.

Choices about childbearing are affected by the wife's career commitment (Spitze, 1988), and employment plans determine childbearing decisions (Waite & Stolzenberg, 1976), so that career-committed women are more likely to postpone or forego childbirth (Voydanoff, 1987). Until they eventually reach a joint decision concerning childbirth (Gilbert, 1988), dual career couples spend considerable time in discussing and analyzing this question (Wilk, 1986). When couples confront childbearing decisions, women have typically been working for about 8 years, have been married about 4 years, and are in their late 20s or early 30s (Wilk), a time when workers are in their most productive years. After childbirth many women choose part-time employment or time-outs (Laws, 1976; Card, Steel, & Abeles, 1980), leading many women, in contrast to men, to experience a distinct, more complex career pattern (Betz & Fitzgerald, 1987; Voydanoff, 1987).

Child-care issues also affect childbearing and work decisions. It has been estimated that 15% to 20% of nonemployed women would look for work if quality, affordable child care were available (O'Connell & Bloom, 1987; Powers & Salvo, 1982), and the availability of child care may mediate childbearing decisions (Stolzenberg & Waite, 1984; Spitze, 1988). Other factors may also affect ultimate decisions about whether or not to have children. For example, women who remain childless reported negative relationships with their parents (Wilk, 1986). Therefore, not employment alone, but a complex interaction of work, couple, and family-of-origin factors are related to women's decisions about whether or not to have children.

Career-committed women have fewer children than do other women. Among career-committed parents, the timing of childbirth may be carefully planned so that parents' career gains are not compromised. Additionally, parents experience increased satisfaction with both family and career roles when they have children at points in their careers when they have greater opportunity for career flexibility (Gilbert, 1988). Despite the demands of career and family roles, parents report an energizing, positive response toward their dual career lifestyles (Guelzow et al., 1991). Furthermore, it seems to be the age of the youngest child, not the number of children or their average ages, that is associated with role strain for both men and women (Hazard & Koslow, 1986; Sekaran, 1986). However, the number of children is associated with disruption in women's career continuity (Pistrang, 1984) and greater family strain in response to maternal employment (Menaghan & Parcel, 1991).

Both men and women expect the father to be involved with his children. Fathers are now playing a greater role in routine child care (Barnett & Baruch, 1987; Volling & Belsky, 1991) and also are participating in the responsibility for periodic, child-related demands like doctor's visits. Greater emphasis is also being placed on the importance of a father's active nurturing (Kotelchuk, 1976; Volling & Belsky, 1991). Participation by husbands of employed wives in routine child care is more extensive. A father's involvement in child care increases with the prestige and importance of his wife's career and her earned income (Gilbert, 1985). However, whether the man views parenting as costly to his career achievement or whether the woman perceives his involvement in child care as important also affects the roles that fathers play in their children's lives (Gilbert, 1985; Guelzow et al., 1991). Although a majority of men report being committed to the idea of sharing in household chores when their wives are employed, current research shows that women still perform the vast majority of housework (Spitze, 1988).

The wife's education and the presence of children at home interact with other factors, such as the attitudes of both partners toward the wife's employment, to predict whether or not she will continue working after she has children. (No study has assessed the factors affecting the continuity of male employment after childbirth.) Women who viewed themselves as more instrumental (see chapter 2 and chapter 4) experienced less work-family conflict and were more likely to work after having children (Betz & Fitzgerald, 1987; Murrell, Frieze, & Frost, 1991). Many women work after their children are born because labor force participation represents a substantial part of their self-definition (Avioli, 1985), and they experience a positive sense of well-being from high-quality work (Adelmann, 1987; Loscocco & Spitze, 1990; Lowe & Northcott, 1988). Moreover, these women worked prior to giving birth and had husbands who were supportive of their careers. (It makes sense to expect that at times when the general economic climate in the country is tighter, more mothers of newborns will work because of financial need.) Housewives who felt personally efficacious in their home roles did not work prior to baby's birth and reported that their husbands opposed their employment (Avioli). When her children were infants, the mother's education was not associated with her employment status. However, among mothers of older children, the mother's higher level of education was associated with her participation in the work force (Voydanoff, 1987, 1988).

Research has shown that it is not whether children are present at home, but the mother's psychological attitude toward her children's need for her that relates to her employment after she gives birth (DeMeis, Hock, & McBride, 1986; Morgan & Hock, 1984). Older mothers are more likely to believe that other caretakers are as capable as she is. Women's experience of motherhood interacts with their attitudes toward work (Pistrang, 1984). "Nonworking" mothers (i.e., Pistrang's terminology for women not employed outside of the home) who reported high work involvement before their babies' birth were less positive toward motherhood. Highly work-involved women who worked after their babies' birth experienced motherhood more positively. Less work-involved women who were at home after their babies' birth also viewed motherhood more positively.

Women's expressed interest in a job or career was highly associated with their labor force participation and was predictive of their level of employment during their children's preschool years (Morgan & Hock, 1984). Women who reported a high degree of investment in caring for others and were committed to the idea that their babies had high needs for their exclusive mothering were less likely to be employed (Morgan & Hock). In contrast, women who were satisfied with their career roles experienced less interrole conflict (MacEwen & Barling, 1991).

A significant problem characterizing research on maternal employment is that children have been viewed as independent or dependent variables that affect or are affected by parent employment. This consistent finding underscores the negative consequences of having children. If the couple decides to pursue a dual career couple lifestyle with children, the drawbacks on their career may be dramatic; however, the rewards of children can more than make up for these difficulties. Apparently, various researchers have often been remiss in not looking beyond the statistics. Giving birth and raising children can be rewarding and satisfying both to men and to women. More concretely, children can introduce a new dimension to the dual career couple relationship, often fostering positive growth in the couple and offering new perspectives on life's priorities.

Impact of Maternal Employment on Children

Research on maternal employment generally has not distinguished among variables related to the kind of work that the mother does, her satisfaction with work, hours worked, or other relevant career features. Children, in turn, have been viewed as outcome measures, or the dependent measures that would determine the impact of the maternal employment variable. The impact of the father's employment on child variables has largely been ignored. Despite early attempts to document the negative impact of maternal employment, the crudeness of the many studies undertaken and the wide variety of maternal employment situations and parenting styles, maternal employment has not been found to have a negative impact on child development outcomes (Bianchi & Spain, 1986; Hayes & Kamerman, 1983; Hoffman, 1989; Kamerman & Hayes, 1982; Spitze, 1988). Additionally, the general finding of studies of children has been that children of employed mothers have secure relationships (Belsky, 1988; Clarke-Stewart, 1988; Moorehouse, 1991; Thompson, 1988). Contrary to expectations that employed women would not have enough time or energy to nurture their children (Maccoby & Martin, 1983), employed mothers participated actively in their children's lives during the time they were home (Hoffman, 1984, 1989). Highly educated employed women spent as much time with their children as did other mothers at the expense of their own leisure and rest (Hill & Stafford, 1980; Spitze, 1988). Moreover, employed mothers compensated for long work hours by spending frequent time in shared activities with their young children, so that first graders with employed mothers who shared frequent mother-child activities matched or exceeded their peers in school performance (Moorehouse, 1991). When shared activities were infrequent, however, children had lower scores in school competence (Moorehouse, 1991).

Children of employed mothers did not feel deprived (Hoffman, 1974), although girls who were left alone and were responsible for more household chores were more likely to resent their mother's employment (Trimberger & MacLean, 1982). Nonetheless, adult daughters of employed mothers viewed their mothers as role models and were more likely to be employed after their own children were born (Betz & Fitzgerald, 1987).

Another reason for the positive findings among children of employed mothers relates to the fact that maternal employment may be a proxy for other issues such as quality of day care, children's relationship to peers, or the children's ability to care for themselves, all of which are associated with maternal employment (Bronfenbrenner & Crouter, 1982). Daughters of employed mothers were more independent (Hoffman, 1974), planned to be employed as adults (Bloom-Feshbach, Bloom-Feshbach, & Heller, 1982; Moore, Spain, & Bianchi, 1984), and did better in school (Hoffman, 1974). Sons and daughters of employed mothers viewed women as competent (Bloom-Feshbach et al.; Moore & Hoffreth, 1979) and had more egalitarian views of adult sex roles (Sorensen & Mortimer, 1988; Wilkie, 1987). Maternal employment may have a negative effect on middle-class sons' academic achievement (Bronfenbrenner & Crouter, 1982; Hoffman, 1979; Moore & Sawhill, 1984; Moore et al., 1984), but this finding may relate to other factors that correlate with maternal employment. Furthermore, quality day care may encourage children to develop various cognitive skills at early preschool ages (Clarke-Stewart, 1991).

Future research on maternal employment would be more enlightening if the dependent variables were changed. Parameters of maternal and paternal employment should be assessed, as well as the family and career balance concerns of the parents. Variables associated with dual career employment such as day care become increasingly important measures related to child outcomes in families where parents are employed.

ROLE CONFLICT

There are significant differences among couples in the way they manage work and career responsibilities. Both partners in dual career couples experience role conflict as they maneuver within their various roles (e.g., Bird & Ford, 1985; Tiedje, Wortman, Downey, Emmons, Biernat, & Lang, 1990). Effective family and career balance is associated with well-functioning in the dual career couple, whereas lack of negotiated balance can result in stress and conflict. Conflict between partners is reduced when roles are effectively balanced and various responsibilities are negotiated. Although this process is highly effective, dual career couples may have a constant need for reevaluating, renegotiating, and replanning their role balance as their work and family demands evolve.

Role conflict is associated with role strain from sources external to the couple such as work demands (Bird & Ford, 1985; Greenhaus et al., 1989) as well as from internal strains of their dual career couple family system (Loerch, Russell, & Rush, 1989). Wives experience greater role strain from child-related variables than do their husbands (Bird & Ford, 1985), even in families where husbands and wives report that they share approximately equally in child-related tasks.

Rapoport and Rapoport (1976) delineated four primary sources of internal strain: (1) social-psychological factors including salience of children and family life, (2) couples' socioeconomic status aspirations, (3) satisfactory division of household chores, and (4) other social-psychological factors. Many dual career couples place a high value on each of their multiple roles in career, family, and parenting, creating strain among the demands of each of these roles (Bird & Ford, 1985). Couples also are highly motivated to work out these conflicts and to maintain positive feelings toward each role (Gray, 1983; Pendleton, Poloma, & Garland, 1980; Poloma, Pendleton, & Garland, 1981).

There are five ways to reduce role strain according to Gray (1983): (1) by rotating attention to roles, (2) by reducing standards within roles, (3) by having family members help out, (4) by scheduling and carefully organizing activities, and (5) by considering personal interests important. Hall (1972) proposed a similar set of behaviors for coping. In addition, partners' attitudes toward role strain are related to the use of effective coping strategies. Wives felt that their husbands' supportiveness was critical to reducing role strain (Bird & Bird, 1986). When partners master time management skills and clearly identify which member is responsible for particular tasks, role strain can be decreased. Perceived control over their employment was also associated with the couple's ability to reduce work/family conflict (Voydanoff, 1988). Finally, workplace flexibility was associated with reduced role strain for both men and women (Guelzow et al., 1991).

Role conflict results from role overload and role interference (Voydanoff, 1987). *Overload* occurs when time and energy constraints prevent the adequate performance of activities associated with distinct roles. *Interference* results when the demands of different roles cannot be fulfilled. This may result from contradictory role expectations involving conflict between role demands, or from role incompatibility related to scheduling conflicts in the performance of multiple roles.

Sequencing work and family roles is the most common choice among women with young children (Voydanoff, 1987). This involves work slow-downs or withdrawal from the work force when children are young, and return to the work force with full employment at some later time. In the past, most fathers have not used sequential strategies for balancing family and career needs. However, as organizational climates change, fathers may also adopt this pattern of working (see chapter 10). Emotion-focused strategies, like cognitive restructuring, can also be used to revalue particular roles and reduce role conflicts (Elman & Gilbert, 1984).

DUAL CAREER COUPLE DILEMMAS

Dual career couples face five major career dilemmas (Rapoport & Rapoport, 1976; Sekaran, 1986): (1) role overload from multiple roles, (2) identity confusion between socially learned roles, (3) role-cycling dilemmas between family and career roles, each receiving priority at different points in time, (4) social network dilemmas because of limited discretionary time, and (5) normative dilemmas that result from environmental sanctions.

1. Role overload dilemmas. Parents in dual career couples share responsibilities at home; each also has career achievement goals. Even if they have hired help at home, a variety of planning, organizing, and coordinating obligations still remain. Partners require emotional support, and children need physical care, love, and support. These demands lead to role overload and stress.

2. Identity dilemmas. Earlier gender socialization of members of dual career couples can lead to particular conflicts about their adult identities, especially if they share household responsibilities equitably. New definitions of what it means to be a "good" mother or wife or a "good" husband or father can help address these identity dilemma concerns.

3. Role-cycling dilemmas. Family life-cycle functions occur within the context of the couple's life spans and their career development stages (see chapter 4). If partners wish to progress in their careers and have children, timing of childbirth can be important. If they wait too long, the woman may be past childbearing age. Having children too early in their careers may introduce difficulties in both partners' pursuing career and family roles. Resolving role-cycling dilemmas requires that partners discuss the relative priorities of family and career issues and agree on when one role takes priority over another.

4. Social network dilemmas. Time for nonwork and nonfamily activities is rare for dual career couples. Therefore, deliberate choices about whom to socialize with and whom to include in a close network of social contacts must be made. These choices can engender stress and guilt in the partners.

5. Normative dilemmas. Partners in dual career couples are often subject to a variety of negative sanctions with regard to social standards. For example, women may be expected to be home with young children. Men may be expected to work full-time and leave household tasks and child care to their wives. Within the dual career couple, these sanctions can create stress. Career-committed women who remain home with young children may irreparably damage their career progress or at least slow it down significantly. Men who do not participate in household responsibilities place an unfair burden on their female partners, and also may jeopardize the future well-being of the couple relationship.

Identifying the dilemmas dual career couples face can help them restructure their priorities and plan creative ways to address these dilemmas and reduce stress. Counselors can assist clients in developing methods to function effectively.

HOUSEWORK CONFLICTS

Fair division of housework is a major concern for dual career couples because of its time-consuming nature (e.g., Coverman & Sheley, 1986; Ferber & Birnbaum, 1980; Hardesty & Bokemeier, 1989; Nelson, 1976, 1977; Nyquist, Slivken, Spence, & Helmreich, 1985). Currently, housework remains primarily a woman's responsibility (Coverman & Sheley; Thompson & Walker, 1989, Loscocco & Roschelle, 1991). Wives at home spend approximately 30 hours per week doing housework, whereas wives employed full-time spend about 20 hours per week doing housework (Berardo et al., 1987; Ferber, 1982). Husbands spend an average of 10 hours per week on housework, whether or not their wives are employed. Employed women will not have time or energy available for career-related educational or professional pursuits if they are solely responsible for the majority of daily household chores. Because of the demands of housework, one author has referred to it as the second shift, and claims that some marriages have disintegrated because of divisiveness over housework responsibilities (Hochschild, 1989). No marriage, however, has broken up because husbands were sharing daily household chores. Higher-earning dual career couples can hire help to perform routine household chores, thereby relieving both partners of some housekeeping responsibilities. For other dual career couples, however, daily household chores still remain the family's responsibility. Housework also reinforces the imbalance of labor force and home roles between men and women (Coltrane, 1990).

Some authors offer dire predictions of the future of dual career couples because of the great burden of household responsibilities. "A shift of responsibility to dual career husbands would not be an effective way to reduce dual career wives' time in housework because it would have negative career implications for them. . . . Hiring household help and foregoing parenthood may be more effective ways of maintaining an equitable dimension of labor between dual career spouses. . ." (Berardo et al., 1987).

Men and women perceive equitable sharing of household chores differently (Benin & Agostinelli, 1988; Yogev & Brett, 1985). Wives feel that household responsibilities are fairly divided when their husbands perform stereotyped women's responsibilities, whereas husbands feel that fair division involves performing responsibilities that don't take too long to complete (Benin & Agostinelli). Husbands may, at times, be unaware that their wives consider household roles as not fairly balanced (Gross & Arvey, 1977). Fostering clearer communication about individual needs and expectations regarding housework can enhance task sharing between partners (Stoltz-Loike, 1991, 1992a, 1992b).

Dual career couples try to establish couple equity or a fair balance of responsibilities as opposed to achieving a quid pro quo (Rice, 1979). This means that rather than expecting that home, family, and career responsibilities can be balanced at all times, partners advocate balance over time and assume that the way responsibilities are shared will feel fair in the long run. When couples delay childbirth until they are in their late 20s or early 30s, fathers were found to be more prepared for housework and child-related responsibilities and mothers were more prepared to relinquish some of these primary role responsibilities (Coltrane, 1990).

Sharing household tasks may be difficult for both men and women because of their gender-role socialization and reluctance to give up traditional roles (Yogev, 1981). When partners' attitudes toward gender roles and roles in the work force change, they also adopt more gender-free attitudes toward men's and women's household roles. Wives who have greater tangible resources, such as income and job status, expect their husbands to help more (Bird, Bird, & Scruggs, 1984). Husbands with more liberal views of gender roles as interchangeable tend to be greater participants in household responsibilities (Barnett & Baruch, 1987; Bird et al.; Ross, 1987). Although the relative income of the husband and wife affect household participation by the husband (Maret & Finlay, 1984; Ross), it may be that the wife's attitude toward her employment and her ability to address her husband's household roles affect the equitability of their household participation (Barnett & Baruch, 1987; Bird et al., 1984; Guelzow et al. 1991).

Truly equitable sharing means that partners do not just perform household chores, but actually take full responsibility for them. The commitment to perform a particular responsibility may be inconvenient, requiring that one stay up late at night, come home early, or leave late for work to ensure that a particular job is properly completed. Thus, equity does not mean that the man "helps" the woman with *her* household tasks, but rather that he oversees a set of daily household chores himself.

Balancing family and career responsibilities is a great challenge to dual career couples. Lack of balance can result in role overload and general marital dissatisfaction. However, blame for lack of equitable sharing cannot clearly be placed on either partner, or on the presence of children. Rather it is the psychological perception of issues like fairness, needs, and the right to ask for change in partners' role privileges that can affect the balance of demands and the satisfaction with the relationship. Participation in multiple roles at home and in the workplace is associated with increased stress, but also with greater life satisfaction among men and women (Crohan, Antonucci, Adelmann, & Coleman, 1989).

QUALITY OF RELATIONSHIP

An important couple goal is to have a relationship of high quality that is meaningful to both partners. This goal will differ among couples according to their needs, self-perceptions, priorities in life, self-concept, and personal identities (Sekaran, 1986). Dual career couples experience a higher quality of relationship when there is equitable participation of both partners in home and family (Vannoy-Hiller & Philliber, 1989). Moreover, when women perceive that their partners are participating equitably in household chores or child care, they experience a greater satisfaction with the relationship. Another factor associated with a high-quality relationship in dual career couples is the sense that both partners' efforts have resulted in relationship success (Gilbert, 1985), and that overcoming their many dual career challenges represents a positive growth experience for the couple (Coltrane, 1990; Gilbert, 1985).

Relationship quality is also related to the sensitivity and supportiveness of the man (Vannoy-Hiller & Philliber, 1989). When he is able to express effectively his concern for his partner's goals and successes, the woman reports a greater contentment with the relationship. The ability to be supportive and sensitive as well as able to take care of one's own personal and career needs represents an androgynous personality that is a combination of "masculine" and "feminine," or instrumental and expressive, behavioral characteristics and is viewed as a positive behavioral goal that characterizes well-functioning personalities (Bem, 1974, 1979). Moreover, the androgynous personality can deal with stress more effectively and functions more capably within a relationship (see chapter 2).

Low-quality couple relationships are associated with specific couple and family issues. The presence of children, especially preschoolers, can diminish the quality of the couple relationship (Vannoy-Hiller & Philliber, 1989). The demands children place on the limited time couples have available and the conflict their presence introduces between the man's and the woman's careers, and their effect on the general family and career balance, contribute to conflict.

Competition is also associated with a lower quality in the couple relationship (Vannoy-Hiller & Philliber, 1989). When partners compete, there is an inability to appreciate one another's independent achievement, a lack of relationship harmony, and an inability to provide the support and safe haven critical to a meaningful relationship. Competition may result when a man needs to be better than his partner, or when he feels inadequate, threatened, or lacks self-assurance (Sekaran, 1986). In other cases, competition may result from not appreciating a partner's career, or one partner's expecting his or her achievement to take priority over the career goals of the other. Counselors can help couples address these nonproductive gender stereotypes.

High-quality relationships, characterized by sensitivity and mutual supportiveness, strengthen the couple bond and are associated with more effective functioning at work and at home. Moreover, the sense that partners have worked at the relationship also has a positive impact. The presence of children and competition among partners are associated with a negative quality in the relationship. Counselors can help foster positive growth within the couple relationship. Moreover, they can train couples in conflict resolution techniques (see chapter 8) to reduce competition. By introducing a life-span perspective (see chapter 9), counselors can help couples address the stress of parenting a young child.

Support Systems

Dual career couples lead complex lives and must rely on one another and accept external assistance to meet many family and career needs. Partners assist one another through enabling that involves "...help, active listening, emotional support, encouragement, boosting the partner's self-esteem and self-confidence, information sharing, offering guidance, and engaging in collaborative efforts to solve problems and achieve goals" (Sekaran, 1986, p. 36). Couples also should foster partner interdependence, which is the ability to be dependent at times and independent at others.

Environmental supports external to the couple include members of the extended families and friends who can pitch in when crises or unexpected career demands arise. Attitudes of these significant individuals may influence how partners evaluate their own family and career behaviors. Men and women may rely on external feedback to validate their own sense of self-worth and may be dependent on the approval of friends and family members who can promote their well-functioning.

Important environmental assistance also involves both the attitude of and support offered by the couple's employers such as parental leaves, flexible benefits, or on-site child care (see chapter 10). Other supports may involve the recognition by coworkers, supervisors, or department chairpersons of the dual career couple's career commitment as well as the demands of their lifestyles.

MEN IN DUAL CAREER COUPLES

Most research on dual career couples has addressed factors related to the female partners or the couple relationship. Rarely has research focused exclusively on men in dual career couples. Gilbert (1985) designed a research project to address that gap and drew a variety of interesting conclusions. Men's roles in dual career couples have changed far less than those of women. Many men in dual career relationships do not participate equitably in household responsibilities. Women who are highly educated or earn a significant proportion of the family income, however, have husbands who do a more equitable portion of household work, suggesting that role balance is slowly changing (Sekaran, 1986).

The high achievement motive of career-committed men is not negatively affected by their dual career couple lifestyles. Moreover, partners in many successful dual career couples are supportive of each other's career goals. The need for support for individual goals varies for men and women. Men need support to be more involved with their children, whereas women may need support to justify their being less involved (Gilbert, 1985).

Three types of men in dual career couples were identified in Gilbert's (1985) study: role-sharing men, traditional men, and participant fathers. Role-sharing men were truly equitable (i.e., household and child-care responsibilities were shared), giving their partners' career an equal value with their own. In couples with traditional men, household responsibilities and child-care responsibilities belonged to the women. Among participant fathers, household responsibilities belonged to the women, but child care was shared.

Four factors distinguished these three groups of men. First, traditional men were in school at the time of the couple's marriage. Couples may have started their relationships with an early imbalance, attributing priority to the career of one partner. This imbalance may have persisted into the couple's later life. An alternative explanation is that women who have not yet pursued their careers may be more timid about asserting their own needs.

Second, level of aspiration can affect household arrangements. All the role-sharing men viewed their wives as having higher career aspirations than the men's own. More traditional and participant men saw themselves as more ambitious. Further study is necessary to ascertain whether the actual aspiration of the wives, or the husbands' perceptions of those aspirations, is the critical factor.

Third, the perception of support was associated with career aspirations. Almost all traditional men viewed their wives as more supportive, but no traditional or participatory man saw himself as more supportive. Many role-sharing and participant fathers saw themselves as highly supportive. Fourth, salary levels were related to balance. Almost all traditional fathers had much higher salaries than their wives. Fewer participant and role-sharing fathers had higher incomes.

In terms of career decisions, no traditional fathers saw their children as influencing their careers, although almost one fourth of participant and two fifths of role-sharing fathers felt that parenting affected their careers. Few traditional fathers had negative feelings about being part of a dual career couple (even if their wives felt differently). Role-sharing and participant fathers faced more difficulties, but viewed the dual career couple lifestyle as beneficial to the couple, their children, themselves, and society.

It is difficult to determine what percentage of men fall into any one of Gilbert's three groups. However, it seems likely that these three types of men are in many dual career couple relationships. Relationships with participant and traditional men are likely to engender stress and resentment in the female partner because of the imbalance of role responsibilities. For each couple, the similarity of perspectives of the two partners on roles, their expectations about their own personal achievement, and their individual sense of what constitutes equity are associated with the responses of each partner to the parameters of the couple's lifestyle.

Recently, other researchers also have expressed interest in the roles men play in family life. Among dual career couples, fathers are more highly involved when their wives have nontraditional attitudes toward sex roles (Barnett & Baruch, 1987) and when they have a high-quality relationship with their wives (Volling & Belsky, 1991). Moreover, men are concerned about both professional and family roles, and they experience lower partner, parental, and career-related stress when they have flexible work schedules, presumably because this allows them to participate in their various roles comfortably (Guelzow et al., 1991).

Work-Family Conflict: New Perspectives

Based on their literature review, Greenhaus and Beutell (1985) derived three antecedents of work-family conflict: (a) strain-based conflict that refers to how time devoted to one role takes away time from another role, (b) strain-based conflict that refers to the intrusion of strain symptoms (e.g., fatigue, irritability) from one role to another role, and (c) behavior-based conflict that refers to the incompatibility of behaviors in one role with those expected in another role. In subsequent work Greenhaus and colleagues (e.g., Greenhaus, Bedeian, & Mossholder, 1987; Greenhaus et al., 1989) distinguished between work pressures that lead to work-family conflict and family pressures that lead to work-family conflict. It is interesting to note that in a recent study of stress-based and time-based conflict, Greenhaus et al. (1989) found both similarities and differences in men's and women's responses. Men and women experienced similar levels of stress-based conflict. Work-role stressors accounted for similar portions of variance in time-based and stress-based conflict among men and women. Characteristics of the work schedule were associated with stress-based conflict for men but not for women. Women, however, experienced great work-family conflict when they were highly involved with their jobs, but did not experience stress when their partners had high work salience. Men's patterns were reversed. Men's work-family conflict was unrelated to their work involvement; their partners' involvement with work, however, predicted their work-family conflict.

Using the forms of work-family conflict derived by Greenhaus and Beutell (1985), Loerch et al. (1989) evaluated the impact of family factors on work-family conflict. No relationship between the number of children, spouse work hours per week, or the couple's employment status was found for time-based conflicts for men or women. However, conflict was related to the frequency of family intrusions and total role involvement for men, and to family conflict for women. Family conflict also was associated with stress-based and behavior-based work-family conflict.

The results of studies by Greenhaus and colleagues and Loerch and colleagues indicated that both men and women experience family conflicts, but in different ways. Further studies are needed to analyze time-based aspects of work-family conflict, the impact of the dual career couple lifestyle on career performance, and partner and family roles. Furthermore, this methodology may yield a fruitful way for teasing apart the distinct ways that men and women experience the dual career relationship.

CONCLUSIONS

Dual career couples experience unique stresses and pressures because of role conflicts and dilemmas associated with their lifestyle. There are also special benefits associated with the dual career lifestyle, including higher financial rewards and the collegiality of partners. Evidence suggests that partners in dual career couples experience a high degree of marital satisfaction. Moreover, the mutual security and support many couples experience reflect the real value that partners place on one another's career. Children can increase the stress among dual career couples and impair the continuity of their careers, but they can also introduce a perspective on employment that is of positive value for each parent. Dual career parents can still be productive and upwardly mobile in their careers despite their young children's needs. Children of dual career couples exhibit few if any adverse affects resulting from dual career lifestyles.

In the past, most of the research on dual career couples analyzed the impact of maternal employment on family outcome measures. The following areas of research would represent significant contributions to the understanding of dual career couples: (a) analysis of the impact of the characteristics of parental employment, the relationship between the parents, or differences in child-care situations on the couple and family relationship, (b) evaluation of the effect of the dual career couple lifestyle on the career paths of men and women, and (c) assessment of the inter-relationship of both family issues on workplace performance and characteristics of the workplace on family stress.

2 Gender Differences

MANY STUDIES HAVE DOCUMENTED the differences between men and women in various cognitive, social, and emotional dimensions of behavior. Moreover, men and women may perceive their environments in distinctly different ways. These fundamental differences between men and women and their implications for interpersonal and work-force performance must be clearly delineated.

A problem that has plagued past research on gender differences is that male performance was taken as the standard for comparison (see Miller, 1973, 1976). Conclusions could ascertain that men and women behaved differently, but only with respect to what was considered typical male behavior. Thus, women were viewed as more emotional than men and less independent. The idea that healthy development among mature women might involve different processes than healthy development among men had never been part of classic theories of human development. Moreover, behaviors characteristic of adult women such as dependence or endurance were labeled as negative adult traits. Because so much past research and theory used only male models, certain behaviors associated with women's adult behavior, like dependence and vulnerability, were not included in the models or were labeled as deviant (Goodrich, Rampage, Ellman, & Halstead, 1988; Miller, 1976), and affiliation and achievement were viewed as mutually exclusive (Travis, Phillippi, & Henley, 1991). Failure to respect women's adult behaviors may relate to the failure of traditional psychotherapy to assist certain groups of women (Brown, 1991). For example, valuations of relational networks over autonomy would reflect respect for women's perspectives in life-cycle theories (Gergen, 1990).

Only recently have therapists articulated the position that various female traits can be viewed positively (Goodrich et al., 1988). Furthermore, recent perspectives have proposed that affiliation and achievement are not distinct categories (Travis et al., 1991) but may both be explained by the same principles (McClelland, 1985; McClelland, Koestner, & Weinberger, 1989) and represent positive aspects of maturity. Additionally, many individuals view achievement as experience in interpersonal affiliation (Travis et al.), suggesting the need for new ways of defining achievement. These examples underscore the necessity of understanding gender differences so that the rich spectrum of human behavior, both male and female, can be described and appreciated (e.g., Bernard, 1966, 1988). The present chapter will review gender differences from the perspectives taken in earlier research within the context of viewing male and female behaviors as constituting mature and healthy examples of human behavior.

OVERVIEW OF GENDER DIFFERENCES: DUAL CAREER COUPLE ISSUES

Gender differences are diverse and pervasive. Nonetheless, they represent socialized human behavior, not the capacity to behave. Men can exhibit and adopt behaviors more typically associated with women, just as women can exhibit and adopt behaviors more typically associated with men. Balancing career and family demands can foster the development of new behavioral repertoires for men and women. Contemporary perspectives reflect the belief that a well-functioning personality is androgynous and integrates behavior typically associated with both sexes (Bem, 1979; Sedney, 1987). With regard to dual career couples, a relevant gender difference is the distinction between instrumental and expressive behaviors, a distinction that characterizes the way individuals interact, perceive others, and view themselves. These differences are also associated with differences in how men and women make choices between career and family demands, which has major implications for achievement in dual career couples. Although many interesting gender differences exist, the focus of this chapter will be on those that have significance for dual career couples.

GENDER DIFFERENCES: DEFINITIONS

Three distinct terms are typically used to refer to sexually related differences between men and women. *Sex differences* refers to the biological differences between women and men. *Sexual orientation* refers to individual differences in orientation with regard to sexual partners. *Gender differences* refers to differences in behaviors between men and women that result from their socialization experiences.

Gender differences can affect how couples perceive, listen, and respond to each other, and gender role attitudes can affect partners' willingness and capability to participate equitably at work and at home. In contrast, gender stereotypes are defined as the attribution of certain behaviors, attitudes, or capabilities to only one sex. Although understanding gender differences enhances the counselor's ability to function in the client-counselor relationship, failure to confront gender stereotypes constrains both the counselor's and client's ability to function.

DEVELOPMENTAL PERSPECTIVES

Some sex differences are exhibited almost from the time of birth. For example, male infants cry more then female infants (Moss, 1967). By the time children reach grade school, researchers report a myriad of differences between boys and girls with regard to communication (Austin, Salehi, & Leffler, 1987; Black & Hazen, 1990; Sachs, 1987; Sheldon, 1990) and children's interactions with peers (Carter, 1987; Maccoby & Jacklin, 1987; Maccoby, 1990; Miller, Danaher, & Forbes, 1986; Thorne, 1986). Differences have also been found with regard to linguistic usage (Graddol & Swann, 1989; Leaper, 1991), spatial ability (Maccoby & Jacklin, 1974), and processing of cognitive information (Carlsson & Jaderquist, 1983; Liben & Signorella, 1980; Martin & Halverson, 1981, 1983).

Significant differences have been found in behaviors of men and women toward male and female infants (Field, Vega-Lahr, Goldstein, & Scafidi, 1987; Lamb, 1977a,1977b; Parke, 1979; Parke & Sawin, 1979; Rendina & Dickerscheid, 1976; Smith & Lloyd, 1978; White & Wollett, 1981). Moreover, Culp, Cook, and Housley (1983) found that adults will treat the same infant differently depending on whether an experimenter has informed the adult that the infant is a boy or a girl. "This finding suggests that sex typing may be quite subtle and adults may be unaware of their own predisposition toward sex stereotyping" (Culp et al., p. 478).

Gender differences are reinforced by parents (Birnbaum & Croll, 1984; Birnbaum, Nosanchuk, & Croll, 1980; Brody, 1985; Jacobs & Moss, 1976; Malatesta & Haviland, 1982; Parsons et al., 1982), teachers (Barnett & Baruch, 1987; Parsons, Kaczala, & Meece, 1982), and playmates (Garvey, 1977). Moreover, gender stereotypes are more rigidly applied to boys than to girls (Archer, 1984; Reckers & Yates, 1976). Parents differ in their reactions to the behavior of boys and girls below the age of 5. After age 5, these parental differences are no longer found. Fagot and Hagan (1991) interpreted these findings as indicating that 5-year-olds may have already incorporated lessons regarding "appropriate" gender types so that parents no longer feel the need to actively reinforce gender differences. Furthermore, separation and independence are emphasized for boys and interpersonal cohesion for girls (Block, 1973, 1984; Chodorow, 1978; Gilligan,

1982; Leaper, Gleason, & Hirsch, 1990; Leaper, Hauser, Kremen, Powers, Jacobson, Noam, Weiss-Perry, & Follansbee, 1989).

The world and the role models to which boys and girls are exposed may be substantially different (Archer & Lloyd, 1980) and further magnify gender differences. Boys' and girls' rooms have different contents and appearance (Rheingold & Cook, 1975), they watch different television shows, read different books, play different games, and play primarily with same-sex playmates (Archer & Lloyd, 1980). Children, however, are able to respond in a manner characteristic of the opposite sex, even though they typically may elect not to exhibit those behaviors (Hargreaves, 1976).

Attempts at changing children's gender-based behaviors through role modeling by adults have yielded mixed results (Katz, 1986). Children will elect to perform those behaviors of actors that they consider gender-appropriate, irrespective of the sex of the person who performs the activity, but will not imitate same-sex actors who perform gender-inappropriate behaviors (Barkley, Ullman, Otto, & Brecht, 1977), and typically do not imitate the behavior of a same-sex child playing with a sex-inappropriate toy (Wolf, 1975; Vieira & Miller, 1978). When studies have reported changes in children's behavior in response to training, these changes often last only as long as the period of the experimental intervention (Sedney, 1987). "Children are not passive recipients of intervention efforts: attempts to influence children's psychological sex role interact with the child's existing preferences, developmental level, and influences from other sources" (Sedney, 1987, p. 319).

The nature of gender differences in adulthood becomes more subtle and more complex. Many gender differences observed in childhood persist, and other gender differences become evident with maturation. However, it becomes difficult to distinguish between gender differences and the knowledge associated with the often distinct context of the work and achievements of men and women.

Although parents contribute to children's adoption of sex-appropriate behaviors, research findings also demonstrate that parental behaviors and attitudes contribute to the development of egalitarian attitudes among children. Non-sex-typed parenting is not solely related to how parents respond to the child's sex or express attitudes regarding acceptable gender roles. Rather, egalitarian parents set an example through their nonstereotyped sex roles, their egalitarian approaches to family power, and their way of balancing family and career issues that communicate the most valuable lessons to children regarding acceptable psychological gender-role development (Sedney, 1987).

Explanatory Theories

Achieving relationship equity is predicated on a sophisticated understanding of the origins and the impact of gender differences on couple functioning. The controversy over whether gender differences are genetic or environmental in origin still persists (Holden, 1991). It is largely irrelevant, however, because of the ubiquitousness of gender differences evident in the psychological research literature and the capacity of men and women for cross-gender behaviors.

A variety of theories have been proposed to explain the origins of gender differences. Social learning theorists assumed that children learned gender stereotypes because they were differentially rewarded for certain actions (Mischel, 1966, 1970) and postulated that imitation, role modeling, and reward and punishment affected gender learning (e.g., Archer & Lloyd, 1980; Mischel, 1970; Perry & Bussey, 1979). Cognitive developmental theorists viewed gender development as a function of the child's comprehension of the meaning and significance of external events (e.g., Kuhn, Nash, & Brucken, 1978; Eisenberg, Murray, & Hite, 1982). Thus, children first identify themselves by the appropriate sex and then decide that they should follow behaviors of others of the same sex.

The traditional theories of gender-role identity assumed that the goal of this development was for individuals to adopt strict gender roles and did not look at gender-role identity past childhood. Recent interest in the development of androgyny, or describing people in terms of ''masculine'' and ''feminine'' behaviors, has led to the investigation of gender-role development beyond childhood (Sedney, 1987). Block (1973, 1984) viewed the goal of development as attaining a functional balance between feminine and masculine behaviors appropriate to the individual. In a multistage, invariant sequence, the end state is perceived as an integration of masculine and feminine personality aspects, or an androgynous gender-role self-definition. In a different, but parallel theory, Hefner, Rebecca, and Oleshansky (1975) viewed gender-role development as progressing from an *undifferentiated* perspective to a *polarized* view of masculine and feminine gender roles to *sex-role transcendence*, characterized by an adaptive, personally appropriate gender-role definition. All individuals do not progress to the stage of gender-role transcendence.

A variety of studies corroborated the hypothesis that life-span development of gender-roles was reflected in less gender-stereotypical gender-role descriptions among older than among younger people (Fischer & Narus, 1981; Katz, 1979; Sedney, 1986). Other work suggests that men become more androgynous with age, whereas women become more feminine (Hyde, Krajnik, & Skuldt-Niederberger, 1991). These findings, and research on children's adherence to sex-stereotyped roles, suggest that androgyny may not be evident until adulthood (Sedney, 1987). Studies indicate that androgynous adults have parents with androgynous personalities, characterized by unconventional sharing of home responsibility, nurturance by both parents, and support for cognitive achievement by both parents (Sedney, 1987). This suggests that modeling of androgynous behaviors might occur throughout childhood, but the impact of this modeling may not be evident until adulthood.

Recently, psychologists and others have postulated that men and women perceive the world differently and it is therefore necessary to develop new theories of psychological development that are sensitive to the distinctions between male and female maturation (Chodorow, 1978; Gilligan, 1982; Miller, 1973, 1976). Gilligan (1982), in her groundbreaking book *In a Different Voice*, discussed the different developmental challenges boys and girls face. Both are raised by their mothers or (almost always) another female caretaker. Thus, girls learn that in order to develop gender-appropriate behaviors, they must be like their mothers or their female caretakers. Therefore, they rely on imitating the caretaker and affiliating with her. Boys, on the other hand, recognize that to develop gender-appropriate behaviors, they must behave differently than the female caretaker and try to function independently of her. As they mature, the developmental challenge for girls is to learn to be more independent, and the developmental challenge for boys is to learn to affiliate with others comfortably. Gilligan claimed that because of their early developmental histories, men and women continue to view the world differently even as adults. Women view the world in terms of interactive issues and the common good, whereas men view the world from a more independent perspective.

Whether gender differences are biological or the result of socialization experiences cannot be easily ascertained, yet these differences persist throughout life. Reinforcement may only underlie the origins of gender differences, and continued reinforcement from society, family, and friends may ensure that these differences become well learned. Thus, gender differences derive from individual developmental histories and are typically reinforced by peers, parents, and teachers. Within domains such as housework, men and women may ''do gender'' by holding rigid standards of what is appropriate, and unconsciously or consciously encourage one another to adhere to these roles (Berk, 1985). Cognitive gender differentiation involves the initial recognition of maleness and femaleness, but may also be associated in adulthood with a continual process of experiential evaluations and reevaluations of how men and women should behave.

Counselors can begin to address gender differences and gender stereotypes by analyzing the positive and negative reinforcement partners receive for particular behaviors, and by listening to clients' rules about what men and women can or should do. When counselors alter reinforcement patterns or present examples that counteract cognitive stereotypes, couples may begin to expand their definitions of maleness and femaleness. By enriching the couple's behavioral repertoire, each individual's ability to function within career and couple roles will be enhanced.

Instrumental Versus Expressive Differences

Scales for Measuring Gender Role Identity

Bem (1972, 1979, 1980, 1981) and Spence and Helmreich (Spence & Helmreich, 1979, 1981; Spence, Helmreich, & Stapp, 1975) developed scales to measure gender identity. Both Bem's Sex Role Inventory (BSRI) and Spence and Helmreich's Personality Attributes Questionnaire (PAQ) assess, by self-report, the masculinity or femininity of a person's behavior. Early work on masculinity and femininity had assumed that these traits were different poles of a continuous scale. The work of Bem and Spence and Helmreich demonstrated that the scales for masculinity and femininity are actually orthogonal, or independent, so that it is possible for a single individual to be high in masculine and low in feminine behavior, high in feminine and low in masculine behavior, high in both masculine and feminine behaviors (androgynous), or low in both masculine and feminine behaviors (undifferentiated). This represented a new way of viewing masculine and feminine behaviors and reflected a respect for the positive aspects of behaviors typically considered feminine or masculine. Results of the parallel masculine and feminine scales on the BSRI and PAQ are correlated and both measure desirable experimental and instrumental traits (Spence, 1991).

The behaviors used on the masculine (instrumental) scale of the BSRI include items like aggressive, ambitious, analytical, athletic, competitive, forceful, independent, makes decisions easily, and self-reliant, and the feminine (expressive) scale consists of behaviors like affectionate, cheerful, compassionate, flatterable, gentle, loves children, sensitive to the needs of others, sympathetic, warm, and yielding. Both men and women can report a prevalence or a dearth of either instrumental or expressive behaviors, although it is more common for women to report that they use expressive behaviors and for men to report that they typically use instrumental behaviors.

Androgynous behavior as measured by the PAQ and the BSRI represents the most flexible characteristics of human behavior and is reflected in reports of high instrumental and high expressive behaviors (see Bem, 1980). This means that healthy personalities would be characterized as sensitive to others, gentle, affectionate, and sympathetic (traditional female stereotypes), as well as self-reliant, forceful, and ambitious (typical male stereotypes). If instrumental behaviors include the ability to get ahead and to take care of oneself, and expressive behaviors include the ability to be concerned with the needs of others, it makes intuitive sense to expect that a well-integrated personality would be characterized as being concerned about others but also able to take care of oneself.

*Scales for Measuring Gender Role Identity
and Dual Career Couple Issues*

Some researchers have questioned the significance of scales measuring gender role identity, arguing that androgyny is an arbitrary, nonsignificant term (e.g., Locksley & Colten, 1979), or that the instrumental or expressive rating on the M (masculine) and F (feminine) scales could be made using only the measure of self-perceived "masculinity" or "femininity" and no other item on the scale (Pedhazur & Tetenbaum, 1979). Additionally, the relationship of androgyny to other concerns like effective parenting also has been questioned (Baumrind, 1982). These criticisms notwithstanding, gender scales have been employed successfully in a wide variety of studies of gender differences and are a popular, widely used tool. They are useful for counselors to assess client couple's gender-related concerns. Also, the vast research related to these scales underscores the greater respect now accorded to masculine and feminine aspects of healthy functioning.

Career progress among dual career couples is more easily pursued when household responsibilities are shared and career aspirations are mutually supported. A variety of studies have assessed the relationship of gender scale performance to household roles and the relationship of personality to gender scale performance. Men who are androgynous as rated by the PAQ, for example, are more likely to participate equitably in household chores (Nyquist et al., 1985). Gunter and Gunter (1990) found interesting differences between men and women, and masculine-typed, feminine-typed, and androgynous individuals. At home, androgynous and expressive individuals, as measured by the BSRI, performed more household tasks than did instrumental individuals. However, women typically performed more tasks than did men, irrespective of gender identity. In couples where the man was androgynous or expressive, both partners performed more household tasks than did couples with an undifferentiated man. Husbands who were high only in instrumental behaviors performed the fewest chores and had wives who performed the most chores. In addition, using the PAQ to measure psychological masculinity, Roos and Cohen (1987) found that individuals high in masculinity (instrumentality) were less affected by negative life events and by trait anxiety than were those low in masculinity. In another study, high instrumental women, as rated by the BSRI, experienced lower levels of work-related strain, were more problem-focused, and had higher levels of personal efficacy (Long, 1989).

In one study, Lemkau (1983) compared the BSRI assessment of equally educated women who were involved in sex-typical or sex-atypical careers, and found an interaction between these assessments and work-role demands. Women in sex-typical occupations described themselves as "feminine" within work and social settings. Women in sex-atypical occupations described themselves as less feminine at work.

The ability of dual career couples to be productive in today's competitive employment market and to function effectively as partners and parents relates to the flexibility of their gender identities. Expressive women may be more intrinsically familiar with mothering roles and instrumental men more intrinsically familiar with other activities. However, men can learn to parent effectively and women can learn to master more instrumental behaviors, resulting in a productive sharing of the various roles family members perform. This sort of crossover learning is essential to the effective functioning of dual career couples and their success in employment and household roles.

Both men and women who are androgynous should exhibit the greatest role flexibility. Because they are high in both expressive and instrumental attributes, androgynous individuals in dual career couples would be able to cooperate most effectively on work, home, and family issues. Androgynous couples would have the easiest time cooperating at home because they do not threaten one another's internalized gender roles. In contrast, couples in which both partners adhere to significantly different, traditional gender roles, may experience anxiety when they cooperate on work and family responsibilities. Both partners may feel that by expanding their self-defined gender roles and taking responsibility for chores normally done by their partners, they diminish both themselves and their partners. Counselors can help couples who adhere to rigid definitions of sex-appropriate behaviors to expand their gender definitions as they master new levels of interaction and respect for their partners.

Impact of Environment and Others' Behaviors

Men and women do not only behave differently (Baker, 1987b), but they are differentially attuned to the environment (Anderson, 1987; Baker, 1987a, 1987b) and situational demands (Redgrove, 1987; Tannen, 1990), and draw different expectations of future performance from past experience (Eccles, 1987; Eccles, Adler, & Meece, 1984; Frieze, 1980; Frieze, Whitley, & Hanusa, 1982; Weiner, Frieze, Kukla, Reed, Rest, & Rosenbaum, 1971).

Different Behaviors

Conversations among men and women reflect the fact that men and women prefer discussing different topics and employ distinct verbiage. Differences have been found in conversational styles of men and women, indicating that conversation of mixed-sex groups is more similar to conversation among men than to conversation only among women (Tannen,

1990). When men talked among themselves, they discussed business or food, whereas women primarily talked about people they cared for, such as friends, partners, and children, and discussed business and health secondarily. In mixed-sex groups, neutral topics were discussed in the style that men use when they converse in a single-sex group. This meant that mixed groups were more likely to talk about activities and plans rather than people or personal health, and that women made a greater adjustment to be part of the mixed-sex group than did men.

It is interesting to speculate that if this adjustment to male conversation existed within dual career couples, it would create tension within the relationship. Women may become expert at tuning into male expectations without ever articulating their own needs, creating great personal stress and, ultimately, psychological dysfunction (Goodrich et al., 1988). Anecdotal reports provide corroborating data indicating that women enjoy women's groups, which provide them with the freedom of discussion uncharacteristic of many of their interactions with men.

Communication

Communication provides the basis for closeness, intimacy, and support in the dual career couple and can be mastered through training and practice (see chapter 7). Because men and women communicate differently, there are many opportunities for misunderstandings between partners (Tannen, 1990). Counselors can assist partners in becoming sophisticated about gender differences in order to become capable communicators and avoid confusion.

In conversations between men and women, men were more likely to interrupt, challenge, ignore the other person's comments, and make more declarations of opinions as facts (Maltz & Borker, 1982). Women, however, used more questions, tried to maintain the flow of the conversation, used more personal pronouns, and were more likely to exhibit silent protest when interrupted. Women were also better than men at decoding overt, nonverbal cues, but less adept with nonintentional cues (Brody, 1985).

Differences in how partners in dual career couples talk about career and family issues may be very pronounced (see chapter 7). At times, communication can be difficult and understanding may be obstructed when partners use different modes of expression. Couples themselves may not acknowledge each other's expertise. Books with titles like *You Just Don't Understand* (Tannen, 1990) or *That's Not What I Meant* (Tannen, 1986) underscore the antagonistic qualities that may characterize couple relationships. Counselors can play an essential role in helping partners to acknowledge expertise and behavior in ways that reflect respect for one another's achievements.

Emotional Responses

Men and women may perceive or try to convey distinctly different images of themselves. Although there were no observable gender differences in emotionality or physiological differences in response to stress (Greene & Peell, 1987), gender differences in self-reported measures of emotionality exist (Durkin, 1987), and men and women report that they cope with stress differently (Cook, 1990). Men also scored higher on measures of fear of failure, whereas women scored higher on hope of success (Durkin). Women are more articulate in discussing emotions and report being more sad, more scared, less angry, and more emotionally expressive than men (Brody, 1985). With age, boys inhibit expression and attribution of emotions, whereas girls inhibit expression and recognition of socially unacceptable emotions like anger (Brody). Women are also more likely than men to show their feelings in their facial expressions, whereas men internalize their emotions (Brody; Hall, 1984).

Theoretically, women experience difficulty in expressing anger (Kaplan, Brooks, McComb, Shapiro, & Sodano, 1983; Lemkau & Landau, 1986) and even recognizing anger (Lerner, 1985), although suppression of anger is associated with mental health problems among women (Kopper & Epperson, 1991). This emotional suppression may be associated with female socialization and cultural taboos that associate anger with unfeminine and inappropriate behaviors (Kopper & Epperson). Little empirical evidence exists concerning gender differences in the expression of anger. Kopper and Epperson (1991), in a well-controlled study involving self-report about proneness to anger and anger expression, found that gender role identity rather than sex was associated with expression or suppression of anger. Thus, individuals assessed as masculine with the BSRI were more likely to get angry and express anger than ''feminine-typed'' individuals.

The lower response of emotionality in men typically found in studies may also be related to the fact that some tests do not measure issues that may arouse anxiety in men (Frieze, Fisher, Hanusa, McHugh, & Valle, 1978) or instrumental individuals. Had studies addressed topics like career or financial issues, men or instrumental individuals might have responded differently.

Impact of Gender Differences on Couple Interaction

Differences in the ''interactive'' style of men and women can create conflicts, misunderstandings, and barriers to equitable functioning within dual career couples. Therefore, knowledge of these differences represents part of the critical corpus of information for those who counsel dual career couples.

Behavioral Style

Women and men exhibit different styles in approaching new tasks. Typically men are overconfident and women are not sufficiently confident relative to their past performance histories (Chipman, Brush, & Wilson, 1985; Linn & Petersen, 1986), and women do not expect to do as well as men on a variety of academic and motor skills activities (Lenney, 1977; Simon & Feather, 1973). In problem solving, women are more cautious and careful in responding to test items. Consequently, they respond more slowly when they are not sure of a correct answer, and they are more likely to indicate that they do not know an answer (Linn & Petersen, 1986).

"Such caution may be realistic in that female respondents may have less information and therefore may simply be indicating a lack of knowledge. Alternatively, such caution may reflect a differential threshold for uncertainty, greater confidence among males, or greater willingness to verify responses to questions among females. This caution seems to reflect an unwillingness to be wrong in these situations—a response that may be reinforced by sex-role stereotypes of women as careful and as attentive to detail" (Linn & Petersen, 1986, p. 94).

Men's and women's behavioral expectations are related to the type of task and experience (e.g., McHugh, Fisher, & Frieze, 1982; McHugh, Frieze, & Hanusa, 1982). Sex-linked tasks interact with women's and men's performance, expectations, and evaluations of performance (Deaux, 1976a, 1976b, Deaux & Kite, in press; Wallston & O'Leary, 1982). Women have low expectations of performance only on unfamiliar tasks (McHugh, 1975), and their expectations are particularly low for stereotypically masculine tasks (Deaux, 1976b, Frieze, et al., 1978; McHugh, 1975). Thus, women may be less confident, more anxious, and more cautious when solving mathematics problems than are men (Linn & Petersen, 1986). Wording of questions is also associated with different responses of men and women (Whitley & Frieze, 1985; Whitley, McHugh, & Frieze, 1986).

Studies of cognitive domains indicate that although experience is important, in most cognitive domains there is a "divergence of expert performance," so that tasks that are performed well may be the result of any of a variety of strategies. Women may focus more on the approach to a problem's solution rather than on the solution itself and, therefore, rate their performance low if they learn of a more efficient way to perform the task.

Self-Concept/Self-Esteem

Women who have the same abilities as men view their skills less positively than do men (Chipman et al., 1985; Stage, Kreinberg, Eccles,

& Becker, 1984). What does this mean concerning how women view themselves? From where do these unrealistic standards derive? How can they be countered? Do women often choose different career paths than men because of an undervaluation of their talents? (see chapter 4). Although women may have a lower expectation for success than men, this does not mean that they anticipate failure. "Women's ratings of their abilities are low relative to men; it is interesting to note that this difference is defined as self-derogation in women rather than as self-enhancement in men" (Whitley et al., 1986, p. 119).

Gender Differences in Decision Making: The Family Factor

Many studies have documented the similarity among particular aspects of men's and women's career orientations, including acceptance of the relationship between work and self-esteem, the recognition of the power and prestige associated with success, and the positive valuation of work (see chapter 4 for a more complete discussion of women's career concerns). No significant gender differences have been found concerning interest in earning high salaries, fringe benefits, and desire for interesting work (Miller, 1980), and both employed men and women exhibited similar responses under the same job conditions (Kanter, 1976, 1977). However, once men and women are asked to make career decisions where both family and career must be considered, pronounced gender differences become evident. Although men and women exhibited the same attitudes toward work and recognized the relationship of work to self-esteem and prestige, they used different criteria in making choices between work and family opportunities (Williams, 1990). Similarly, the anticipated occupational plans of adolescent girls are strongly affected by whether or not they expect to combine family and work responsibilities (Aneshensel & Rosen, 1980).

Women experience significant role conflict when they try to accommodate both family and work roles (Laws, 1976; Osipow, 1975; Card et al., 1980; Falk & Cosby, 1978), although they evaluate their dual role structure positively (Gilbert, 1985, 1988; Guelzow et al., 1991), and many women even find working in jobs with routine responsibilities to be associated with enhanced self-esteem (Crohan et al., 1989; Gove & Tudor, 1973; Loscocco & Spitze, 1990; Lowe & Northcott, 1988; Voydanoff, 1987; Wright & Hamilton, 1978). Marriage and the presence of children may have disruptive effects on the continuity of women's employment and may increase their involvement in part-time work (Card et al., 1980; Falk & Cosby, 1978; Felmlee, 1984; Moen, 1985; Sewell, Hauser, & Wolf, 1980). Women's work orientation and job satisfaction may also be associated with the compatibility of their work with family needs (Mortimer, Finch, & Maruyama, 1988).

Gender differences in job satisfaction may be based on different socialization experiences of men and women (Mortimer et al., 1988). For career counselors, in particular, it is instructive to note that ". . .if women's work orientations are substantially affected by family variables such as [husband's attitude or presence of preschool-age children], it might be the case that women's job satisfaction is less responsive than that of men to important features of work like autonomy and extrinsic rewards" (Mortimer et al., 1988, p. 113). Additionally, the fact that women typically select careers below their aptitude and not necessarily in accordance with their interests (Fitzgerald & Crites, 1980), may also contribute to the degree of satisfaction they derive from their employment.

Other gender differences are displayed in the work arena. For example, women place greater emphasis on work hours and commuting time between home and work (Quinn, Staines, & McCullough, 1974). Women report that primary job concerns involve work pressures, how tiring the work is, and employment hours, whereas men are more concerned with work characteristics associated with authority, such as leadership opportunities for upward mobility and decision-making opportunities (Miller, 1980).

Gender differences also have been found to characterize the job search strategies of adolescent men and women (Borman, 1988a, 1988b; Finch & Mortimer, 1985). Young men were far more likely than women to obtain a job through contact with a friend. Men were also more likely to stay in the job that they had found longer than women. Moreover, young men used fewer job search strategies than did young women, but had greater success. Male adolescents who stayed at their jobs tended to have families on whom they could rely for financial support and advice and to have close work relationships with a mentor/supervisor. That men and women have different experiences in the workplace is well documented. Partners can learn to play significant roles in supporting one another's career aspirations.

Ambivalence About Pursuing Successful Careers

Although both women and men recognize that self-fulfillment may be associated with a successful career, women often express ambivalence about their desire to pursue a career. For example, Gilligan (1982) cited one woman's attitude toward aborting her second pregnancy: "[Abortion] would be an acknowledgment to me that I am an ambitious person and that I want to have power and responsibility for others and that I want to have a life that extends from 9 to 5 every day and into the evenings and on weekends, because that is what power and responsibility mean. It means that my family would necessarily come second. There would be such an incredible conflict about which is tops, and I don't want that for myself'' (p. 97). Such attitudes reflect that women may be "caught in a matrix of irresolvable conflicts of ideology and social role. . . .The resulting internal conflict stems from her knowledge that success means performing as an 'ideal worker,' which, as a lifestyle, precludes the worker's ability to meet children's daily needs for care and affection" (Williams, 1990, p. 351).

Women's attitudes toward decision making and career pursuits represent a distinct pattern. Concern with family issues does not represent a lack of orientation to career achievement, but rather the complex and normal way that healthy adult women evaluate their various life roles. It is important that male partners not interpret women's focus on family issues as nonconcern with career achievement, but recognize it as a real conflict that men may not face as they focus on independent rewards and high achievement, rather than on affiliation with partners or children.

GENDER STEREOTYPES: SOME LABORATORY FINDINGS

Much of the research investigating gender stereotypes uses a common design. A group of evaluators, or raters (adults, students, managers, etc.), are presented with a packet that describes an individual stereotyped as either masculine or feminine. Then, evaluators are asked to rate the hypothetical individual on a variety of measures that may include attractiveness, competence, appropriateness for employment position, and so on. In studies of gender bias in hiring, the job may be described as traditional, progressive, or neutral, or may be selected as a stereotyped masculine job, stereotyped feminine job, or gender-neutral job. Research on gender stereotypes within a laboratory setting has yielded important information on commonly held gender stereotypes and how men and women are perceived differently. An important question, which is not easily addressed, is whether laboratory findings can be generalized to perceptions of men and women within the work force.

A significant concern for dual career couples is how gender issues affect their careers. Men and women differ in their attitudes toward male and female workers and supervisors, a finding that can have profound implications on women's upward mobility. Moreover, when making decisions about the interface of work and family issues, men and women use different sets of information as the basis for their decisions. For dual career couples, this may not only lead to an impasse in the decision-making process but to a variety of misunderstandings about the relative importance to each partner of either career achievement or family issues.

Gender Stereotypes in the Laboratory and Workplace

Women are judged as less competent than equally qualified men (see reviews in Arvey, 1979; Lott, 1987; Wallston & O'Leary, 1982); however, situational factors and characteristics of the raters or individuals being rated can affect the results. Hypothetical female job candidates are judged more favorably by mixed-gender groups in the presence of a female experimenter, whereas hypothetical male job applicants are judged more favorably by mixed-gender groups in the presence of a male experimenter (Etaugh, Houtler, & Ptasnik, 1988). Additionally, men were more influenced than women by the sex of the experimenter, so that they gave applicants higher ratings in a presence of a same-sex experimenter (Etaugh et al.). Although college students evaluated both women and men positively, they rated women more positively (Eagly, Mladinic, & Otto, 1991; Eagly & Mladinic, 1989). Whether these results are related to the positive valuation the authors gave to feminine traits, like "helpful, gentle, or kind," or whether attitudes toward women may parallel positive changes in the status of women, should be further explored.

Rosenwasser and Dean (1989) varied the sex and gender behaviors of hypothetical presidential candidates resulting in four candidate descriptions: "Masculine" female, "Feminine" female, "Masculine" male, or "Feminine" male. Both men and women reported that the "Masculine" and the male candidates would be better at dealing with crises like terrorism, whereas the "Feminine" and female candidates would be more competent at solving issues relating to domestic education. Both men and women thought men would be more likely to win the election.

Although women currently represent more than half of the work force, the fact that they earn only 70 cents to every dollar that men earn reflects the direct relationship between gender and earning power. Moreover, the recognized phenomenon of the glass ceiling continues to exist at many institutions and prevents women from moving into the top ranks of employment, also reflecting gender constraints in career opportunities.

Women may follow a different career path than men to achieve career success. The corporate model of achievement assumes that the primary goal of the employee's family is the worker's success. Therefore, for men being a family man is viewed as a positive sign, reflected by the fact that 95% of corporate executives are parents (cited in Schele, 1991). In contrast, for women, being a member of a family may be considered detrimental to career progress, reflected by the fact that only 30% of executive women are parents (cited in Schele). These observations indicate that women experience and receive profoundly negative messages about the possibility of pursuing family roles and being successful in their careers. Men, in contrast, draw different conclusions and receive different messages about work and family issues.

Attitudes Toward Male and Female Workers

In the 1970s few women with positions of power were in the workplace, and researchers found a generally negative attitude toward female managers by male managers and a negative evaluation of female job applicants by male personnel managers (Hartnett, 1978). In more recent studies, changes in attitudes toward female managers are apparent, and managers seem to evaluate applicants on merit rather than sex. Male and female middle and upper level managers are similar across traits like nurturance, succor, and aggressiveness; however, women seem to be greater risk takers and more independent than their male peers (Hatcher, 1991).

With regard to technical jobs, managers show no preference between male and female applicants (Gerdes & Garber, 1983). This finding may relate to the ambiguity of the job description and applicant-job fit, or the type of jobs investigated (Plake, Murphy-Berman, Derscheid, Gerber, Miller, Speth, & Tomes, 1987). With stereotypically masculine jobs like engineering, bias against hypothetical women applying for managerial positions is evident (Gerdes & Garber), whereas it is not apparent in studies with gender-neutral occupations like counseling psychology (Plake et al., 1987). Female students did not stereotype managerial positions; male students, however, were more likely to think that men possessed more attributes necessary for career success (Schein, Mueller, & Jacobson, 1989). Similarly, male undergraduate business majors expected women to be poorer managers and less knowledgeable, but to possess better interpersonal skills than men, whereas female students preferred male bosses (Frank, 1988). Women, in contrast to male college students, had lower expectations for their own performance in male-dominated occupations, but higher personal expectations for their performance in female-dominated occupations (Bridges, 1987, 1988). Men, however, had similar self-expectations across fields.

Researchers have reported different responses toward male and female employees in the workplace. Katz (1987), for example, had business students compare applicant fit in two hypothetical companies. One was stereotyped as progressive (women in positions of power, team management approach) and the other as traditional (only men in positions of power, management hierarchically organized). Student evaluators expected that women would perform less well than men and be less satisfied in the traditional environment. In contrast, women were viewed as fitting better than men in the progressive company. Despite these findings, a growing body of contemporary research suggests that gender stereotyping of job fit is decreasing (Stake & Rogers, 1989; Vodanovich & Kramer, 1989).

Perception of Women and Men in Laboratory Settings

In a laboratory setting, when performing a task with women, men were more likely to turn away, make negative comments, and not attend to the woman's ideas than when they were in a same-gender pair (Lott, 1987). In a much-cited study by Megargee (1969), which was partially replicated by Nyquist and Spence (1986), men and women were rated on dominance and then paired so that a high dominant individual was paired with a low dominant individual. Half of the groups were of the same sex, and half were of the opposite sex. Pairs were then asked to choose a leader. In the same-sex pair, the more dominant individual was chosen as a leader 70% of the time. In the mixed pairs, if the more dominant individual was male, he was chosen as the leader 90% of the time; if the more dominant individual was female, she was chosen as leader only 20% of the time. Exploration of these findings in Megargee's study suggested that when women were dominant, they decided who should be the leader, so that in the 80% of cases where they were not selected as leaders, they still pulled the strings for the pair's performance. Although Nyquist and Spence found the same results, they did not receive the same explanations as Megargee. Therefore, the implication of differences in leadership attribution in the mixed-sex pair remains unclear.

Some important derivative questions based on these findings are relevant for dual career couples. Are differences in behaviors seen in the lab also observed outside of the laboratory setting? What sorts of differences are found in the workplace and in expectations for performance in the workplace? Does knowing that someone is an expert override gender stereotypes? How do these stereotypes affect interactions of men and women within dual career couples? Do their gender-based expectations affect what they may offer or request from their significant others?

Within a laboratory setting, the only information an individual has about another performer is the person's sex, rather than any issues of ability (Durkin, 1987). Therefore, sex could routinely determine a set of expectations for the performer (Deaux & Kite, in press). In the "real world," individuals have information about the performer's and observer's social categories as well as the sex-typing of the tasks, both of which affect expectations about performance.

Different Perceptions

In both laboratory setups and in the real world, gender expectations and perceptions can influence performance. Therefore, the generally reported finding that women may be more easily influenced than men can affect how women are viewed and how their behaviors are interpreted. How people play games in same-sex and mixed-sex dyads has been particularly useful in highlighting differences in perception-related behaviors to members of the opposite sex. Findings on adults indicated that how people played games depended both on their purported ability and the sex of the competitor (Wyer & Malinowski, 1972). Boys were more competitive and girls more cooperative; however, in mixed-sex groups, boys became more cooperative and girls became more competitive (Maccoby & Jacklin, 1974).

Jacobson and Effertz (1974) compared reports on group interaction among four adult groups of three people: (1) all male, (2) all female, (3) two men with a female leader, and (4) two women with a male leader. All groups attempted to perform a difficult problem-solving task (and performed equally poorly), and then rated the leader and fellow group member. Results revealed that male leaders were rated more poorly than female leaders, and that female leaders rated female team members lower than male group members. Further data are required to evaluate whether this same pattern is found with men and women outside of the laboratory.

Perceptions of the nature of women and men differ. As cited earlier, a substantial literature has shown that women are thought to be more influenceable than men, as evident from the fact that they were more easily persuaded than men and were more conforming than men in group situations (Eagly & Carli, 1981). However, in studies on the ability to be influenced that were authored by women, sex differences disappeared, suggesting that gender differences in the conformity literature were strongly associated either with the sex of the investigator or other factors (Eagly & Carli). Type of subject, outcome, and research method can also affect the research findings (Becker, 1986). Related analysis of the association of conformity to occupational status revealed that when occupational status was controlled, there was no significant difference between men's ability to influence women and women's ability to influence men (Eagly & Wood, 1982; Eagly & Steffen, 1984). This suggests that findings of earlier studies may have confounded gender differences with assumed differences in occupational status of men and women. "Gender stereotypes, then, appear to be a relatively accurate reflection of one's experiences with men and women. If these experiences change so that the distribution of people into social roles becomes less sex-typed, we can expect the gender stereotypes that result from this distribution to become less pronounced" (Eagly & Wood, pp. 927–928).

Data presented earlier in the chapter indicated that women were more likely to underestimate their performance than men. Perhaps in areas where women do not have experience, they may behave with uncertainty, which is interpreted as their being easily influenced. Within the dual career couple, if a male partner were to interpret the woman's expression of uncertainty as the ability to be influenced, and her agreement with his perspective as her willingness to adhere to his perspective, the couple might operate under a principle of one-upmanship rather than equitability, where the man assumes the role of leader and the woman the follower. This could create serious barriers for healthy couple functioning.

DIFFERENCES ARE NOT IMMUTABLE

Although many gender differences exist, it does not mean that men or women cannot adopt behaviors characteristic of the opposite sex. Instrumental men can be supportive and nurturant fathers, and expressive women can fire an employee who performs poorly. Within the workplace and at home, it seems likely that individuals who can be sensitive to others and can take care of themselves will enjoy the richest repertoire of functional behaviors.

Knowledge Versus Capacity

Some gender differences in skills are robust and significant whereas others may be quite small (Anderson, 1987) or relate to experimental procedures (e.g., Eagly, 1986; Hyde, 1986). Both men and women may exhibit many behaviors typically associated with the opposite sex. "One of the most striking phenomena encountered in the study of psychological sex differences is that research generally fails to substantiate the sex differences that people perceive in everyday lives" (Eagly & Wood, 1982, p. 915).

These findings are particularly significant for dual-career couples. Many couples may believe that women are more nurturant. However, it may need to be pointed out to these couples that with a little practice men may be able to nurture just as effectively, and that not all women are equally capable or competent in nurturing roles. Moreover, men's different ways of nurturing, which may involve more rough-and-tumble play, are equally valid. For couples attempting to achieve couple equity, it is important to recognize that different style or knowledge does not represent lack of competence.

An important demonstration of the distinction between knowledge and capacity is available in the literature on science and math performance among children and adults. Gender differences in mathematics and science performance may be related to large gender differences in out-of-school participation in mathematics and science-related activities (Linn & Petersen, 1986) and to the different reinforcement offered to men and women by some teachers, school counselors, parents, and society (Parsons et al., 1982; Linn & Petersen). Also, boys' extracurricular activities, such as basketball (where scoring is by 2 points) or collecting and remembering baseball statistics, encourage greater comfort with number functions. Gender differences in attitudes and confidence with regard to mathematics are also evident among high school and college students and adult women (Hyde, Fennema, Ryan, Frost, & Hopp, 1990).

Gender differences also have been found with regard to the acquisition of scientific knowledge. Women are more likely to acquire information in the biological and health sciences, whereas men have more physical and earth science knowledge (Linn & Petersen, 1986). It is not that girls and women cannot reason scientifically in every domain, but that they lack the basic scientific knowledge essential to particular areas of scientific analysis (Linn & Petersen).

Women who have taken a variety of mathematics courses are more likely to subscribe to the career advantages associated with mathematics (Armstrong, 1979). Experience with mathematics and science increases achievement in these areas. Because educational opportunities and experiences have been shown to affect task performance, gender differences may be diminished by encouraging equal participation among men and women in these various domains. Equally significant is that lack of experience in math and science has important implications for career achievement among men and women. Girls begin to fall off in math performance by the end of high school (Chipman et al., 1985). Because so many college majors require some mathematical background, women without it will not be prepared to pursue majors in the natural science or social science areas, which are associated with greater occupational prestige and higher salaries.

Just as experience with scientific and mathematical problems affects performance in science and math, it is reasonable to expect that women's experiences in other domains can also affect their performance. Women may exhibit greater preferences for careers in the sciences, engineering, or high tech industries if they have had greater exposure to courses, toys, play, and learning experiences that allowed them to feel familiar, knowledgeable, and comfortable in these domains. Similarly, men's interest in children and in more nurturant professions like social work or nursing might also relate to experience and comfort. Creating cross-gender opportunities for learning would be well pursued in the future. For men and women in dual career couples to function effectively in both career and family roles, they must feel capable in both sets of roles. Partners may consciously or unconsciously undermine each other's ability to break out of gender role stereotypes and to allow the partner opportunities to practice a variety of behaviors. With a counselor's help, couples can plan opportunities for practicing broader gender roles.

CONCLUSIONS

Gender differences exist. The relevant question for counselors concerns the implications of those differences for individual and couple functioning. Gender differences may be separated into two categories: gender differences in skills and gender differences in styles. Gender differences related to skills have been demonstrated in a variety of areas. Experience, however, affects the ability of men and women to perform equally. Thus, when men and women have taken similar courses and have had similar exposure to nonclassroom learning experiences, differences are diminished.

Because of these differences and the fact that women tend to underrate their achievements and men overrate theirs, counselors might recommend and women may select careers other than science. In reality, research indicates that women who have similar experiences to those of men in science and math perform comparably with men (Holden, 1991). Therefore, experience directly affects gender differences in skills and performance.

Other skills characterized by gender differences may also be influenced by training and experience. Men and women may be expert in specific and different household responsibilities, child responsibilities, or business roles. Experience will affect their performance in each role. Counselors can assist dual career couples to offer one another the opportunity to gain experience at multiple roles.

What is interesting about the gender difference literature is how pervasive the reports of perceived gender differences are, even when no gender differences can be detected by researchers. Accordingly, researchers have begun to argue that reports of differences between men and women might be related to gender difference issues among the scientists conducting the study, rather than to meaningful differences between the men and women studied. Rather than focus on finding gender differences, a more productive plan might be to focus on situations that diminish gender differences. For example, there is little perception of difference in expectation of influenceability among career successful women and equally successful men with whom research participants are familiar. This suggests that expectations of gender differences may be related as much to the knowledge of the typical status of men and women in our society than to any real gender differences.

It is difficult to imagine that gender differences in style would affect individual performance negatively. Even within a corporation, as executives become more focused on management for quality and personal achievement, individual style becomes less relevant. Couples can also benefit by recognizing particular differences in style between men and women. Both male and female ways of perceiving and interacting with the world are valid and enrich couple life. Greater sensitivity to these differences as well as to differences in communication (see chapter 7) can be critical to couple functioning. A counseling goal might be to educate dual career couples about these differences, rather than working to homogenize male and female functioning. Thus, the style that men use in performing skills at work and at home and that women use at work and at home should be respected, because this diversity of style enhances and enriches both work and family environments.

Counselors can assist dual career couples by acknowledging the constraining impact that gender-stereotyped expectations can have on individual performance and on the way that men and women interact in dual career couples. Dual career couples' adherence to stereotyped gender role behaviors for the two partners may constrain the woman's ability to perform effectively in her career and the man to perform effectively in family roles. It is the job of the creative counselor to help clients expand their gender definitions and to make available to them new ways of behaving. Couples can also benefit from discussions about instrumental and expressive modes of functioning. Functioning well in career and family roles is most directly facilitated by the mastery of both instrumental and expressive aspects of gender identity.

Respecting differences in style between men and women while encouraging a goal of equity in skills critical to the couple relationship can result in balance within the dual career couple. The sophisticated counselor can achieve this goal by helping each couple achieve their own ideal balance as partners and as men and women.

3 Couple and Family Counseling

UNRESOLVED QUESTIONS RELATING To family and career balance can lead to marital tension or dissolution in dual career couples. Two general areas can create particular problems for the couple. First, marital tension may be expressed in overt ways, such as anger or resentment, and in more covert ways, like unavailability to the partner both psychologically and physically. These reactions diminish the couple's satisfaction with home life and may lead to dissatisfaction with their work lives as well. Second, dual career couples need to communicate effectively to reach a balance among their many competing career- and family-related demands. For example, both partners may be offered different relocation packages during their careers, or be expected to work late or on weekends on a regular basis. Unless couples can plan their work schedules together, there will be repeated conflicts between his needs, her needs, and family needs. This may require mastery of communication, negotiation, and empathic listening skills through counselor modeling and training. Even in well-functioning and well-meaning couples, the balance of responsibilities may be nonequitable because couples feel unable to discuss family and work issues directly. Negotiation and compromise may be critical to resolving differences between the distinct styles and standards of each partner.

This chapter reviews a variety of approaches to couple therapy and marriage and family counseling. Both the underlying theory and the methods of counseling are reviewed and analyzed. Examples of how methods from this literature can be used with dual career couples are presented. [1]

---

[1]The couple and marriage and family literature typically addresses couple issues in terms of marital relationships. Nonetheless, these concerns are equally applicable to long-term nonmarital couple commitments.

46

FAMILY SYSTEMS THEORY—OVERVIEW

Underlying family systems theory is the assumption that the family functions under the same laws as other systems. Systems try to maintain homeostasis or balance and attempt to reestablish this balance when disturbed. Similarly, families function as balanced systems that operate to maintain equilibrium. When the balance is disturbed, the family changes its way of functioning to reestablish homeostasis.

Families differ in the way they cope with environmental stresses and social strains, and how they maintain equilibrium between career and family. If the family's method of dealing with stress is effective, the family functions well. However, in dysfunctional families the inability to deal with stress becomes apparent as the family adopts counterproductive methods to cope with crisis situations and reestablish equilibrium. Because family and individual functioning are linked, when the family does not function effectively, one or more family members will exhibit psychosocial difficulties. Family-related problems that are addressed within the family context are solved more effectively. When these problems are addressed instead in individual therapy, outside the family context, the family "problem" cannot be resolved and the dysfunctionality will continue in the individual client or appear in another family member.

The goal of the family is to support both individual expression and membership in a functional family unit. Families support growth and development of their members, evolve rules concerning family interactions, and require flexibility in dealing with "normal" stresses throughout family life cycles, such as children's growing up and leaving home, or parents' aging. Each new demand may lead to familial stress, imbalance, and disequilibrium which, when properly addressed, will lead to positive growth in family functioning.

The family systems approach to family functioning is particularly relevant for dual career couples who may experience pronounced stress as they balance multiple roles and require flexibility to function effectively. If family equilibrium is based on equity and fairness, then when one partner changes his or her family or career roles, creating a systemic disequilibrium, family rules will reestablish couple/family homeostasis. This will result in a new, equitable way of functioning for all participants. If the balance is not based on equity and if one partner changes his or her roles, the couple may lack effective coping mechanisms and be unable to reestablish equilibrium, or may establish a new equilibrium again characterized by nonequity.

Family Stresses

The stresses families experience throughout their life spans may be differentiated into three crisis situations (Goldenberg & Goldenberg,

1980): *Acute situational stresses* are crises that all families experience during the family life cycle. These stresses include the death of family members, the birth of a baby, and relocation, and require immediate changes in family functioning. *Interpersonal stresses* involve the lack of harmony within the family and may be due to competition between career-minded partners, disagreements over money, or problems with children. *Intrapersonal stresses* are the conflicts that occur within an individual. These may be due to a variety of external concerns, including factors related to family of origin and current familial situations, and also include decisions about balancing family and career demands. Although no two families have identical ways of functioning, patterns of effective and ineffective interactions among family members are evident to the experienced family therapist.

Well-functioning families respect the individuality and autonomy of each family member. For example, Lewis, Beavers, Gossett, and Phillips (1976) assessed the functioning of ''healthy'' families and found that ''no single thread'' defined their interactions. Rather within the functional family, members were able to express thoughts and feelings and parents were able to function effectively as a subsystem. In other words, personal autonomy was respected and individuality and separateness among family members were tolerated (Goldenberg & Goldenberg, 1980). Moreover, family members expressed their own opinions comfortably even when this led to disagreements with other family members. Thus, negotiation and discussion rather than authoritarian control were the effective means of resolving family conflicts.

To counsel a family effectively, the ''rules'' of family behavior must be ascertained. Couples operate within a set of rules (also referred to as expectations or contracts) that define what they are willing to bring to the relationship and what they expect from their partners. Family rules are learned within the context of family interaction and are viewed as determining individual patterns of behavior, so that each person's behavior is associated with, and depends upon, the functioning of the rest of the family. These rules may be overt, clearly admitted and discussed, or covert, not admitted or known and not openly discussed.

Dual career couples can benefit by overt, agreed-upon family rules regarding employment and family responsibilities. Without rules, family responsibilities are performed haphazardly and families become overwhelmed by normal dual career couple responsibilities. Therefore, rules are necessary to determine who cooks and cleans, who takes care of unexpected household demands or a sick child, or who makes the kinds of preparations necessary for partners working late or traveling. When family rules are covert and when dual career couples have demanding lives both at home and at work, each partner operates with a different set of expectations about the family, leading to stress, disappointment, and dissatisfaction with the family. Thus, without articulating their assumptions about interdependent family roles, individuals may be disappointed when their significant others do not fulfill their expectations. An important goal of family therapy is for couples to verbalize these covert expectations as a first step in resolving their conflicts (e.g., Rice, 1979; Sager, 1976; Satir, 1972).

Families consist of subsystems that may be formed by age, sex, or interest (Minuchin, 1974), and fulfill many roles related to socialization and education. Family members may simultaneously belong to a variety of different subsystems within the family and learn different skills and possess different levels of power within each subsystem. Parental, spouse, and sibling subsystems are the most significant within the family (Minuchin & Fishman, 1981). Mother and daughter can also simultaneously form another subsystem within the family. Problems within the spouse or parental subsystem are associated with dysfunctionality that reverberates throughout the rest of the family system. Lack of respect for boundaries or distinctions between different subsystems can lead to stress that can result in intrafamilial dysfunctionality. For example, when the boundary between the spouse and parent-child subsystems is not distinct, each relationship suffers and the family does not function effectively, leading to opportunities for children to manipulate and control parents, rather than parents functioning in their powerful parental roles (Minuchin & Fishman, 1981).

Relationship difficulties between partners in dual career couples can arise from resentment over rules for balancing family and career roles, or dissatisfaction with rules about the priorities given to each partner's role. These difficulties can lead to problems in other interactions within the family system. If the couple lacks opportunities for nurturing the continual growth and development of their relationship, there may be a breakdown in the couple/parent subsystem that can greatly affect the partners and their family. When boundaries are clearly defined and rules are overt and supported by family members, both the family and its subsystems function effectively and interactions are healthy and provide support for individual growth and development.

The "how well" of family functioning is more important than the "how," underscoring the importance of the therapist's responding to family needs and not his or her own standards. The goal of therapy is to help families become better able to function within the possibilities that exist for them. For dual career couples this means that the goal is not to avoid conflict but to address conflict in productive ways that can lead to individual growth and development. Thus, counselors should work together with couples to set standards of family and career balance that feel fair to the couple and can be achieved.

Dysfunctional Patterns

A variety of communication and family subsystem difficulties characterize dysfunctional families. Families may communicate but may not accept responsibility for feelings or actions. Shaky parental coalitions are common, making it unclear where family power resides and permitting stereotyping of family members. In severely dysfunctional families, members tend to be chaotic and rigid and exhibit little interaction with the external world, demonstrating that change represents a difficult challenge for these families. When counselors who work with dual career couples encounter dysfunctional families, then couple issues must be addressed with a trained family therapist. The need for change may be extremely threatening for some families because standard patterns of behavior may preserve covert dysfunctionality within the family, and any attempts at change may threaten to expose hidden problems. Furthermore, lack of family flexibility can by itself cause stresses for family members trying to achieve change.

Family members communicate their support and emotions as well as dysfunctional patterns both verbally and nonverbally. Nonverbal messages may include facial expressions, body rigidity, tone of voice, and eye contact. Verbal communication may involve negative or impossible messages, such as double-bind messages, which contain two messages that are inherently contradictory but must both be addressed. It is impossible to respond to both messages because the truth of one message is dependent on the falseness of the other. As an example, a woman may return home from work looking extremely angry. When her husband asks her what is wrong, she claims to be quite happy. He believes both his perception and what his wife says. However, if she is not angry, his perception is wrong. If his perception is accurate, she is lying. Accepting one message means that the other message is not true, which results in a problematic, double-bind contradiction.

Communication in dysfunctional families can be constricted by family rules concerning the expression of family information. Only certain members may be permitted to offer opinions, and these opinions may be valid only when expressed in specific ways. Moreover, children can play special roles in dysfunctional families, articulating messages that parents cannot express, or having problems that deter parents from confronting aspects of their own problematic relations. One child carries the pathology of the dysfunctional family, and he or she along with other family members perpetuate that role to ensure that the real family problem is not expressed.

FEMINIST FAMILY THERAPY

A major goal of feminist psychology is to engender social change regarding how men and women are viewed. The family plays a critical role in this reformulation because family has traditionally been "women's domain" and because families are responsible for transmitting social norms. It is the goal of feminist family therapy to restructure contradictions between gender, power, family, and society (Goodrich et al., 1988).

Within this framework, feminist writing has cautioned that counselors who work with families must reexamine some of the basic assumptions of systems theory relating to how families are organized (Walters, Carter, Papp, & Silverstein, 1988). First, feminist therapists distinguished between role complementarity and role symmetry. Complementarity suggests that men and women have different domains, but power in the relationship resides with the man. In contrast, role symmetry indicates that both sexes are involved in instrumental and expressive roles, representing an egalitarian power model. Second, the traditional view of mature adults was that they would become autonomous (see also Gilligan, 1988). In fact, within a context of egalitarian power for men and women, the adult goal for development would be interdependence or "autonomy with connectedness." Third, systems theory assumes that family members play reciprocal roles within the family in maintaining family dysfunctionality. This, however, is true only when the family members have equal power. When family power is not egalitarian, it cannot be assumed that there is a reciprocal balance.

Within this context, feminist therapists like Walters et al. (1988) cautioned that therapy can be genderless only if the rules of the family system are genderless. For example, therapists may focus on balance of power in the family; however, this assumes that all members have equal access to family roles. When the woman chooses a role in response to one already chosen by or assigned by society to a man, the family balance cannot be egalitarian. These writers also encourage therapists to avoid blaming the mother for any child dysfunctionality.

Although many clinical case studies reflect deep respect for individual goals of men and women, therapists may not actively advocate gender-sensitive approaches in their counseling, which can undermine the effectiveness of treatment for both members of the couple. Walters et al. (1988) outlined a number of guidelines relevant to practicing more effective feminist family therapy:

1. Consider the impact that gender may have on the couple/family.
2. Recognize the limits of women's access to social and economic resources.
3. Understand the social constructs that constrain women's ability to direct their lives.
4. Address the implications of women's socialization to take the central role in family responsibility.

5. Evaluate the challenge for women who have children because children create a conflict between women's role as mother and other roles.
6. Consider the meaning of the fact that women typically derive power through their relationships with men.
7. Validate women's values of connectedness, nurturing, and emotionality.
8. Respect women's roles outside of marital and family roles.
9. Assume that interventions are not gender-free and will have different meaning for members of each sex.

For the dual career couple, a feminist perspective would mean valuing both home and career roles of both partners. Moreover, it could provide a framework for traditional couples to adopt more gender-fair methods of functioning. Although achieving egalitarian gender roles can require a great deal of work on the part of the therapist, the benefits to the partners with respect to increased opportunities for functioning would be well worth the time and effort.

PSYCHOTHERAPEUTIC TECHNIQUES

Basic to family therapy is the belief in the institution of marriage and the commitment to the positive value of a good family life.[2] Related to the positive value placed on marriage is the assumption that partners had a reason for choosing one another, that the strength of the couple is greater than either individual's strength, that both partners have overt and covert expectations of benefits and contributions to their relationship, that partnership survives only through the conscious decision of each member to remain together, and that because of individual resistance to change, couples who divorce and remarry often choose a reasonable facsimile of the first spouse and eventually have similar problems (Goldenberg & Goldenberg, 1980). The goal of family therapy is to develop a functionally appropriate framework so that these positive relational aspects can be expressed.

A particular difficulty for the dual career couple is the contradiction between this model of couple functioning and the corporate model of the ideal employee, which assumes that institutional needs take priority over couple concerns. In many corporations today, there is a growing concern

---

[2]These various therapists refer to the couple relationship of marriage. Therefore, I have used terms like husband, wife, and spouse in reviewing these diverse approaches. Again, the theories would be equally applicable to partners in a long-term nonmarital commitment.

with the impact of employee mental and physical health on productivity. Therefore, greater attention is being paid to the demands of work and other roles, including family roles (see chapter 10). It is still largely assumed, however, that reaching the executive suite requires single-minded devotion to corporate success.

The varied therapeutic approaches of five major couple/marriage and family therapists will be reviewed to benefit those counselors who work with dual career couples. This section presents the therapeutic approaches of Ackerman (1938, 1954, 1956a, 1956b, 1958, 1960, 1965, 1968, 1970a, 1970b; Ackerman & Behrens, 1974; Bloch & Simon, 1982), Minuchin (1974; Minuchin & Fishman, 1981), Papp (1983), Haley (1970, 1976), and Satir (1967a, 1967b, 1972; Satir, Stachowiak, & Taschman, 1975). Additionally, Rice's (1979) use of family therapy techniques in his work with dual career couples will be discussed. Although all these theories share some common ideas, they reflect differences in outlook, technique, and the role of the therapist. In Table 3.1 many differences and similarities among these theories are outlined.

Ackerman

Nathan Ackerman (1938, 1954, 1956a, 1956b, 1958, 1960, 1965, 1968, 1970a, 1970b) was one of the founders of the contemporary family therapy movement. He explored the inclusion of the family in therapy because he found that it was not unusual in individual therapy for a person to improve and then for others in the family to get worse. Individual therapy had not solved the family pathology. Therefore, he developed new techniques for therapy that were problem-oriented, not technique-oriented, and that were directed to assist the individual within the context of the family.

The basic function of the family is related to security, child raising, socialization, and the development of the partners as a couple and as individuals. Family functions are sexual, reproductive, social, economic, and educational. Stability of the family is a function of the emotional interaction between members. Because family members are interdependent, problems in one family member result in the dysfunctionality of other members.

To understand family behavior, several issues need to be considered and assessed, including the integration of members into the family, the interrelationship and interdependence of family members, and the impact of adaptation in one family role to functioning in another family role. Family roles are interdependent and reciprocal, and each family member can take on multiple roles simultaneously. Moreover, each family member affects family functioning, and overall family functioning affects the well-being of each family member.

TABLE 3.1

Summary of Differences Among Couple/Marriage and Family Therapeutic Approaches

Therapist	Role of Therapist	Role of Family	Dysfunctionality	Therapeutic Intervention
Ackerman	1. Reorganize, reeducate, and resolve couple conflicts 2. Induce change via diagnostic plan 3. Act as participant/observer	1. Security, child raising, couple development, socialization of children	1. Family conflicts 2. Failure of complementarity	1. Use psychoanalytic techniques 2. Assess family history 3. Clearly delineate roles
Minuchin	1. Join the family 2. Understand reality they experience 3. Develop with family way of functioning	1. Define interaction between family and outside world 2. Define boundaries and space between family subgroups 3. Adults model appropriate behaviors for children	1. Lack of adherence to family structure 2. Crossing of boundaries between subsystems	1. Realign family organization to produce change and ultimately achieve appropriate structural alignment within family
Papp	1. Define meaning of change for family 2. Regulate rate of change 3. Connect symptom with dysfunctional behavior	1. Create significant interrelationships among family members 2. Develop functional system where the whole is greater than the individual parts	1. Ineffective responses to stress 2. Identified patient presents symptoms	1. Identify family themes 2. Use cotherapeutic group 3. Direct intervention using logic and advice

Haley	1. Solve the problem client presents 2. Increase problem-solving possibilities for approaching family 3. Therapist does not reveal hypotheses about family dysfunctionality to client	1. Develop effective system of communication 2. Develop functional hierarchies of power within family	1. Symptom protects other family members 2. Inappropriate hierarchies within family	1. Give directions for change 2. Reassert family rules 3. Reestablish appropriate family hierarchy
Satir	1. Model and foster effective communication 2. Evaluate receptiveness of family to change 3. Assess congruence between verbal and nonverbal communication	1. Model effective means of communication 2. Provide positive support to family members	1. Poor communication 2. Lack of accurate perception of self and others	1. Model good communication 2. Reinterpret negative in positive terms
Rice	1. Help partners verbalize and achieve goals 2. Make marriage contract and expectations overt 3. Point out positive benefits of change	1. Establish equity 2. Manage time and organize family functions	1. Competition between partners 2. Power struggle 3. Lack of support structures	1. Use psychodynamic methods involving historical perspective 2. Discuss marital contract 3. Model communication, negotiation, and empathic listening

Family therapy is designed to affect family relationships directly rather than to change family interactions indirectly, as in classical psychotherapy. By developing rapport with the couple, the therapist ''catalyzes'' conflicts, stimulates new methods of coping within the family, and exposes the ''real context of the conflict'' within the family, which leads to the dissolution of barriers and obstacles to conflict resolution. This enlightens marital partners about their problems, and stimulates the partners' ability to empathize and communicate with one another and develop essential problem-solving skills. Another aspect of the reciprocal interplay of the family and the individual is the fact that individuals derive support from the family for growth and development while the family relies on individual members for continuity and functioning. The nature of this relationship between the family and the individual varies both as the family group progresses through developmental stages and as the individual matures. Family therapy is therefore oriented to the different needs of the family and its individual members at different stages of the life cycle. A primary goal of the family is to deal effectively with conflict within a context of shared family experiences and normal family functioning. When the family's ability to deal with conflict is impaired, the family's ability to grow and develop is also affected.

In the course of therapy, the family's emotional life is expanded and the perceptions of family relationships are altered. These changes lead to new levels of family intimacy, sharing, support, and identity, which enhance the possibility of growth in family interrelations. The job of the therapist is to simulate closeness and sharing by challenging and questioning conflicts and disassociation within the family. Moreover, the therapist makes the family aware of new ways to share identity and form alignments, and assesses the family's resources for developing effective solutions to conflicts.

Understanding both the history of the couple and their individual past within their families of origin is necessary to comprehend current marital crisis. Therapeutic processes involve verbal and nonverbal methods to challenge unrealistic family and individual beliefs. Because symptoms within the family are functions of unresolved family conflicts, the therapist moves the symptom from the individual to the family arena, where conflicts may be resolved.

When family members can delineate their roles, relationships become smoother and more meaningful. Reeducation, reorganization of communication, and resolution of conflicts are associated with family well-functioning and the opportunity for change and growth within the family. Thus, the therapist helps family members to understand the working dynamics of the family and to develop new skills in conflict resolution and familial functioning.

Many elements of Ackerman's theory are directly related to some dual career couple issues that will be discussed throughout this book. His perspective on the interdependence of individual, couple, and family functioning is comprehensive. Partners take on many roles, and each role affects all other aspects of family functioning. For dual career couples, this relates to overlapping demands and responsibilities of each partner within family and career domains. Ackerman views creative conflict resolution as a goal of family well-functioning. Both this idea and the notion of recasting conflict as a problem to be solved are essential to growth in the dual career couple and will be discussed extensively in chapter 8.

Minuchin

Transcripts of Minuchin's therapy sessions read like novels, and his technique is colorful, spontaneous, and flexible. Minuchin argued for mastering technique so well that the therapist can transcend technique and function spontaneously in each therapy session. Family therapy requires the ability ". . .to join a family, experiencing reality as the family members experience it, and becoming involved in the repeated interactions that form the family structure and shape the way people think and behave. The goal of the therapist is to become an agent of change who works within the constraints of the family system intervening in ways that are possible only with this particular family to produce a different, more productive way of living" (Minuchin & Fishman, 1981, p. 2).

Families may initially resist change. When therapists are able to enter into the client's family context, they can agitate for change in a way that is tolerable to the family. Although Minuchin's success with his methods is legendary, it is difficult to imagine all therapists having the capacity to put themselves within a particular family framework. In the therapeutic setting, therapists build common ground with client-families, but leave space to join and distance themselves from the family as necessary. When therapists join the family, they participate in family experiences and emotions along with family members. Joining the family, however, requires that therapists know their own resources and limitations. As therapists accommodate to the family, they also expect the family to accommodate to them. By challenging dysfunctional behaviors, therapists give families confidence that change can occur.

Minuchin's work is distinguished by his deep respect for each client-family and its individual members. Every family has something positive to offer its members and every member possesses unique potential because of his or her specialness. Therapists assist families and individual members in expressing that potential.

A "holon" refers to the unit of intervention in family therapy. The holon may be an individual, the family, or the community, and is simultaneously a whole and also a part of some nonconflicting larger entity. Each holon strives for independence as a unit and affiliation with the larger system of which it is a subunit. At the time of couple formation, the spouse holon, whether it consists of legally bound individuals or two mutually committed partners, requires that each partner give up some of his or her individuality to belong to the new system. Within the new couple transactional patterns develop, and, eventually, any deviation from these accustomed transactions will lead to a sense of disappointment or betrayal. The spouse holon also develops boundaries while establishing psychological and physical space for the partners and warding off intrusion by friends and other family members. Minuchin views these boundaries as ". . .one of the most important aspects of the viability of the family structure."

Ideally the spouse subsystem offers a basis for dealing with the external world and perhaps a way of personal protection from external stressors. Individuals must also develop independent identities. When spouses cannot incorporate independent external experiences into their subsystem or cannot achieve diversified self-expression when alone, the spouse holon becomes impoverished and dysfunctional and cannot provide a source of growth to the couple. Dysfunctions within the spouse holon are evident in family problems.

The parental holon involves socializing children, educating them about authority, informing them about how their needs are met, and training them in effective communication, negotiation, and rules concerning appropriate and inappropriate family interactions. Parents model interactions and affective behavior for their children, and wide variations in parental holons are typical. The parental holon must be flexible so that it can change as children develop and their abilities for mastery and self-control evolve. In the parental holon, parents have rights and duties to make decisions to protect the total family system and to guard the privacy of the spouse holon.

Problems in the parental holon are often solved by trial and error, and the dynamics of effective solutions change throughout family life stages. Difficulties in dealing with common family problems represent a cue for the therapist that family members may be part of a dysfunctional unit, and underscore the need for the family to develop problem-solving techniques. Dysfunctional parental holons are associated with various children's problems. Deviant parental models can affect the child's values and expectations. Moreover, children can be scapegoated or drawn into alliances with one spouse against the other.

Couple formation involves defining the boundaries between couples and the outside world. Questions arise about how partners will relate to members of their families of origin, friends, coworkers, or neighbors. To achieve intimacy, a functional balance between external contacts and couple privacy must be reached. Individual differences in expectations, emotional expression, and relationships with other adults must be negotiated. Also, couples must decide on rules for closeness, responsibilities, and cooperation, and also evolve common values, learn to listen to each other, and decide how to handle their differences and deal with conflict. Minuchin considers couple formation as a complex transition from functioning as an individual to functioning as part of a new couple unit. Therapy may help couples to appreciate the value of this complementarity.

Couples with children. Immediately upon the child's birth, new holons of parental, mother-child, and father-child subsystems are formed. Reorganization and redefinition of the spouse holon is required so that parents can care for the dependent newborn with his or her own personality. Couples must establish new definitions to preserve their relationship but expand their family boundaries to include their child. Parents must negotiate new relationships with neighbors, friends, and extended family. Moreover, as the child grows, rules must be established that give parents space together, yet maintain safety and parental authority. As additional children are born, family patterns and subsystems are renegotiated.

Minuchin's approach to family therapy has significant implications for dual career couples. First, Minuchin underscores the close connection between the individual and the family. Positive family relations are viewed as integral to individual functioning. Within dual career couples, partners' goals should not be viewed as antagonistic but rather should result from couple negotiation so that they are mutually respected and supported (see chapter 7). When the family functions well, individual members can express their greatest potential. Second, conflicts between partners should be viewed as problems to be solved that will strengthen the integrity of couple functioning. Third, Minuchin views flexibility as a key to the family's accommodating to change. Dual career couples who can function flexibly are the most successful at supporting partners' various career and family roles. Fourth, Minuchin underscores the importance of the couple's establishing boundaries between themselves and the outside world. For dual career couples, an important boundary may be the couple's ability to separate themselves from the demands of work. Using cellular phones and beepers during nonbusiness hours may compete with couple well-functioning. Instead, couples sometimes need impermeable boundaries to ensure couple intimacy. Fifth, Minuchin also underscores that couples must be able to negotiate for roles and responsibilities within the family and appreciate rules established by the family. Negotiation (chapter 7) is an essential skill that dual career couples must master to function effectively.

Papp

According to Peggy Papp (1983), the family functions as a highly interrelated system in which the whole is greater than the sum of its parts and which is regulated by feedback loops. Thus, during therapy, individual functioning can be understood only in the context of the entire family, and change in any part of the family results in changes throughout the family system. Although therapists may advocate change in the family, they must also ensure that change occurs at a pace the family can accept. This means that advocating change is not a solution but rather represents a dilemma for the therapist. If the symptom is eliminated, what will replace it to regulate the family system? Only by ensuring that the family is prepared to change can the therapist support altered patterns of family behavior.

In the course of the family life cycle, families are exposed to many sources of stress. Families may manifest a variety of behaviors in an attempt to balance unacceptable stresses. Some behaviors may have adaptive value; however, families may also adopt dysfunctional patterns in response to stress. It is the job of the therapist to identify problems within the family and change dysfunctional, stress-related patterns of interaction.

Rules governing the family are defined by members' many intersecting beliefs. Dysfunctional rules involve family themes, or a "specifically emotionally laden issue around which there is recurring conflict" (Papp, 1983, p. 14). When partners become disenchanted with each others' way of enacting a theme, they may turn elsewhere for a solution. A child, for example, may then occupy the position formerly held by the partner, a sign of dysfunctionality in the family. Therapists deduce family themes by listening for metaphorical language, tracking behavioral sequences, and picking up key attitudinal statements, but they cannot assess themes by direct questioning. Once they recognize family themes, therapists form hypotheses about family symptoms and the effect of change in the family system.

With some problems, direct interventions, including logical explanations and rational advice aimed at altering the family's rules and roles, may be effective. Therapists can work with clients to train them in effective, open communication, in controlling children, or in managing family life. In addressing complex cases, Papp employs more complex approaches to therapy. One technique involves a partnership between the therapist and a cotherapeutic group, called the consultation group, that watches the session from behind a one-way mirror. (A single cotherapist in the consultation room may be used instead of the cotherapeutic group.) This group provides commentary to the therapist on the course of therapy. The consultation group is preoccupied with change and comments on how change will occur, what its consequences will be, which family members will be affected, and what the alternatives to change are.

Messages from the consultation group are sent into the therapy room. The therapist then decides how to use the content of the messages to create the strongest impact on individual family members and the course of family therapy. The group can be used "to support, confront, confuse, challenge, or provoke the family," and the therapist can support or oppose the group's message.

An essential way to use the group is as part of a therapeutic triangle where there is a planned conflict between the therapist and the group. The therapist encourages the family to change, whereas the group warns the therapist about the dangers of change for the family system and underscores who or what subsystem is the antagonist of change. The therapist regulates change within the family by agreeing or disagreeing with the group.

Two particular aspects of Papp's therapeutic program are relevant to dual career couples. First, Papp's notion of themes relates to the recurring maladaptive behavior patterns and areas of conflict characteristic of some interactions within couples. Such themes may involve financial issues, career-career balance, household responsibilities, or other concerns. Only when couples master skills related to communication, negotiation, and conflict resolution can they begin to address and resolve these themes. Second, change leads to a behavioral vacuum that may result in a new dysfunctional pattern of behavior. Counselors can assist dual career couples in resolving partner conflict and planning creatively for change. Additionally, follow-up with the couple can ensure that creative approaches that change dysfunctional couple patterns and solve problematic couple themes do not result in new couple or family problems.

Haley

From the perspective of Jay Haley (1970, 1976), families face a variety of adjustment periods throughout life. Early in their marriages husbands and wives must develop ways of separating from their parents. When children are born, partners extend the couple dyad into a family triad. Thus, flexibility is the necessary hallmark in a well-functioning relationship. Families are characterized by hierarchical structures and rules governing who is primary and secondary in status and power. When family subsystems are organized within defined hierarchies and when executive subsystems are in control, the result is autonomy, responsibility, and cooperation. Symptoms, however, result when this hierarchical structure is not clearly defined and family members are not sure about who is their peer and who is their superior. Dysfunctional confusion can also result from coalitions between members at different levels of the hierarchy and may lead to a power struggle within the family. The therapist's job is to reestablish hierarchical family power structures within the family context.

Families typically come to therapy with one member of the family as the identified patient. In fact, the symptom is carried by this one person to protect the other family members and is maintained by ineffective family organization. Haley sees members of the family together because he believes that interviewing individual family members is like functioning in the dark. Only when family members are brought together can they learn how to differentiate themselves from the family successfully. Therapists can solve client problems only within the context of the family because relationship problems are viewed differently when partners are seen individually or conjointly. By seeing an entire family initially, therapists can grasp problems and perpetuating social conditions. Couples often cannot see how they elicit and respond to each other's behaviors; instead, they see behaviors out of context. For example, individuals may report that their partners criticize them with no apparent reason. In fact, the "nonoffending" partner may use a variety of nonverbal signals that elicit the other partner's behavior. Neither partner's behavior is correct, and both sets of behaviors would need to be addressed in therapy.

Therapeutic change occurs in sequential steps. Initially, behaviors that maintain problems are identified. Next, the goal for therapy is specified. Then, change proceeds by a series of steps that transform family dysfunctionality into resolvable problems. The job of the therapist is to help solve clients' problems by initiating, planning, and expediting appropriate changes during the course of effective counseling.

Therapists use spontaneity and flexibility as part of their therapeutic approach. Intervention highlights the family problem and relationships that need to be changed. Problems must be specified precisely before they can be solved. Therefore, psychodynamic language or terms like "low self-esteem" or "unhappiness" are not used. A well-defined problem, like a child who will not go to school or a husband who does not participate at home, is identified, and clear therapeutic goals are specified.

Successful therapy, according to Haley, involves changing the way that families communicate. Change within the family therapy context can result in positive change for all members when it occurs under the supervision of a therapist who sees the family through a period of stabilization and accommodation. In contrast, change in a single family member can lead to disastrous consequences for the family. Therapists help clients develop alternate modes of relational interactions so that symptoms can be abandoned. Therapists are attuned to how family members speak about themselves and other family members and how attentive each individual is to the statements of other family members. In these statements, individuals provide both overt and covert messages concerning family interactions and the presenting problem.

An important therapeutic task is giving directives. The therapist encourages the family to adhere to directives by underscoring the positive gains for each family member. Directives support the relationship between therapist and family by making families think about the therapist between sessions, thereby helping to stimulate change. Client responses to directives provide important information for the therapist. Directives may involve asking a husband to do something special for his wife and asking the wife to be gracious in her reception of it. This encourages the husband to begin something new in the relationship and to think about the wife and her needs and desires as he decides to do something unique for her.

Like Ackerman, Haley focuses on couple dysfunctionality as a problem to be solved. For dual career couples, this is a productive approach to conflict, especially because their problem-solving skills may already be well developed through a variety of work-related experiences. For example, by listening to and observing couple behaviors, a counselor may highlight a variety of aspects of the couple relationship the clients have not yet verbalized. Couples can also reenact particular conflict situations, and counselors can prescribe specific behaviors to encourage alternate patterns of behavior and to further develop positive aspects of the relationship. Effective couple communication is the critical aspect for dual career couple functioning. As Haley indicates, no change can occur without the couple's ability to communicate effectively. Moreover, clear communication is a prerequisite for assessing the impact of change on the couple relationship (see chapter 7). Identifying the significance of change for the couple and training couples in negotiation skills are critical to ensuring that these changes will be implemented and will lead to productive couple growth.

Satir

According to Virginia Satir (1967a, 1967b, 1972, 1975a, 1975b, 1975c; Satir, Stachowiack, & Taschman, 1975; Stachowiak, 1975a, 1975b, 1975c; Taschman, 1975), the family is a system that constantly changes, sometimes slowly, sometimes quickly, as it attempts to maintain homeostasis. Because of the balance in the family system, changing one element of the system will affect all constituent parts. Each individual in the couple must learn to process the continually changing environmental input so that he or she can address problems openly. Satir does not subscribe to a democratic model of the family, believing instead that families need leaders to direct decision making. Functional families are more comfortable expressing direct, open conflict and both positive and negative emotions. Moreover, well-functioning families can achieve a significant structural goal by helping family members develop self-esteem and self-worth. Because partners of the couple are the ''architects'' of the family, any problems they experience have repercussions throughout the entire family. During family therapy, family members are treated "conjointly," or together, using transactional communication techniques rather than discussion of thoughts and feelings.

Satir focused on four critical issues that distinguish functional and dysfunctional families. First, functional families can use their time effectively for family tasks like decision making. There is also a balance between work or task effort and family members' social and emotional needs. Maladaptive families have an imbalance of attention to task and emotional needs. Second, family leadership is important to the functioning of the family. A matriarchal or patriarchal structure is necessary for effective family functioning, so that one parent operates as leader and the other partner and family members can cooperate with that role. In adaptive families, different members take on leadership roles at different times. Maladaptive families are characterized as being autocratic or inept and have no leader. Third, the family must support expression of differences in a way that can be discussed and resolved. The critical issue for the family is not how much conflict is expressed but how the family supports and reacts to conflict. Fourth, clarity of communication also distinguishes functional and dysfunctional families. In functional families clear communication is encouraged and supported. Members of dysfunctional families often communicate with no one, making speeches instead of speaking to one another.

Because the way people communicate is a reliable indicator of their interpersonal functioning, the goal of the therapist is to foster communication between partners as a prerequisite for individual growth and development. *Clear* communication is necessary for effective interactions. When words become abstract, communication becomes obscure. Even nonverbal information can be used to bolster clear messages.

Family growth is related to individuals' ability to alter ineffective ways of communicating. When family members can communicate congruently, they recognize that all feelings are valid and may be expressed. Thus, a further goal of effective communication involves learning to get in touch with how people look and sound when they speak to one another. Effective functioning means that the individual recognizes the vast repertoire of behavioral options available and is not constricted by a single way of doing things. Each family member learns to recognize differences among individuals as the therapist encourages each person to speak for him- or herself, accept differences in opinions and perceptions of the same situation, and say what he or she feels, thinks, and sees. Individual capacity for change is related to the skill of the therapist. Therefore, the job of the therapist is to train clients in new ways of feeling and thinking. Partners must learn how to assert their own thoughts and feelings while paying attention to each other's thoughts and feelings. The result is clear communication—characterized by direct requests and supportive communication. Poor communication is associated with covert requests, failed expectations, accusations, and recriminations. Partners in dysfunctional couples suffer from low self-esteem, which derives from relationship difficulties in their families of origin. Couple problems develop when individuals focus on what they get (which leads to failed expectations) rather than what they can give to the relationship.

Therapists act as resources and models of communication for the family. Their clarity of communication and ability to reveal themselves may be the first experience the family has had in clear communication. By using congruent verbal and nonverbal communication, therapists can exemplify and teach clients how to behave. Developing such communication skills takes time, so that lessons should be repeated and conclusions explained. Because the goal of couple therapy is to communicate directly, recognize the boundaries between self and others, and ask clear questions and make clear statements, ". . .treatment is completed when everyone in the therapy setting can use the first person 'I' followed by an active verb and ending with a direct object" (Satir, 1967a, p. 177). In addition, successful therapy, according to Satir, is related to family members' ability to handle "the presence of differentness" in planning for family responses to change. In a functional family there is congruence between what people say and how they look.

Satir used her personal experience to understand client needs more effectively. If the other person backed away, she reflected on whether she was sending a double-level message, where what she said and what she was projecting were different, in order to explain what made the other person draw back. Recognizing the significance of self-reflection, Satir advocated the use of videotape as an essential therapeutic tool for helping people see themselves as others do.

Therapists create a setting where people feel secure in taking the risk of looking at themselves and their actions objectively. Because the therapist requests and responds to information in a straight, nonjudgmental way and offers statements that reflect the positive values of family, clients develop self-esteem. Family members are encouraged to do things that bring pleasure to one another and set effective rules for family interactions to foster healthy functioning and self-esteem at home.

Satir's focus on communication parallels the focus of this book on the need for good communication skills within dual career couples. Clear expression of individual needs is prerequisite to the couples' effective functioning. Counselors can assist clients in reaching a high level of mutual trust, which stimulates comfortable discussion about goals and values. Satir's focus on verbal and nonverbal aspects of communication is critical for achieving meaningful couple communication (see chapter 7). Just as therapists can encourage positive self-esteem through communication skills, dual career couples can foster their own healthy functioning by using direct, supportive statements about positive regard for a partner to foster that individual's self-esteem. Satir's techniques for developing listening and speaking skills and using videotapes to develop congruence between verbal and nonverbal messages can be helpful for counselors.

Rice

David Rice (1979) views the establishment of equity as the guiding principle for marriage and believes that "the achievement of a perceived equitable relationship is enhanced if the individuals manifest flexibility and relative freedom from the constraints of gender-role prescribed behaviors" (p. 103). Most theories about couple and family therapies focus on relationships between family members, but do not evaluate the impact of career roles on family functioning. Recently, family counselors have begun to advocate the recognition of the interdependence of work and family life (e.g., Ulrich & Dunne, 1986). Rice's approach is unique because he applies psychodynamic techniques directly to the conflicts and stresses of dual career couples and includes discussion of the interdependence of family and career roles in the application of his therapeutic techniques.

The dimension of couple equity changes over the family life cycle as family and individual parameters evolve. Effective functioning among dual career couples is characterized by couple equity, or the expectation that responsibilities balance over time. According to Rice, if couples perceive that there is nonequity, they will attempt to re-achieve equity through changes in one partner's behavior, or try to achieve psychological equity through distorting reality and perceiving a nonequitable task distribution as fair.

Dual career couples have different marital structures than more traditional families. Rather than their roles being complementary, dual career couples have overlapping roles. Responsibilities within each of these roles must be negotiated and addressed so that couples can establish rules about caring for children, managing family and personal time, and handling relationships with other people. Dual career couples may experience particular conflicts when they have children because they have few role models for fulfilling parent and career roles simultaneously. Planning, discussion, and negotiation are fundamental for establishing appropriate role expectations of dual career couples who become parents.

A particular problem Rice highlighted involves the relationship between members of dual career couples and other individuals. Dual career couples may experience less need for one another and for outside social contacts because of a high degree of association at their place of employment with like-minded people. Although this can be personally satisfying, couples may feel threatened by their partners' close relationships with coworkers. High involvement in work may indicate individual satisfaction or may mask specific problems. Open discussion about relationships, employment, and boundary issues within a counseling setting increases the couple's ability to balance family and career demands.

Benefits of the dual career couple lifestyle include enhanced intellectual partnership, increased income and resources, and a greater intellectual fulfillment and contentment of each partner. Roles and expectations are flexible within a healthy relationship. Partners in dual career couples may also experience stress associated with their lifestyles (see chapter 1), and particular developmental events in the family life cycle may lead to relationship stresses or problems. For example, partners may experience significant personal growth at different points in their relationships. Berman, Sacks, and Lief (1975) found that wives experienced significant growth in self-esteem a few years following professional training. Husbands at that point were focusing on the positive sense of establishing stability within the marriage. These distinct developmental patterns can result in couple conflict and strain as the partners address different priorities. Rigid adherence to socially approved gender role norms also constrains well-functioning in dual career couples.

Therapists form a therapeutic alignment with the couple. The initial agenda of therapy is related to helping couples address their past experiences so that they can learn to function effectively. Issues like money management, decision making, relationship to family of origin, and permeability of couple boundaries are relevant because the couple's current attitudes to each of these issues are associated with the way they addressed these concerns in their families of origin. Because the couple constructs boundaries to outsiders, partners may exhibit pronounced resistance to change, so that the therapist should be more active in counseling dual career couples than clients in individual therapy. Partners learn through therapy how to relate to one another with regard to negotiation, communication, empathic listening, and offering emotional support. The goal of therapy involves dissolving a family's defensive behaviors, which may make clients anxious until they learn new cognitive skills. Dual career couples may offer particular challenges to the therapist because of their unique demands and because behaviors for which they have been rewarded in the past may be counterproductive to the success of current therapy. To progress in counseling, dual career couples need to address cognitive issues, like working out a schedule, and affective issues, like not sidetracking the therapist by using verbal repartee, because dual career couples may use verbal means and intellectualization to resist therapy. Expressing affect and achieving change may be difficult for some dual career couples because tuning out affect and adhering to their own beliefs may have been highly rewarded in the past. Therapists can help couples develop ways for expressing personal needs and offer supportive verbal feedback.

Many family members behave as if they derive positive gains from family dysfunctionality. When therapists underscore the apparent positive benefits as well as the more realistic drawbacks of dysfunctional behavior, the family can be restructured in a more positive fashion. Later in therapy, partners might address issues of competition and power struggles and the difficulties of arranging a support structure. By discussing these issues, couples gain additional channels of communication as well as opportunities to redefine their relationship. In this way, therapists help partners develop trust and respect for each other. By focusing on earlier positive experiences within the couple, partners regain positive perspectives on their relationship.

Marital Contract

A marital contract, as viewed by Rice, represents both the verbalized and nonverbalized expectations about the relationship and is revised throughout the life cycle as partners mature. Within dual career couples, partners are motivated by goals of career success and personal and marital fulfillment. Clear communication about these expectations increases the satisfaction individuals can offer to partners and derive from their relationship. When the marital contract is not discussed, both partners may be dealing with different sets of unstated, but conflicting expectations and be frustrated by their inability to achieve important family and career goals within their relationship.

Dual career couples may benefit by developing an effective marital contract. The counselor can help partners elaborate the evolution of their expectations from the time of relationship formation to the present. A counseling goal involves developing a single, agreed-upon contract characterized by reciprocal equity and appropriateness to the couple's current demands and lifestyle. Issues relevant to the development of a marital contract include the husband's and wife's anticipation of support and reinforcement for occupational efforts and successes, expectations that partners will buffer external stresses and provide support, or the assumption that parenting roles will be shared. Because of the often stressful and highly demanding nature of their work, dual career couples may at times be unable to fulfill these expectations effectively, a condition that may also need to be addressed within the contract.

CONCLUSIONS

Several underlying themes emerge from the various theories of marriage/couple and family counseling that are directly related to relationship success. First, couples must establish boundaries between themselves and others in the outside world. Second, partners must be able to express emotional and physical supportiveness for each other. Third, good couple relationships depend on direct and sophisticated communication skills. Fourth, couple functioning depends not on the absence of conflict, but on the couple's mastery of effective conflict resolution techniques. Fifth, couple dysfunctionality can be viewed as a problem to be solved. Sixth, couple development depends on the process of change, which couples often resist and fear. Counselor-guided change can enhance the couple relationship.

Each of these aspects of couple functioning is of special relevance to dual career couples. Because of the pressures and demands of their lives, dual career couples are more vulnerable to stress and must master sophisticated communication and negotiation skills. These various skills enhance the couple relationship and lead to opportunities for individual and couple growth. Counselors play critical roles in training couples and encouraging them to incorporate these skills into their behavioral repertoire. By recognizing the interdependence of individual choices within the family system, counselors can assist couples in individual decision making and in anticipating the impact of independent decisions on the partner and on other parameters of family life.

4 Life-Span Development

CHANGES IN THE INDIVIDUAL, the couple relationship, and career progress are integral components of life-span development in dual career couples. Progressive stages in couple and family relationships are associated with different demands and opportunities for personal, couple, and career development. The development of mature cognitive and physical capabilities facilitates the successful resolution of psychosocial crises, which propels the individual toward more integrated stages of functioning. These maturational changes affect both the nature of the couple relationship and the productivity of the career-minded individual. Counselors can enlighten clients about various life-span changes typical of human growth and development at different ages, which offers dual career couples a perspective for appreciating their past and future challenges and achievements. Furthermore, the life-span approach can help couples appreciate the interdependence of developmental milestones and how different rates of development in one domain, or by one partner, may enhance or curtail other aspects of development.

Until recently, most of the literature concerning human growth and development dealt with how the innocent infant developed into the knowledgeable, informed adult. This literature described the minutiae of language acquisition (Callanan, 1989; Gleitman, Newport, & Gleitman, 1984; Nelson, Denninger, Bonvillian, Kaplan, & Bakes, 1983; Shatz, 1984), cognitive development (Kohlberg, 1975, 1976; Piaget, 1950, 1954, 1962, 1969, 1970; Smetna, 1989; Rose, Feldman, Wallace, & McCarton, 1989), social development (Ainsworth, Blehar, Waters, & Wall, 1978; Eckerman & Didow, 1989; Keller & Wood, 1989; Gavin & Furman, 1989; Matas, Arend, & Sroufe, 1978), and emotional development (Lewis, Stranger, & Sullivan, 1989; Thomas et al., 1970; Worobey & Blajda, 1989) from birth to early adolescence. There was an implicit assumption, however, that

70

nothing very interesting happened developmentally after adolescence, and perhaps that is true relative to the rapid rate of developmental changes characteristic of the person's first decade and a half of life. Nonetheless, researchers more recently have begun to consider that development is a lifelong process and that childhood growth and development represent one phase of an ongoing process of change that characterizes the human life span.

This chapter will address life-span development in three separate domains: individual development, couple development, and career development. Particular attention will be given to the reciprocal interplay between the individual and the environment across the life span.

INDIVIDUAL GROWTH AND DEVELOPMENT

A variety of studies has shown that the newborn infant is not a helpless individual, but rather is actively involved in shaping his or her earliest interactions. Although behavioral repertoires change over time, continuity in development can be seen by the baby's repeatedly using similar interactive forms in a variety of different situations (Sameroff, 1975). This interaction of human behavior and environmental conditions is found at all ages. People do not perform actions in isolation, rather they act in concert with their environments. When characteristic behavior patterns change in one member of a couple, the interaction with the other partner will be altered.

Two classic theories of human development were written by Erik Erikson (1950, 1968a, 1968b) and Jean Piaget (1950, 1954, 1962, 1969, 1970); both offer concrete lessons for dual career couples to help them better understand life-span development. Erikson dealt with development throughout the life span, whereas Piaget addressed development from birth through adolescence. Erikson offered one of the earliest discussions in the psychological literature on life-span development. Human progress from birth through old age, according to Erikson, consisted of eight stages of life, each with its own developmental challenges and crisis periods, encompassing potential for vulnerability as well as growth and strength. Erikson's psychosocial theory describes how individuals develop within a social environment and how the crises they experience within the social context affect their future development. Erikson's eight stages, and the crises and goals of each stage, are summarized in Table 4.1.

The main lesson to be learned from Erikson's theory is that crises are not necessarily negative events but rather critical junctures for developing psychosocial strength. Psychological dysfunction, according to Erikson, occurs when normal psychosocial crises are not properly resolved.

TABLE 4.1

Summary of Erikson's (1950, 1968a, 1968b) Eight Stages of Development, and the Crises and Goals of Each Stage

Stage	Age	Crisis Situation	Normal vs. Pathological Event	Psychosocial Strength
1	Infancy	Feeding	Trust vs. mistrust	Hope
2	Early childhood	Muscular control	Autonomy vs. shame	Doubt, willpower
3	Play age (preschool)	Comprehension	Initiative vs. guilt	Purpose
4	School age	School, tool use	Industry vs. inferiority	Competence
5	Adolescence	Integration of self-definition	Identity vs. identity confusion	Fidelity
6	Young adulthood	Affiliation	Intimacy vs. isolation	Love
7	Maturity	Communication to next generation	Generativity vs. stagnation	Care
8	Old age	Facing death	Integrity vs. despair	Wisdom

Erikson's theory highlights how early events can continue to affect individuals throughout the life span in both positive and negative ways. It is critical for dual career couples to recognize that poor resolution of current crises can continue to affect their relationship throughout its duration.

Erikson's theory is based on his perspective of men's psychosocial development (although the claim is made that it represents the way all people develop). Women may progress through development in a different order or experience different crises (Gilligan, 1982; Vannoy-Hiller & Philliber, 1989) than men. More research is needed to verify the significance and accuracy of different paths of psychological development for men and women.

Another approach to human growth and development is represented by the cognitive-developmental theories of Piaget (1950, 1954, 1962, 1969, 1970) and Kohlberg (1975, 1976), which address the impact of individual experience on cognitive development. Cognitive developmental theory created a revolution in the way that scientists and educators thought about the developing child, leading them to recognize that children are intelligent beings who affect and learn from their environments. These theories highlight how children's view of the world varies with their developmental stages.

Piaget and his students described the child's development from birth to adolescence, demonstrating that until individuals are in complete control of higher cognitive functioning, they view the world as magical and find it difficult to understand naturally occurring physical events. Piaget's theory has implications beyond the domain of child development, namely:

- People of all ages interact intelligently with their environments.
- The way that people think is affected by their views of how their actions affect their environments.
- What individuals, at different cognitive-developmental stages, conclude from observing the same event is different, because each observer perceives environmental events based on his or her previous experience. Thus, different past histories are associated with different levels of understanding.

Although the rapid rate of cognitive acquisition may decelerate after the teenage years, growth of specialized knowledge can continue throughout the life span as individuals change careers, participate in adult education, or pursue new domains of knowledge.

THEORETICAL MODELS OF LIFE-SPAN DEVELOPMENT

Familiarity with theories of life-span development can influence counselors' conclusions about how the environment affects individual development and how individual change and environmental factors interact. Clients' interactions with their environments affect their development and their ways of thinking. For dual career couples who are searching for new modes of interaction, discussions of the plasticity of human development offer hope that their relationship can also be altered.

Three perspectives of life-span development illustrate different ways that individuals interact with their environments (Vondracek, Lerner, & Schulenberg, 1986): (1) a mechanistic perspective, (2) an organismic perspective, and (3) a developmental-contextual perspective. Each is associated with different views on how change is possible in dual career couple relationships.

The mechanistic perspective assumes that individuals' responses to the environment differ with regard to the presence or absence of elements of the behavioral repertoire acquired according to the laws of conditioning.

In principle, one could predict the behavior of a person in any given environment by assessing his or her behavioral repertoire through applying known behavioral response laws (Reese & Overton, 1970). Individuals operate as a machine, receiving and transmitting signals, which leaves a trace or connection. Dual career couples' choices about career or family would be related to past reinforcement histories, meaning that adopting new lifestyles would be particularly difficult. Changes in reinforcement contingencies would be associated with new modes of behavior, so that relationship equity could be achieved only by changing the environmental responses to different behaviors of each partner. From this perspective, change among dual career couples would represent a major effort, because their family-of-origin environment and employment environment may support traditional family models.

The second perspective is the organismic model, which assumes that individuals interact actively with their environments. Environmental events can only accelerate or decelerate development, but cannot affect the ultimate sequence or quality of the developmental process. Development involves attributing meaning to one's behaviors and integrating new behaviors into old behavioral repertoires. Development is goal-directed, so that change brings individuals closer to a defined end state.

Development in dual career couples could involve changing existing gender beliefs relating to concerns like "maleness" or "femaleness," or changing the association between household responsibilities and its attribution of maleness or femaleness. Change in couples' beliefs and behaviors would occur through discussion and exposure to alternate role models. The organismic model highlights the interdependence of each partner's diverse roles in dual career couples.

The third perspective is the contextual model, which assumes that people function on multiple levels concurrently. Change occurs regularly because both the individual and the environment are constantly changing, sometimes at different levels or rates. Individuals are viewed as changing systems that interact with other changing systems, or with systems embedded in other systems (Jepsen, 1990). Transactions, which are interactions that elicit other multileveled interactions, lead to changes in individual system organization and represent psychological development. A focal point of interest in the contextual perspective is evaluating how the timing of significant events affects development. For dual career couples, because individuals function at multiple levels, change in role parameters for either partner would have repercussions for that partner's behavior in every other role. Moreover, couples should reevaluate balance across the life span because change occurs regularly, and accommodating to change-related development requires routine renegotiation of couple roles and balance.

Contemporary Theories

A number of theories have introduced novel approaches to understanding life-span development. Counselors may find these theories useful in their practice because identifying factors that affect individual growth and development can lead to greater understanding of the challenges dual career couples face. Moreover, one partner's career achievement may be slowed down because of the career demands of the other, or because of other couple or family demands. Knowledge of these theories can help counselors suggest interventions to address these interdependent responses. Also, by analyzing the dynamics of person/environment interactions across the life span, counselors can help couples anticipate the impact of career slowdowns or subsequent achievements on the dynamics of their relationship.

Two theories will be reviewed. The theory of Vondracek, Lerner, and Schulenberg (1986) has specific implications for interactions at different points throughout the life span. Bronfenbrenner's (1979) ecological theory addresses the interrelationship of the many roles individuals play at any particular time.

DEVELOPMENTAL CONTEXTUALISM—VONDRACEK, LERNER, & SCHULENBERG

Developmental contextualism is viewed as occurring within the context of individuals' interactions with their environments, resulting in changes in how individuals organize their environmental concepts. Additionally, transactions between individuals and the environment occur continually, so that the environmental context produces changes in individual behavior and is reciprocally affected by it. Therefore, individuals are characterized as having a great degree of control in both determining the environments they experience and in controlling their own future development within those environments.

Two other theoretical concepts, embeddedness and dynamic interaction, must be defined to understand life-span approach to development. Embeddedness refers to peoples' abilities to function at multiple levels at any one time. For example, an adult can experience events on biological, psychological, interpersonal, work-related, and community-related levels simultaneously. In turn, these levels may be either developmental or nondevelopmental phenomena, and may affect and be affected by other levels of functioning. Individual plasticity and the dynamic interaction of individuals and environment at multiple levels of functioning are associated with individual change, which can occur at any time throughout the life span. It is this dynamic interaction, rather than a single developmental factor, that explains outcome variables.

Three implications of developmental contextualism are relevant for dual career couples. First, because of the plasticity of human functioning, the nature of the relationship between partners in dual career couples can change at any time. Second, career choices of one partner can affect career and other roles of the other partner. Third, partners have multiple ways to achieve career, family, and personal goals because individuals experience dynamic interactions and function on multiple levels. Each of these theoretical implications is important for counseling interventions with dual career couples.

PERSON-ENVIRONMENT INTERACTION—BRONFENBRENNER

Bronfenbrenner's (1979) theory of person-environment interaction focuses on the individual in his or her ecological environment, defined as a series of interconnected systems. These systems are (1) the *microsystem*, the system containing the developing individual, (2) the *mesosystem*, the interrelationships among different microsystems, (3) the *exosystem*, systems that may affect the developing individual but remain external, and (4) the *macrosystem*, those cultural belief systems that are evident in the other subsystems (see example in Table 4.2).

These hypothesized subsystems are interconnected and interactive. During development each system changes, and the system's modifiability is transformed. Individuals retain their ability to change as they remain part of each of these interacting systems. Thus, individual change affects each system just as systemic or global transformation affects the individual.

With regard to dual career couples, Bronfenbrenner's theory underscores the ability of individuals to be involved in overlapping roles simultaneously. Because these roles are interconnected, they directly affect

TABLE 4.2

An Example of How the Child May Simultaneously Be Involved in Various Subsystems According to Bronfenbrenner's (1979) Theory

Ecological Environment	Subsystem
Family and school	Microsystem
School and home	Mesosystem
Parent's workplace and volunteer activities	Exosystem
Stereotyped beliefs about parental roles or child labor laws	Macrosystem

individual functioning and couple relations. For example, a woman who is a mother may also be a part of a couple relationship as well as part of her employment environment (microsystems). She is also part of her family and the larger corporation (mesosystems), is affected by her children's school performance and her significant other's career demands (exosystems), and her roles are affected by generally held beliefs about mothering or beliefs about women and work (macrosystems). This example highlights the interdependent roles of dual career couples and their employers. When the employer functions effectively, the employees are satisfied; reciprocally, when employees are satisfied, the employer is healthy. When family and career needs are not met, neither the employer nor the employee will exhibit optimal levels of functioning or productivity.

Significance for Dual Career Couples

Both the theories of Bronfenbrenner and Vondracek and colleagues underscore that human functioning is characterized by multiple levels of simultaneous functioning, and the involvement of both partners in multiple roles reflects the interdependence of family and career roles for dual career couples. Small, individual change can result in complex alterations in many other roles of both partners. Thus, one person's role involvement, for example, affects the opportunity for the significant other's role achievement.

WOMEN'S CAREER DEVELOPMENT

The 1970s marked a significant change in women's attitude toward employment. Until that point, relatively few women held positions of high earnings or high occupational prestige, and relatively few women attended postgraduate professional programs in traditionally male fields. Moreover, until the 1960s most women did not expect their careers to play a primary role in their lives (Regan & Roland, 1982). Associated with the advent of the women's movement has been a variety of changes in women's employment, including changes in the timing of women's participation in the work force, types of careers pursued, and personal expectations for combining family and career roles.

Despite these many changes, the career development of women is viewed as more complex than that of men because of their concerns with family issues. Whether traditional career development theories like those of Levinson (Levinson & Gooden, 1985; Levinson, 1986) and Super (e.g., 1983) characterize women's career development has been questioned (Ornstein & Isabella, 1990), and the need for empirical studies comparing female and male career development has been underscored. First, the generalization from male career development to female career development is questionable (Betz & Fitzgerald, 1987; Jenkins, 1989). Second, specific questions with regard to career preferences and plans of women still remain unanswered (Betz & Fitzgerald; Ornstein & Isabella). Third, it is important to comprehend women's career development from the female perspective because of the large number of anticipated female entrants into the work force and the importance of ensuring their career progress (Schwartz, 1989; Johnston & Packer, 1987).

Research over the last 20 years has revealed a dramatic shift in women's perspectives on their careers. In the 1960s and early 1970s, women were typically viewed as having different educational goals than men and viewing careers as less salient in their lives (Greenhaus, 1971; Masih, 1967). Currently, the vast majority of college women intend to combine work and family roles (Baber & Monaghan, 1988; Bridges, 1987; Covin & Brush, 1991; Harmon, 1981; O'Connell, Betz, & Kurth, 1989), anticipate that their careers will be an important future role (Covin & Brush, 1991; Gilbert et al., 1991), and that their careers will be part of a life-span process (Osipow, 1991). Statistics support these empirical findings. Women currently represent half of the work force and 39% of the professional labor force (Gilbert, Dancer, Rossman, & Thorn, 1991), and over 60% of mothers are employed.

Despite women's current levels of high career interest, their career paths remain discontinuous (Voydanoff, 1987), on average they earn 70 cents to the dollar of male wages (Maret & Finlay, 1984), they are less likely to achieve occupational status commensurate with their educational attainments (Betz & Fitzgerald, 1987), and they experience significant interaction between family and career roles (Betz & Fitzgerald; Loscocco, 1990; Loscocco & Roschelle, 1991; Williams, 1990). These various findings led researchers to investigate whether the career development of women may be different than that of men. Part of the difference in earnings between men and women can be accounted for by past gender bias in hiring and promoting men as compared to women. Women, however, begin work in jobs of higher occupational status relative to men, but by midlife, men's occupational status is higher because they have continually moved up, whereas women have gone down in occupational status (Sewell et al., 1980). Women's career progress is affected by the fact that employed women tend to cluster in a smaller number of lower-paying jobs than men, with fewer opportunities for upward mobility (Betz & Fitzgerald, 1987; Sewell et al., 1980). However, even highly career-committed women with jobs of high occupational prestige experience differences in career progress from those of men (Williams, 1990).

Women's career development, it seems, is more complex than the career development of men (e.g., Fitzgerald & Crites, 1980; Betz & Fitzgerald, 1987). Specifically, women are viewed as first deciding about family perspectives and then making career decisions, as compared with men who directly focus on career concerns (Betz & Fitzgerald). For women who choose to be parents and partners, this creates a true challenge to lifetime career achievement. To understand the differences in career achievement of men and women, women's gender differences in career motivation, achievement or attitudes, types of jobs they pursue, and family/child issues must be evaluated.

Achievement

Earlier work suggested that men and women have different attitudes and achievement motivations (e.g., Ace, Graen, & Dawis, 1972). Recent studies contradict these earlier perspectives. Both men and women have basic needs for self-fulfillment through meaningful work (Fitzgerald & Crites, 1980), and there is an increasing convergence of vocational needs among men and women. Both sexes value accomplishment, job security, income potential, and coworkers' respect (Beutell & Brenner, 1986). Women work for the same reasons as men: to earn a living and function as productive and competent members of society (Chester & Grossman, 1990; Grossman & Chester, 1990). Moreover, women and men are both interested in the power associated with work (Grossman & Stewart, 1990), and there is no difference between achievement goals of men and women, although those goals may be expressed in different domains (Chester, 1990) and have different meanings to men and women (Travis et al., 1991). Thus, differences between male and female career issues are evident when career choices and careers decisions are explored within the context of women's anticipated parental roles.

Career women experienced job dissatisfaction when they worked overtime; derived a sense of primary well-being from nonwork pursuits; and derived self-valuation through feedback from work (Sekaran, 1986). In contrast, men who worked overtime experienced greater work satisfaction, derived well-being from both work and nonwork pursuits, and derived their self-concept from work role identity (Sekaran, 1986). These career women may have experienced conflict as they attempted to balance work and family roles.

Among members of the work force, sex differences in occupational roles are not evident at higher occupational levels, although they are apparent at lower, midcareer levels (Diamond, 1971). Members of both sexes experienced adjustment problems when they pursued occupations stereotypical of the opposite sex (Osipow & Gold, 1968; Roe & Siegelman, 1964). These findings led one researcher to conclude that ". . . the career of the woman functioning vocationally at very high professional levels and the woman at the unskilled level may bear more similarities to their male counterparts than the large mass of women in the middle-level careers'' (Osipow, 1983, p. 271).

Careers Women Pursue

Women are more likely to pursue careers in traditionally female jobs like teaching, nursing, social work, or office work, which pay less than comparable traditional male jobs, despite similar educational and other requirements for job entry (Murrel, Frieze, & Frost, 1991; Olson, Frieze, & Detlefson, 1990; Treiman & Hartman, 1981). Women generally select careers from a narrower range than men (Hesse-Biber, 1985), view fewer careers as suitable (Poole & Clooney, 1985), and choose careers less consistent with their vocational interests (Swaney & Predeger, 1985).

Although women typically enter the work force at higher salaries than men, their advantage quickly falls off, so that men's lifetime earning and occupational prestige are higher (Heckman, Bryson, & Bryson, 1977; Ferber & Kordick, 1978; Sewell et al., 1980). Women's lower levels of achievement compared to men also relate to the types of careers they pursue. Women's work typically has less autonomy, authority, and opportunity for advancement. In 1982, according to U.S. Department of Commerce figures (cited in Sorensen & Mortimer, 1988), full-time employed women earned $241 and men earned $371 per week, meaning that women had to work 7½ days to gross what men earned in 5 days. Furthermore, men's income benefits more directly from work experience and education than women's (Barrett, 1979; Featherman & Hauser, 1976).

Throughout all stages of education, girls outperform boys and women outperform men, yet women lag behind men in career development (Betz & Fitzgerald, 1987). In mathematics, however, women are disadvantaged relative to men even in high school (Chipman et al., 1985), because they take fewer courses and have generally weaker backgrounds (Betz & Fitzgerald). Furthermore, girls avoid math because they have less confidence in their mathematical ability, not because they perform more poorly than boys (Chipman et al., 1985). This finding signifies the constriction of career opportunities for women because the vast majority of college majors may require math backgrounds (Sells, 1973), and because math is required for effective performance in many careers in our highly technological society (Betz & Fitzgerald). Women with higher education degrees in math-related fields, however, are more likely to be in the labor force. One study found, for example, that 51% of women with BAs and 91% of women with PhDs in science or engineering were employed (Vetter, 1980). Although educational attainment is an important correlate of career achievement among men, it does not have a similar salutary effect on women's salary (Betz & Fitzgerald). Nonetheless, more educated women are more likely to be in the work force, and plan on continuous lifetime employment.

Family Issues: Impact of Children

Women's careers are viewed as more discontinuous than those of men because of the role that family plays in their lives (Loscocco & Roschelle, 1991; Voydanoff, 1987). Studies have documented that college women anticipate satisfaction from both future career and family roles (Baber & Monaghan, 1988; Covin & Brush, 1991; Gilbert et al., 1991; Regan & Roland, 1982). Similarly, even career-committed employed women consider family issues when they decide among career options (Williams, 1990).

The simultaneous role of employee and homemaker affects women's labor market performance and involvement, and their entry into and level of work (Goh, 1991; Psathas, 1968; Zytowski, 1969). Moreover, marriage, timing of childbirth, and spouses' attitudes to their employment are important considerations for women's career development (Psathas). Social factors also affect women's career development in different ways than they affect men's career development (Osipow, 1983; Williams, 1990).

Although married women may change careers after matrimony (Philliber & Hiller, 1983; see chapter 1), the presence of children may not be directly related to career continuity. Other factors, including parents' attitudes toward maternal employment (Morgan & Hock, 1984; Pistrang, 1984) and the mother's attitude toward her children's need for her (Hock et al., 1984; Morgan & Hock, 1984), are more directly related or interact with child factors to predict women's career continuity. In fact, both fathers and mothers with employed spouses were reported as more highly involved in their careers (Gould & Werbel, 1983), presumably because of the greater financial need among those families (George & Brief, 1990). Career women who choose to remain single have higher levels of education and are more likely to pursue traditional male careers. Moreover, career-oriented women are less likely to have children or want to have them, and will have fewer children than other employed women (Betz & Fitzgerald, 1987).

One of the few studies of women of color found that Black women were more likely to work than White women, but have positions that were more discontinuous, less secure, and lower paying than those of White women (Crohan et al., 1989). Black women perceived little conflict between high career aspirations and working outside of the home (Heaston, 1976). Instead, they viewed providing well for their family as reflecting their strong family orientation (Allen & Britt, 1983) and were therefore more likely to choose traditionally male occupations than their White counterparts (Murrell et al., 1991).

Understanding Women's Career Development

There is an apparent contradiction in the literature relating to women's career development. There are statements like, "Relatively few women work continuously over their entire work history" (Voydanoff, 1987, p. 25), and also statements like, ". . . both husbands and wives considered their careers to be equally central to their lives" (Sekaran, 1986, p. 45). How can these differences in perspectives be resolved? Are women career-committed or do they have different goals than men?

In analyzing these differences, Betz and Fitzgerald (1987) underscored that no single distinction can adequately describe women's career development: ". . . a woman pursuing a traditionally female occupation such as nurse or elementary school teacher could be as strongly career oriented as a woman pursuing a nontraditional occupation such as medicine or law. Conversely, female role innovators (e.g., physician) undoubtedly differ in the extent to which marital and family roles are salient to their life plans" (p. 21).

Inherent in this statement is the resolution to the apparent contradiction. The individual's gender role identity (see chapter 2) is significantly related to individual career plans, career commitment, and plans to pursue a traditionally male or female career (e.g., Fassinger, 1990; Gaddy, Glass, & Arnkoff, 1983; Mazen & Lemkau, 1990; Murrell et al., 1991; Strange & Rea, 1983). Consistent with this perspective, factors with positive relationships to women's career development include instrumentality, androgynous personality, high self-esteem, strong academic self-concept, high ability, and nontraditional sex-role attitudes (Betz & Fitzgerald, 1987).

Plans to combine family and career are associated with lower career aspirations (Ragins & Sundstrom, 1989; Rix, 1982) only among women who plan careers in traditionally female professions (Murrell et al., 1991). Among women who plan careers in traditionally male professions, there is less of an association between career aspirations and anticipated family concerns. Moreover, women in male-dominated jobs have lower traditional attitudes and gender stereotypes (Murrell et al.).

Gender role identity is related to career choice (Strange & Rea, 1983; Terborg, 1977). Women in nontraditional majors like math and science had higher instrumental scores (Hackett, 1985) and women with instrumental gender role identities were employed more frequently in typically masculine careers (Betz & Fitzgerald, 1987). In contrast, women in female-dominated careers had lower achievement orientation and less education (Lemkau, 1979).

The Work and Family Orientation Questionnaire (WOFO) (Helmreich & Spence, 1978) was designed to measure (1) *mastery,* or the desire for challenging tasks and the desire to do well, (2) *work,* or the desire to work hard, and (3) *competitiveness*, or the enjoyment of competing with other people. Men score somewhat higher on mastery and competitiveness, whereas women score higher on work. When instrumentality, as measured by the PAQ, is held constant, gender differences in work and mastery disappear.

These results taken together indicate that apparent gender differences in male and female career issues may actually be differences in "masculine" and "feminine" personalities toward career issues (Betz & Fitzgerald, 1987; Murrell et al., 1991). Thus, women with masculine gender role identities are more likely to pursue male-dominated careers, and may follow similar career development paths to men. In contrast, women with feminine gender role identities are more likely to pursue female-dominated careers and experience greater conflict between family and career issues. This suggests that counselors who wish to advise their clients effectively may need to consider both the results on career development indices and client gender role identities. In the past, women often selected careers inconsistent with their aptitudes and vocational interests (Fitzgerald & Crites, 1980) because of their focus on pursuing careers consistent with family needs. If, in the future, counselors can focus on career plans and gender role identity, they may be able to assist women to pursue careers consistent with their talents more effectively (Ornstein & Isabella, 1990). Women with masculine gender role identities could be advised to pursue traditional career paths. Women with feminine gender role identities might be encouraged to explore employment in businesses that are sensitive to family and career needs and offer flexible work options (chapter 10), or to plan ways of sequencing work and family priorities while still retaining critical business contacts. Women whose decisions focus on family and career concerns also may have partners, or sensitize their partners, to focus on these dual concerns. Therefore, feminine individuals, both male and female, may advocate one parent's using flexible work options to address family needs.

Although women may have been socialized at one time to remain at home, current evidence suggests that they now expect to combine family and career responsibilities. Within the dual career couple, the careers of both partners play significant roles, yet women who care deeply about their careers may also utilize various flexible work options because they also care deeply about their families. Anecdotal evidence suggests that these flexible options are viewed as temporary and that career-oriented individuals plan to pursue full-time work at a later time. Counselors can assist partners in understanding the significance of women's different career paths. If a woman's significant other thinks that flexible work reflects a lack of career commitment, this assumption will affect both partners' decisions and the balance of family and career responsibilities. Additionally, a woman may experience challenges and difficulties when she eventually returns to a full-time work commitment and requires greater flexibility on the part of her partner so that she can reintegrate into the work force. Counselors can help couples plan for this eventual transition so that it can be smoother and more rewarding for both partners.

COUPLE DEVELOPMENT

In the foregoing section, a life-span developmental approach to individual change was presented. This section will deal with a life-span approach for the couple, focusing on changes that occur within the couple from the earliest stages of couple formation to the more mature "empty nest" stage. The presence or absence of children, as well as their ages and birth order, can affect career progress among dual career couples. Furthermore, counselors can educate their clients about the relationship between couple development and career progress throughout the life span.

Classical theories that specified stages of psychological growth used male models of development. Gilligan (1982) postulated that female development may be distinct from male development. During early stages of development, Gilligan postulated that children in the Western world are raised by female caretakers. From this experience, girls learn that successful psychosocial development involves being like the caretaker, whereas boys learn that successful psychosocial development involves being different than their caretakers. This leads girls to form strong attachments to their female caretakers, to family members, and others, whereas boys develop a sense of independence from the caretaker and others (Gilligan, 1982). As they age, boys and girls face distinct developmental challenges. Girls must learn to be independent and boys must learn to be interdependent.

Men and women also may experience developmental challenges differently. If Gilligan's postulates are accepted, it may be hypothesized that girls experience the crisis of intimacy in early adolescence and identity in young adulthood, which is the opposite of Erikson's order of psychosocial stages. If men and women pass through psychosocial stages of development in different orders, this may have profound implications on the couple relationship. At the same time that women are forming relationships and pursuing early career stages, they may be facing the challenge of consolidating their identity, which may hamper their ability to establish equity. In early adulthood, men may, instead, be consolidating their ability to form relationships. Incomplete consolidation may affect men's ability to interact with their significant others or to nurture their children.

Corroborating research indicates that men and women report different levels of self-esteem as graduate students and in their first jobs (Berman et al., 1975). Men experience a rise in personal self-confidence during graduate school, whereas women report a significant increase in self-confidence in their early postgraduate employment years, suggesting that developmental progress may differ for men and women. Data from other studies indicate that men and women both recognize the importance of career-related achievement, but use different criteria for making decisions about family and career balance (Williams, 1990). Women, in contrast to men, usually include family issues in their decision-making criteria. Anecdotal stories suggest that middle-aged men value family issues highly and may consider them equally important to career concerns.

Many couples may choose not to have children at all, but how their development differs from couples who elect to have children has not been adequately examined. Because there is at best a scant literature on couple development without children, the present section will not focus on these couples. (See chapter 3 for greater detail on aspects of couple functioning unrelated to children.)

Stages in Family Development

Six major stages in family development can be identified (Hazard & Koslow, 1986; Sekaran, 1986). At each stage the couple is confronted with organizational issues concerning balancing family and career needs, managing time, providing mutual support in the relationship, using available resources effectively, determining family levels of functioning, and expressing their commitments to the relationship. Because early development affects later stages, choices made at any one point may have pronounced effects on later family decisions. However, because of the plasticity of human development, routine assessment and discussion of couple and career issues can alter some of the negative consequences of these early decisions.

The first stage of family development is called "couple launching dual career lifestyles" (Sekaran, 1986). This stage begins when couples consider marriage or long-term commitments. Couples who had comprehensive discussions about family and career priorities and future lifestyles before they agreed to a long-term relationship had higher levels of job satisfaction (Sekaran, 1982) and more successful dual career couple lives (Holmstrom, 1972). Although currently most female university graduates claim that family and career will both be important elements of their future lifestyles, many men prefer lifestyles that give precedence to male career pursuits (Rosen, 1985; Sekaran, 1986; Yogev, 1981).

Counselors can play critical roles in encouraging honest discussion about future relationship expectations. Moreover, they can work with couples to broaden and define the meaning of a dual career couple relationship in a gender-free context. Choices made before and after the relationship commitment can be readdressed, renegotiated, and altered because of the plasticity of development. Decisions are made to be changed, and human flexibility is such that even multiple changes can be accommodated. The embeddedness of human behavior also affects counseling strategies because decisions of one partner have repercussions on the availability of other career and family roles. Partners can plan career and family paths actively to accommodate the career needs of their significant others, allowing them the opportunity to construct couple goals that maximize the individual goals of each partner. When couples passively ignore discussion of couple goals, family or career decisions will alter the balance among the couple's various roles, but will have negative implications for the couple's relationship.

The second stage is called "young childless couples" (Sekaran, 1986). During this period, partners focus on building their careers and defining the characteristics of their relationship. Couples establish patterns for relating to one another and to people outside of the nuclear family. Also, rules for providing or requesting emotional and intellectual support between the partners are developed during this stage. This stage often lasts 4 to 10 years, or until women are in their early 30s when partners in most dual career couples plan to have their first children. When couples decide to remain without children, their couple development may differ from that of couples who choose to give birth to children.

Some critical family concerns at this stage involve both negotiation and renegotiation of the meaning of the relationship, handling finances, making decisions, and setting goals for family and career. Counselors play critical roles at this stage in addressing competitive feelings between partners. Because of the distinct career demands in different fields, different career patterns, or different abilities, partners may progress up their career ladders at different rates. Counselors can help couples to express emotional and physical support for the independent career achievements of their partners and to appreciate their career success. An example of physical support may involve one partner agreeing to take on extra household responsibilities for a short or extended period of time to enable the other partner to take on an important, but demanding project at work.

During this stage, couples think about children and need to address how children affect their dual career couple life and the attitudes of their companies toward family concerns. Additionally, traditional men and women may not want to share child-care responsibilities and may experience gender-socialized conflict when they do share. These traditional roles may be meaningfully addressed in counseling where the goal of couple equity can be discussed.

The third stage is called "early-stage families" (Hazard & Koslow, 1986) and begins when the couple's first child is born and continues through the time that the youngest child enters school in preschool or kindergarten programs. Once partners become parents, a critical concern involves child-care arrangements, back-up plans for emergencies, time scheduling, and developing a functional perspective on the relative career and family losses and gains of different family and career decisions. Raising preschoolers involves balancing family resources (financial, psychological, and physical) with other family and career concerns. Moreover, decisions about planning for more children and reaccommodating the family to its own possible growth in size becomes another challenge. The strains of raising preschoolers can also lead to crises in functioning within the couple.

Couples may experience particular stress at this stage because it often coincides with the time when employees have the least control over job demands and yet experience the greatest demands at home and at the workplace (Sekaran, 1986). Moreover, because couples typically have little time for outside interests or for friends, they may have few opportunities for unwinding or reducing stress (Rice, cited in Sekaran, 1986). How individuals experience the presence of preschoolers may be related to their personal perspectives. For example, in contrast to older mothers, younger mothers are more wedded to the belief of the baby's exclusive need for them rather than of other caretakers (Morgan & Hock, 1984). Therefore, younger mothers may experience a greater degree of guilt if they do not remain at home with their preschool children.

Counselors can assist partners in addressing guilt over leaving young children. Partners may be cautioned not to overindulge children when they return home from work (Sekaran, 1986) and encouraged to participate fully in child-care responsibilities. Couples may experience the "young parent syndrome" (Humphrey, 1983), characterized by low energy and loss of interest in partner intimacy. To address these problems, couples can be encouraged to spend time together on a regular basis and to plan relationship-building activities.

The fourth stage is called "middle-stage families" (Hazard & Koslow, 1986), which begins from the time that the youngest child is in school and continues through the time that this child reaches adolescence. For parents of school-aged children, major family issues involve socializing the children, finding time to interact with the children's school, and deciding on how to manage career and family needs, including concerns like the level of children's participation in extracurricular activities and attendant carpooling. For the couple themselves, important issues revolve around maintaining their own lives, which may mean participating in both couple and separate, personally meaningful activities, coping with the demands of work and family effectively, and forming meaningful couple-to-couple relationships.

New challenges regarding the issues of generativity and stagnation (Erikson, 1968a, 1968b) may also begin to present themselves to the couple. Identifying the significance of both family and career achievements in defining success will affect how individuals and couples perceive their life-span roles. Furthermore, the relative ability of men and women to pursue career goals may differ significantly at this and the earlier stage of couple development. Women are more often involved in the primary care of young children. Therefore, they may not show significant career advances during this stage, whereas their significant others, even if they are the same age, may have exhibited successes at an earlier stage in the couple relationship. Without the stress of caring for a preschooler, the couple relationship and individual career patterns now flourish at a more rapid pace.

Counselors can encourage partners to relearn the pleasures of communication and intimacy. Additionally, counselors can play important roles as clients plan methods for pursuing future career progress. If women have taken time-outs or work slowdowns for child care, discussions with clients can focus on building work-related skills, developing business contacts, and planning ways to become retracked into the workplace.

The fifth stage, referred to as "late-stage family" (Sekaran, 1986) begins when children are adolescents. In this stage, the parents' relationships to their children involve setting limits, communicating openly with children, simultaneously providing supervision and freedom for their children, helping children develop plans for their future, and establishing a new balance between work and home demands. During this stage, one partner may be offered a relocation possibility, presenting major challenges for the other partner's career decisions and for the dimensions of family functioning. Parents may experience additional burdens as they become more responsible for the care of their own aging parents. When their children leave home, couples may fine-tune or reorient their relationship. Both partners in the couple may also begin to confront issues regarding their own mortality and the possibility of eventual widowhood.

Couples at this stage may move further into the psychosocial crisis about generativity and stagnation, evaluating their various goals for life-span achievement. Furthermore, they may redefine their connections to various family, individual, and couple systems. Counselors can help clients address conflicts and stresses by assessing each partner's stage of development. Counselors can help couples focus on family building activities and consolidation of career and family achievement.

The sixth stage is referred to as "the empty nest" (Sekaran, 1986) and occurs when all the children have left home. Partners may have allowed children's problems to mask their own concerns and problems at earlier stages, meaning that this period may be a crisis for those couples who have used children as a buffer to intimacy. For other couples, this stage represents an opportunity for couple renewal. Women, in particular, may experience this period as a time of autonomy (Gerstel, 1977) because they can devote themselves to their careers by working longer hours, attending more actively to their work lives, or accepting a relocation offer. Counselors can help dual career couples plan for retirement at this stage to enable couples to view the postemployment years as a time of growth and development, not dysfunction and stagnation.

CAREER DEVELOPMENT

Many aspects of career development parallel stages of human growth and development (Beilin, 1955; Osipow, 1983). In contrast to developmental psychology, which focuses on the first two decades of life, however, the time focus in the career development literature generally begins in adolescence and continues onward through adulthood. Career issues have particular significance for dual career couples, and individual stages of personal development may significantly affect career achievement. For example, career achievement is associated with self-esteem, positive self-image, and self-respect (Barnett & Baruch, 1978a, 1978b; James, 1990) and has significant implications for personal growth and development within dual career couples. Couple issues affect career progress because of the interdependence of partners' career and family choices. With regard to life-span development, three major issues concerning career development are relevant:

1. *Career development theories.* General theories of career development highlight the interrelationship of personal development and the individual's ability and readiness to make career choices.
2. *Career perspectives in adult development.* Mature stages in career growth are associated with different opportunities for flexibility in work schedules. Flexibility is a hallmark of reducing role stress and of balancing family and career needs for both men and women in dual career couples (Guelzow et al., 1991). Particular career skills, like the ability to make career decisions, are related to life-span achievement in dual career couples. Individuals who cannot master these career skills will have a more difficult time balancing their career needs with those of their significant others.
3. *Life-span career development.* New approaches to life-span career development directly focus on how career needs vary throughout both partners' work lives.

Each of these issues will be addressed in separate sections below, and their impact on individuals and client-couples will be discussed.

Career Development Theories

The career development theories of Ginzberg (1972, 1984; Ginzberg, Ginsburg, Axelrad, & Herma, 1951) and Super (1951, 1953, 1964, 1980,

1983, 1986) elucidate the interrelationship between career development and other developmental phenomena and are excellent models for counselors to incorporate into their own strategies. It should be noted, however, that researchers have questioned whether these career development theories are equally characteristic of women's career development (e.g., Ornstein & Isabella, 1990). With respect to the dual career couple, each partner's career stage affects the career opportunities and achievement potential available to the other partner. Understanding how individuals arrive at their career decisions may help counselors facilitate clients' future career progress.

Ginzberg's Theory

Career choice involves a set of career decisions first made in early adolescence and continuing until the early 20s (Ginzberg et al., 1951). These career decisions require compromise among the individual's many options. Career choice progresses from a *fantasy stage*, where career choice does not have a rational basis, to the *tentative stage*, where the individual already has an orientation to reality, time perspective, and self-knowledge, to the *realistic stage*, where the adolescent/young adult progresses from exploring different careers to identifying a major field for pursuing a specific vocational path. Throughout development, the individual increasingly differentiates personal vocational interests from those of his or her parents. Moreover, personal considerations, knowledge of external reality, and potential for social contribution all become more salient in the choice of a career path as the individual matures.

Occupational choice continues from adolescence throughout the life span (Ginzberg, 1972, 1984). Although early decisions may shape later career choices, career choice is not irreversible. Important career phenomena like work experience and personality issues may shape the direction of career choices for the mature individual. Major changes in career direction after a certain stage, however, can involve substantial career and personal costs.

The goal of career choice is to optimize the fit between reality and personal goals, and between preferred career and available opportunities (Ginzberg, 1972, 1984). Therefore, career decisions throughout the life span reflect an attempt to match individual goals with the realistic opportunities and limits inherent in the work world. Furthermore, occupational choice is a lifelong process, whereby individuals who view their work as a primary source of satisfaction try to match their developing career goals with employment opportunities (Ginzberg, 1984).

Ginzberg's theory has significant implications for dual career couples. First, career choice is based on the balance between available opportunities and external reality. Dual career couples' relationship and family demands represent significant elements of external reality. Thus, different career choices might be made depending on whether an individual is single or a member of a couple. Career-committed women marry at a relatively mature age (Voydanoff, 1987) and are more likely to postpone childbirth or to decide not to have children (Yogev, 1981). Second, some women continue in full-time career pursuits throughout their life spans, whereas other women may take advantage of flexible work schedules (see chapter 10), switching careers or taking work slowdowns when they have young children (Voydanoff, 1987). Ginzberg's theory would predict that women who use flexible benefits would be able to return to the work force and may be successful, but only at significant career and personal costs.

Super's Theory

Career choice can be viewed as reflecting individuals' attempts to implement their personal self-concept by selecting a career track where they have the greatest opportunities for self-expression (Super, 1951, 1953, 1964, 1980, 1983). Behaviors chosen to express the career self-concept are a function of the person's stage of development. Super's theory represents a merger of developmental psychology and psychology of careers, which he refers to as vocational psychology. Vocational guidance is "the process of helping a person to develop and accept an integrated and adequate picture of [him/herself] and of [his/her] role in the world of work, to test the concept against reality, and to convert it into a reality, with satisfaction to [him/herself] and benefit to society" (Super 1951, p. 92).

Career development is also influenced by responses of peers and others to individual role choices. Super identified five stages, or maxicycles, that characterize the development of the self-concept as part of career development (see Table 4.3). These are growth, exploration, establishment, maintenance, and decline. Progress through these career development stages is associated with specific career activities referred to as vocational development tasks. People's self-concepts reflect their ability to view themselves as unique, yet also understand the similarities that they share with others. Role rehearsal may be used to facilitate the development of the vocational self-concept. Differential abilities, interests, and personality characteristics are associated with attitudes toward various occupations. Reciprocally, successful functioning in different occupations requires particular patterns of abilities, interests, and personalities. Individual career patterns may be closely related to the family-of-origin phenomenon, including parental socioeconomic level and lifestyle, and personality issues, mental ability, and the availability of opportunities. Career patterns are also affected by changes in individual interests as well as external issues like technology or the economy. Career choice evolves through a series of stages involving the development and implementation of the personal self-concept, which requires a compromise between the self-concept and reality. Individuals might satisfactorily choose a variety of related occupations rather than experiencing a single occupational choice. The eventual career choice is reflected in the interchange of developmental tasks and individual behaviors. Vocational interests and abilities, lifestyle and work involvement, and self-concept are usually fairly stable from late adolescence through adulthood.

Various scales have been developed to assess both clients' level of career development and their orientations to other life roles (Nevill & Super, 1986, 1989; Super & Nevill, 1984; Super, Thompson, Lindeman, Jordaan, & Myers, 1981; Super, Thompson, & Lindeman, 1984). Information such as life stage, performance on specific developmental tasks, career maturity, work salience, work values, and career adaptability have been measured. Counselors can use these measures to assist clients in assimilating knowledge about their career development stage, information about future stages, and the personal significance of work and other life roles. Personal satisfaction is dependent on establishing a lifestyle related to earlier growth and exploration, and finding a balance between work and other life roles. A goal of dual career couples is to identify satisfactory work roles that allow personal growth without diminishing opportunities for growth in a significant other.

Specific predictions from Super's theory are relevant to dual career couples. First, self-concept is related to career choice, and may also influence the relationship between partners in a dual career couple and the anticipated balance of family and career. Thus, career choices represent an integrated expression of personality, rather than a set of isolated choices. Second, career choice will be a function of relationships and family issues. As the demands of families change, career decisions may also evolve. Third, Super emphasizes the embeddedness of roles, much as Vondracek and colleagues. Therefore, individual career choices will affect other areas of individual and couple functioning and the career choices of the partner. Fourth, choices in one life role will affect choices available in other life roles. However, role balance may show considerable change across the life span.

Career Perspectives in Adult Development

Each stage of career development offers unique challenges to the individual and the dual career couple. Different opportunities are available for career growth, but these can also constrain the couple's ability to address family concerns and to nurture their relationship. Four separate issues related to career development and their association with challenges at different career points will be reviewed. These issues are (a) career skills, (b) intellectual challenge and work satisfaction, (c) occupational experience and aging, and (d) midlife career issues. Life-span progress involves assessing the stage of career development of clients, evaluating

TABLE 4.3
Summary of Super's Five Stages of Career Development

Stage	Approximate Age	Career Activity	Career Task	Self-Concept
Growth	0–14 years	Self-image development Orientation to work	Work habits & attitudes Future orientation Sense of agency and self-esteem	Developing self-concept Related educational decisions
Exploration	15–24 years	Self-analysis Self in context	Crystallization Specification Implementation	Self in environment Identifying and implementing vocational preferences
Establishment	25–44 years	Adjustment and advancement in career	Consolidation Stabilization Advancement	Developing skills and priorities
Maintenance	45–64 years	Preserving position achieved	Holding on Innovating Breaking new ground	Using talents and abilities in field
Decline	65 years and older	Disengagement from work roles Pursuit of other roles	Deceleration Disengagement Retirement	Pursuing new roles

their readiness for moving forward in their careers, and assisting that forward movement (Ivey & Goncalves, 1988; Super, 1983).

Career Skills

Career decision making and career maturity are two career skills relevant to the individual's ability to make an effective occupational choice. Degree of mastery of each of these skills will affect the dual career couple at "the couple in formation stage" and at later stages.

Career decision making. Decision making is viewed as a developmental process that proceeds from initial stages where information is accumulated and integrated to an end state where this information can be analyzed and utilized for career choice (Phillips & Pazienza, 1988). During evaluation, individuals make tentative career decisions. Decision-making theory focuses on transitions from one career stage to another. Tiedeman and O'Hara (1963) described a stage model where progressively increasing individual differentiation and complexity were reached through a decision-making process involving anticipation, implementation, and adjustment. Differentiation of the career objectives occurred as individuals employed problem-solving approaches to career issues (Dudley & Tiedeman, 1977).

Individual differences exist in decision-making styles and abilities (Phillips & Pazienza, 1988; Jepsen, 1974; Dinklage, 1968). Harren (1979) described three decision-making styles: *The rational style* involves the individual's awareness of how earlier decisions affect subsequent ones, *the intuitive style* involves the individual's acceptance of responsibility for past decisions without anticipating future implications or considering alternatives, and *the dependent style* involves projecting responsibility for a choice onto others. Rather than the individuals' using a single style across situations, the situation may influences the decision-making style (Krumboltz, Scherba, Hamel, Mitchell, Rude, & Kinnier, 1979). Some empirical work has found distinct career exploration patterns associated with each decision-making style. Rational decision-making style was related to greater environmental exploration and users had more fully formed personalities (Blustein & Phillips, 1990). Dependent-style individuals did not explore sufficiently (Marcia, 1966), and intuitive-style individuals were not more decisive than any other group (Apostal, 1988).

Betz & Hackett (1981) applied Bandura's (1977) self-efficacy theory to vocational psychology. Efficacy refers to persons' belief that they have the competence to perform behaviors that will achieve a desired goal. Self-efficacy is directly related to career decision making, which means that students with greater self-efficacy are more likely to be confident that they can complete training necessary to achieve specific career goals (Meier, 1991). Despite similarity in abilities, women were found to view themselves as less efficacious for nontraditional careers than were men.

For dual career couples, it is particularly important that both partners master decision-making skills and learn how to make career decisions together, incorporating their different styles to solve problems. Because effective decision making can facilitate the career choices of both partners, counselors can help couples take responsibility for their career decisions and identify the implications of those decisions for family and career functioning. In this way, couples can benefit by discussing career issues together even when only one partner is facing a current career choice issue. This can provide a career sounding board to the other person and offer emotional support that is a prerequisite to new career moves.

Career maturity. Career maturity is a measure of individual level of development with regard to career issues. Two measures of career maturity can be identified and can be measured using instruments developed by Super and Crites (see Chartrand & Camp, 1991, for review): Career Maturity I (CM I), which measures the client's achievement on career development tasks, and Career Maturity II (CM II), which measures individuals along a variety of dimensions and compares them to age cohorts on specific developmental tasks. CM I can be measured using the Career Development Inventory-Adult Form (Super et al., 1981) or the Assessment of Career Decision Making (Harren, 1979, 1980, 1984). Career counselors who work with "career-immature" clients will help clients to acquire information about the world of work. Counseling more mature clients involves reality testing and implementation of career decisions. Counselors can help clients develop career skills like problem exploration, clarification, and career exploration.

Career maturity has particular relevance to dual career couples because lack of self-knowledge or cognitive immaturity are associated with poor implementation of career goals. Specific career choices affect both partners, therefore one individual's poor career choices can derail the career plans of the significant other as well. Effective career counseling can assist the career-immature partner to grow careerwise and eventually pursue a career path with potential for success. As another example of the interdependence of partners' career issues, individuals who are unsuccessful in a chosen profession because of career immaturity will experience disappointment, and their lack of achievement may lead to competition with a more successful partner. Counselors can assist career-immature clients to gain relevant career skills that will lead to greater probability of career success and decreased pressure on the couple relationship.

Popular measures of vocational maturity include the Career Development Inventory (Super et al., 1981), The Adults Career Concerns Inventory (Super et al., 1984), The Career Maturity Inventory (Crites, 1973, 1978), and The Career Mastery Inventory (formerly, the Career Adjustment and Development Inventory, Crites, 1975, 1982). Vocational maturity assessment has also addressed the relationship of vocational planning to self-knowledge (Gribbons & Lohnes, 1968, 1982), decision-making ability (Dilley, 1965), and cognitive factors associated with vocational maturity (Westbrook, 1976).

Individual psychodynamic histories (Watkins & Savickas, 1990) or opportunities for social reinforcement (Krumboltz & Nichols, 1990) can affect career maturity. Watkins and Savickas assessed the interrelationship of psychosocial development as measured by Erikson's fifth stage of development (identity vs. identity confusion) and career readiness: "An occupation. . . is a means by which individuals express who they are, how they see themselves in relation to others, and how they see themselves as contributing to the world about them" (Watkins & Savickas, p. 84). Unresolved identity crises or identity confusion could therefore interfere with each aspect of occupational expression. Because Erikson suggests that women's identity crisis occurs after they are partners, one is left to question the logical implication of Erikson's theory that women without a partner never establish a fully formed identity (Barnett & Baruch, 1978a).

In comparison with individuals with poorly crystallized identities, people whose identities are sharply crystallized are more likely (Watkins & Savickas, 1990):

1. to have successfully passed through earlier stages of development;
2. to have more significant information for making career decisions;
3. to choose a more appropriate career;
4. to make career choices more decisively;
5. to be more career-mature;
6. to benefit from self-directed activities and other career interventions that use their identity development;
7. to be more satisfied with their careers; and
8. to have more efficient work behavior and be more productive.

Counselors use a variety of measures to assess career development as well as attitudes toward family and career roles. The job of the career development counselor then is to help clients integrate these multiple roles into one goal-oriented plan within the constraints of individual and partner concerns.

Intellectual Challenge and Work Satisfaction

Much of the research on work satisfaction and associated antecedents has used middle-class White men as the target group. Job conditions affect intellectual development in men of various ages (Miller, Slomczynski, & Kohn, 1988). Specifically, job situations that allow the use of self-direction in work can increase intellectual flexibility, open-mindedness, and non-authoritarian orientation at all worker ages. "There is thus a notable continuity not only of the effects of job conditions on intellective process, but also of the effects of intellective processes on job conditions. Men continue to learn from their jobs and to generalize those lessons to outside-of-job reality, and men continue well into their careers to select and to mold their jobs to fit their intellective proclivities'' (p. 101).

Studies of women's work conditions have found that there is a significant association between work satisfaction and related psychological functioning (Miller, Schooler, Kohn, & Miller, 1980). Women are affected by their job conditions in both positive and negative ways. Miller et al. (1980) underscored the error of the ''. . .belief that large segments of the female work force are somehow immune to occupational circumstances— that, for example, mothers of young children or women who do not think of themselves as having careers, or women who are ''only working to supplement the family income'' are insensitive to the deleterious effects of routinized work or are unresponsive to the mind-stretching experience of doing substantively complex work'' (p. 94).

Work experience is related to the occupational values employees attribute to their jobs (Mortimer & Lorence 1979a, 1979b, 1985; Mortimer, 1988). Jobs with feedback and autonomy that encourage the use of a wide range of skills are positively related to career motivation and to the centrality of career in a person's life (Noe, Noe, & Bachhuber, 1990). Similarly, jobs characterized by challenge, meaning, and variety are most satisfying to employees (Glisson & Durrick, 1988; Loscocco & Roschelle, 1991). Those employees who work at jobs where they can request and accept feedback and interact with coworkers have the highest enthusiasm, greatest interest in career goals, and most active participation in activities designed to maintain technical and professional vitality (Noe et al., 1990). Work autonomy (Greenberger, Strasser, Cummings, & Dunham, 1989; Lorence & Mortimer, 1985; Sekaran, 1989) and the known opportunity for upward mobility are also related to worker satisfaction (Lincoln & Kalleberg, 1985; Loscocco, 1990).

Because managers today serve as career advisors, referral agents, coaches, and performance appraisers (Leibowitz & Schlossberg, 1981), their interpersonal skills are related to their workers' developing intellectually on their jobs (Noe et al., 1990). Therefore, job satisfaction is related to matching employee and supervisor on work values (Meglino, Ravlin, & Adkins, 1989). Additionally, upper-level managers, who are usually male, play an important role in mentoring younger employees. Women are less likely to be mentored, which can affect their opportunities for upward mobility (Carden, 1990; Noe, 1988). It might be advantageous to train male managers to mentor female subordinates (Goh, 1991).

Job satisfaction seems to be greatest among older workers (Adler & Aranya, 1984; Campbell, Converse, & Rodgers, 1976; Janson & Martin, 1982; Kalleberg, 1977; Quinn et al., 1974; Rhodes, 1983; Schwab & Heneman, 1977). However, prior to preretirement ages, satisfaction may increase (Mortimer & Borman, 1988) or exhibit a curvilinear effect so that satisfaction increases until about age 40, then plateaus until about the mid-50s, and then increases again at older ages (Kalleberg & Loscocco, 1983). Three interpretations of these results are possible. First, workers revise expectations to fit the realities of their employment at different career stages (Loscocco & Roschelle, 1991). Second, workers reflect the increasing fit between themselves and the job because of the greater opportunities more mature workers have to shape their jobs, and because their needs and values may have evolved in response to job constructs to fit organizational demands more closely at more mature ages (Mortimer & Borman). A third explanation involves age cohort effects. Younger workers may have unrealistic job expectations and therefore may be less satisfied with their employment relative to older workers (Loscocco & Roschelle).

In one of the few studies of people of color, the satisfaction of Black and White women with their work and their lives was found to be directly related (Crohan et al., 1989). In another study, women's attitudes toward the organization, job satisfaction, willingness to leave the company, willingness to relocate, or desire for promotion did not differ with career stage (Ornstein & Isabella, 1990). Men were found to exhibit differences in career attitudes and plans across career stages (Ornstein, Crohn, & Slocum, 1989). It is interesting to speculate that career satisfaction among women who are mothers may be different from that of childless women because of their different career paths. At the ages when men's career pursuits are plateauing, many mothers are first able to devote significant, unconflicted time to career achievements (Gerstel, 1977). Because of these and other gender differences in the career paths of men and women, Ornstein and Isabella stressed the need for further study of these parallels and differences. For dual career couples, important considerations involve achieving balance in a couple where one partner is retired and the other is still employed. Women may continue working many years after their male significant others have already retired because of age differences between partners or time-outs for child care.

Occupational Experience and Aging

In early stages of employment, usually when the worker is young, job selection may be largely determined by psychological factors, values, abilities, and needs (Mortimer & Borman, 1988). Personality characteristics differentially affect perceptions about careers and associated successes or failures (Mortimer & Borman). At later points in employees' careers, these psychological factors may become less important as workers reach their career ceilings. Age is associated with varying patterns of reward values. Younger workers are more concerned with opportunities for promotions as they consider the increasing financial needs of growing families, whereas older workers are more concerned with retirement benefits (Wright & Hamilton, 1978). Yet, it would be erroneous to think that the aging worker does not actively interact with his or her organization.

With regard to dual career couples, the implications of selection factors on job choice are critical. Psychological and values issues are related to organizational policies of the employer and may determine career selection among single workers, and affect the career choices of dual career couples at all points in their careers. When children are involved, family-friendly policies in companies have significant implications on worker recruitment and retention among employed parents (see chapter 10). Dual career couples may follow a different career path than other workers, achieving career milestones at later ages (see chapter 9).

Midlife Career Issues

Employment is associated with increased positive self-esteem for both men and women (Barnett & Baruch, 1978a, 1978b; James, 1990); however, career changes at midlife may affect self-esteem concerns. At midlife, couples may still be experiencing career progress or may already be preparing for eventual retirement. Thus, the needs and satisfaction of midlife career employees may be distinct from other workers'. Common concerns of midlife employees include decreased self-esteem, feeling that their job security is threatened by younger workers, and that their highest career possibilities have already been reached (Murphy & Burck, 1976; Williams & Savickas, 1990). Specific developmental tasks are necessary to address these experiences, such as setting new goals and reevaluating control over the future. Individuals may select horizontal career moves, vertical career moves, or multiple vertical changes (Sarason, 1977) to re-energize their careers. Career change at midlife may result from self-generated pressure, from life changes such as divorce or widowhood, from the desire for greater income, or from external pressures such as job loss, relocation, or corporate takeover.

Career development at midlife consists of the positive perspective associated with maturity, such as increased knowledge and information as compared with younger workers (Osipow, 1983). However, there is also an associated decline with progressive maturation in both resources and physical capacity, which may have a negative impact on work performance. Furthermore, opportunities for life-span development in different careers may vary because of differences in age of entry, expected length of productivity, and mandatory age of retirement. In careers that are dependent on being at the technical cutting edge, more mature workers may be concerned about their ability to adapt to change (Williams & Savickas, 1990). Individuals who seek counseling often need to feel that they can develop an awareness of self and the world of work throughout their life spans (Dorn, 1990).

The interaction of work experiences and age ("often considered as a proxy for stage in the work career") has a differential impact on individual occupational choices at different phases of the life cycle: ". . .do the effects of work on psychological development vary as workers move through their careers? When do the processes by which work affects the personality begin? Do they taper off, continue with the same strength indefinitely, or increase with longer exposure to the job environment? Do work-related attitudes stabilize with age, or is psychological development in response to work a life-long process? Do jobs have psychological effects of the same kind throughout the worklife, or might work conditions that are deleterious in one phase have more salutary consequences in another?" (Mortimer & Borman, 1988, pp. 3–4).

For dual career couples, midlife may involve a reevaluation of career choices and career directions. Couples who do not have children or who may have already "launched" children may be ready to begin the maintenance and decline stages of career growth. Other couples may have chosen to have children later in life and be facing middle-stage child-care issues during the later stages of their careers. In still other couples, the male and female partners may be at significantly different stages of development. The men in these couples may have pursued more direct career paths and be at later stages of career development. In contrast, the women may have taken time off, or work slowdowns for child care, and may be at an earlier stage of career development. Women may have the flexibility to devote effort to their career endeavors that they had not had at earlier times. In each of these cases, the career issues partners face will be distinct and the challenges to career counselors will vary. Also, at midlife, individuals may have progressed far enough in their careers to command greater flexibility so that they can pursue outside interests and become more involved in volunteer pursuits.

Lifespan Theories of Career Development

Jepsen's Theory

Work or career is embedded within other aspects of the person's life history and represents one aspect of the multidimensional changes that define human development (Jepsen, 1990). Development reflects change in behavioral organization and content, as well as the mode or structure for organizing that information. The relationship of the developmental counselor to the client extends over a long period of time and involves intermittent reviews and responses to current work roles, so that developmental career counselors have the opportunity to influence simultaneously many interrelated client behaviors, rather than affecting only one decision process. Clients, however, are expected to play an active role in their own career development.

Career development counselors emphasize factors that facilitate the transition of individuals from one stage to another. Because counselors work with clients throughout their life spans, dual career couple issues are particularly significant. Balance between partners and varying demands of family roles each affects client career issues throughout the life span. Moreover, developmental career counselors can play significant roles in assisting dual career couples to plan for career achievement, because these clients' success in couple, career, and family roles may require a higher degree of strategic planning than necessary among other clients.

CONCLUSIONS

Dual career couples are affected by the developmental stages of the individual, the couple, and their careers. First, with respect to the individual, stage of development will affect career performance. The family and career choices of each partner may restrict or expand the opportunities available to the significant other. Second, with respect to the couple, different stages of development will pose different challenges to individual and career achievement. When couples are parents of preschoolers, each individual may have few opportunities for pursuing other roles. Moreover, the pressures both for achieving within a career and for effective parenting may be acute. As children mature, their needs for parents diminish, so that parents may pursue different roles more easily. Third, career choice is affected by external reality, which involves decisions about family and career equity among dual career couples. Career counselors can play a significant role in facilitating this equity to encourage client career success. Fourth, because of the plasticity of human behavior, the nature of the relationship between partners in dual career couples can change when they avail themselves of opportunities for establishing equity at any stage in the couple relationship.

Part II

Part II

5 An Integrated Approach to Counseling Dual Career Couples

THE NEED FOR A NEW COUNSELING APPROACH

Dual employed couples today represent approximately 60% to 70% of employees at major corporations (Johnson, 1990), a far greater proportion of American working couples than the 7% represented by single earner families (Sekaran, 1986). Among college students, women anticipate being involved in work throughout their life spans, and both men and women expect to be part of dual career couples (Baber & Monaghan, 1988; Bridges, 1987; Covin & Brush, 1991; Regan & Roland, 1982; Sekaran, 1986; Spade & Reese, 1991). Therefore, innovative strategies in counseling dual career couples will be relevant to the future needs of many clients.

The second part of this book represents an innovative approach to counseling dual career couples by addressing their distinct counseling needs. Mastery of sophisticated strategies for balancing redundant roles and overlapping responsibilities of career, home, and family expected of each partner in the dual career couple is a central element of this counseling strategy. Much of the early literature on dual career couples focused on the distinctiveness of their lifestyles and the belief in the "motherhood mandate," which specified the importance of mothers' availability to their children. This literature focused on characterizing the particular stresses and strains dual career couples experienced and on identifying the negative impact of maternal employment. So certain were early researchers of finding this negative effect that they used maternal employment as a dependent variable. However, parameters of maternal employment, the woman's attitude toward the number of hours employed, or her education were rarely assessed. No negative impact of maternal employment in children's cognitive, emotional, or social development was detected (Bianchi & Spain, 1986; Hayes & Kamerman, 1983; Hoffman, 1989; Kamerman & Hayes, 1982; Spitze, 1988) and, more importantly, children and their employed mothers were found to have secure relationships (Belsky, 1988; Clarke-Stewart, 1988; Moorehouse, 1991; Thompson, 1988). Parameters of paternal employment also were ignored, and the dynamics of the couple relationship were not considered (see chapter 1 for a comprehensive review).

Innovative ways to look at the dual career couple lifestyle involve assessing various aspects of parental employment and parents' interaction with children to understand more completely the roles parents play in career development and the stresses or strains partners experience. Examples of such studies include assessing the quality of parents' work lives, the balance of responsibilities between partners in a dual career couple, one partner's attitudes toward the significant other's employment, or the difference in family role patterns among dual career and single earner couples. Moreover, it seems likely that development among children of dual career couples will relate to the parent-child relationship, the types of schools children attend, peer groups, or factors associated with the cognitive growth of children in other families. Additionally, different characteristics of the relationship within the parent couple, the quality of time each parent spends with the child, and other similar variables will affect the child's development, rather than this development simply being a function of whether or not a mother works outside of the home.

The integrated approach presented in the second part of this book represents an action agenda developed to address the unique demands of dual career couples. Rather than grafting the needs of dual career couples onto counseling approaches used with individual clients or single career families, this innovative counseling approach integrates information presented in earlier sections of this book relating to dual career couples, gender psychology, career counseling, marriage/couple and family counseling, and life-span development. The fundamental objective for dual career couples is to achieve relationship equity, which is a distinct balance between various aspects of partners' responsibilities that feels right to each member of the couple. The integrated approach described in this book will enable counselors to assist dual career couple clients to negotiate an equitable balance among their family and career roles.

Dual career couples face challenges and rewards that distinguish them from other couples. The partners, by definition, are highly involved in their careers and consider their employment roles as integral aspects of their self-definitions. In fact, it is the high value given to women's careers that distinguishes dual career couples from other couples (Wilk, 1986). Couple and family success also takes high priority. Because of their commitment to their careers, their relationship, and their family, members of dual career couples may often find themselves overburdened. By sharing household responsibilities among other family members, or hiring household help, partners can reduce some of their role demands. This will increase available time for the more rewarding aspects of partners' roles in the family and in their careers. Although every couple differs in ability and inclination to perform various obligations, couples will function more effectively once they address strategic balance among these roles.

The lifestyle of dual career couples is characterized by a complex interdependence of their family and career roles. These couples do not represent variants of traditional couples where the career responsibilities of the woman are simply added on to her family roles, and the man's family commitment is added on to his career role. Assuming that either men's couple or family roles can be denied, or that women's career roles can be neglected, ignores the realities of the successful dual career lifestyle.

The Difficulty of Achieving Success as Dual Career Couples

Successful dual career couples claim that their roles as partners take priority over their career roles (Wilk, 1986). Although this is evident when they make major decisions, on a day-to-day basis, each partner is highly involved with career demands, often obscuring the primary role of the significant other. Therefore, partners need good communication skills to make each other feel significant and appreciated even when a great deal of time is routinely given to career pursuits rather than to building the couple relationship.

Dual career couple clients should be counseled within the context of the multiple responsibilities associated with their many roles. A primary concern for counseling is the establishment of family equity, which is the negotiated balance of various family, couple, and household roles. Family parameters and career demands, as they evolve, reverberate throughout the family and are related to changes in role dimensions. Counselors may advocate change in role parameters and evaluate the implications of individual career transformations or relationship role changes on each partner's career, couple, and family potentialities.

Dual career couples experience a higher level of stress and pressure than other couples. Time is always at a premium. Once family and career obligations are attended to, little time remains for socializing with friends, family, or business associates. If couples take time to socialize with friends, they may feel frustrated by the insufficient time available to spend with their children. Stress is also associated with the high level of organization necessary to function effectively on a daily basis, and the limited amount of time available for performing many routine responsibilities. Couples also face the stress of continually setting priorities among the many things they would each like to do alone and together.

Impact of Dual Career Couple Lifestyle on Achievement

Despite these many stresses and pressures, many couples claim that the dual career couple lifestyle has many rewards and is worth its many difficulties (Sekaran, 1986; Wilk, 1986). Opportunities for individual growth, companionship, and intellectual development apparently outweigh other drawbacks dual career couples face.

How does the dual career couple lifestyle affect the career achievements of male and female partners? Women have different career paths than men because of their child-care concerns (Betz & Fitzgerald, 1987; Hall, 1987; Voydanoff, 1987). In the past, many women interrupted their careers to attend to family roles (Betz & Fitzgerald). Contemporary research is beginning to focus on the impact of family concerns on men in dual career couples. Anecdotal evidence also indicates that men are more involved in child-care demands like dressing children for school or day care, picking them up at day care, and bringing them to medical or dental appointments. This involvement may affect, directly and indirectly, the long-range career achievement of men. As more men become increasingly involved in equitable sharing, parallel effects of dual career couple lifestyles become evident in the careers of both men and women. It is likely that the career paths of both partners in dual career couples may be distinct from those of other couples because of the commitment of each partner to home, child-care, and couple concerns. Partners may maximize the benefits of any career decisions by making choices that help the career progress of both partners. Promotions that require additional business travel or longer work hours might be turned down because of concern for the other partner's career demands. Relocations also may be rejected because of consideration for a partner's career progress and development. Couples may experience increased stress if an alternative career decision would have had dramatic benefits for one partner's career at the expense of the career progress of the significant other.

Two major effects of the dual career couple lifestyle on career achievement can be anticipated. First, partners in dual career couples will achieve career objectives at a slower pace than other corporate employees. This may be related both to child-related work slowdowns, such as time-outs, flexible work schedules, and part-time employment, as well as to nego- tiated choices about career priorities made to benefit each partner at different points in his or her career. Keohane (1984, cited in Hall, 1986) advocated the development of a new career model for "flexible success" that assumes that careers will be interrupted and advances will be slower. This model is particularly relevant to the career choices dual career couples with children make, and it is related to their plans for life-span success.

Second, dual career couples require home and career flexibility to achieve success. Because compromises are made between both partners' career goals, creative planning is crucial to achieve success. If either partner has taken time off for child care, he or she may face many obstacles in reentering the work force and achieving success. Flexibility in consid- ering how to achieve goals and in deciding on what goals can be achieved can reduce the frustration of partners' attempts to compensate for time-outs from the work force.

Dual career couples can evaluate their achievement most effectively when they view it across the life span. Because of slower paths to achieve- ment and alternate routes to success, achievement may not be evident across small spans of time. Only over many years and with attention to the interplay of family, career, and couple roles can dual career couples begin to evaluate their life successes.

THE INTEGRATED APPROACH

Given the unique demands of dual career couples, the integrated ap- proach to counseling them focuses on a novel way to view family respon- sibilities. In traditional models, it was assumed that the wife would take care of the home and that the husband would work outside of the home. If the wife wanted to work, she would add that responsibility to her housework, and if the husband were generous or egalitarian, he would assume *some* household responsibilities. Today, approximately half of the entering classes at some of the most competitive educational institutions in this country are composed of women. Moreover, based on demographic, sociological, and economic forecasts, women will represent the majority of new entrants into the future work force (Johnston & Packer, 1987). Therefore, new models that respect the career, couple, and family roles both men and women must play in dual career couples signify the most forward-thinking approaches for counselors as they enter the 21st century.

The integrated approach is characterized by three distinct parameters:

1. The goal of dual career couples is to achieve balance and negotiate family and career equity.

2. Counselors can use innovative approaches in integrating knowledge related to gender issues, family/couple counseling, and human development to design appropriate assessment techniques and to encourage couple development.
3. Counselors can help couples recognize how family and career concerns and role conflicts evolve over the course of the life span. Both rewards and challenges will differ over time.

It is important to note here that I am discussing dual career couples, or couples in which both partners are serious about their careers and view their employment positions as essential to their self-definitions. As I have stated previously, career commitment does not reveal whether people work in any particular field. I have met managers, physicians, and lawyers who view their jobs as something temporary until they find more congenial work. On the other hand, I have met office managers, technicians, and hourly workers who are serious about their jobs, take great pride in their work, and view their jobs as an essential part of who they are as well as an important step in their progressive life-span career paths. Thus, "dual career couples," within the context of this book, refers to couples who view their careers as important, significant, and progressive and as an essential element of their self-definition, irrespective of the kind of work they perform.

The new attitude toward dual career couples that I propose would assume that the couple and their family are a unit that must divide a variety of responsibilities. Money must be earned, household chores must be accomplished, children may need to be cared for, and individual needs must be met. Outdated assumptions about whether men or women are best at earning money or caring for children are irrelevant in this model. Instead couples are viewed as negotiating responsibilities based on talents, inclinations, abilities, interests, and what needs to be done. Even when couples take on traditional responsibilities, they will feel more in control of their situations and more capable of renegotiating unbalanced responsibilities. Furthermore, there is a difference between negotiating for responsibilities and negotiating away responsibilities. Traditionally, women in dual career couples were seen as negotiating away responsibilities for cleaning, cooking, general housekeeping, and child care. Every responsibility negotiated away could become a chit that she owed her significant other. In the integrated model, couples negotiate for a part of the total responsibilities that must be done for the family to function as a cohesive unit.

People have different skills and preferences with regard to performing various family responsibilities and vary in their orientation to their employment. Maintaining communication with friends and members of their extended families, cooking, cleaning, shopping, paying bills, managing home repairs, and caring for the car or home are all essential to family well-functioning, and just a few of the many tasks that need to be done. One goal of the family is to meet individual needs, which may involve a variety of psychological and psychosocial parameters. Of particular psychological significance for dual career couples is the self-actualization associated with pursuing a satisfying career successfully. Career-committed individuals derive many positive aspects of their self-image from their careers, and self-esteem and self-confidence are higher among women who are employed (Barnett & Baruch, 1978b; James, 1990). Moreover, for all individuals, career development is an essential aspect of psychological growth.

Couples negotiate around the personal meaning of employment and its associated demands as well as the parameters of other home and family responsibilities (see chapter 7). These negotiations must accommodate each partner's goals for success as defined by the individual, and by the institution where the individual is employed. Ranking their goals is critical to dual career couples because success is generally possible in only a few areas. Couples can use a life-span approach to plan intermediate steps on their way to ultimate success and retrospectively to evaluate the success they have achieved.

EXAMPLE OF DIVERSITY AMONG DUAL CAREER COUPLES

The following is an example of how a hypothetical dual career couple planned an equitable balance to reflect their abilities, interests, and talents. Cullee, a professor, is older than his wife, Joyce, who has just graduated from law school and has been offered a position at a very demanding, high-paying law firm where she will immediately make a salary substantially in excess of Cullee's current salary. The demands of each job are different and her job is more demanding, providing little personal free time for performing home-related chores. She will be expected to work 80 to 90 hours per week on a regular basis, and any kind of work slowdown would signify lack of career commitment. Cullee has a less demanding work schedule than Joyce, and has a more positive inclination to care for the basic needs of babies and children. Their expectation for household role responsibilities is that Cullee will run the household in addition to meeting his career obligations. If and when they decide to have children, Cullee will take primary responsibility for their care. In this situation, it would be erroneous to expect the husband to perform the role of primary breadwinner and the wife the role of primary household and family caretaker. Instead, other roles, more appropriate to their skills, life-span stages, careers, and inclinations are advocated.

ACHIEVING EQUITY WITHIN THE RELATIONSHIP

Within the family, roles and responsibilities are undertaken and decisions are reached through communication, negotiation, and conflict resolution. Therefore, couples must learn to communicate their feelings about
different chores to one another and master negotiation skills, discuss career
needs, and plan for dividing household responsibilities equitably. Both
scientific studies and popular literature support the idea that men do not
often participate fully at home. Therefore, wives may be routinely coached
about how to encourage their husbands to participate. The new female
fantasy involves having a relationship with the "perfect man" who is
willing to be totally supportive and participatory, as reflected in a wide
variety of popular romance novels (Stanley, 1991). Husbands receive no
similar coaching to participate, suggesting that couples may reach an
impasse.

Counselors can adopt a new model for addressing the needs of dual
career couples that views family responsibilities as the requirement of
both partners (cf., Miller, 1976). Women who are seriously involved in
time-consuming careers will be unable to progress in their careers if they
alone shoulder the burden of daily home responsibilities. Continually
relying on the largesse of a husband or significant other to "help out" at
home is demeaning and counterproductive and breeds resentment. Moreover, if counselors who work with dual career couples operate with the
assumption that the home is the woman's domain, the negotiation for
equitable balance will be hampered, and the woman will negotiate from
a position of weakness as she tries to diminish her responsibilities while
her partner agrees or refuses to assume those responsibilities. A variety
of contemporary models for gender-fair couple counseling are available
to expand counselor functioning (cf., Miller, 1976; Walters et al., 1988).

CONSTRAINTS ON DUAL CAREER COUPLES

It is impossible for men or women to pursue a career successfully and
move up in their career while putting in 20 to 30 hours of household work
per week. Moreover, it is difficult for individuals to continue pursuing a
career without anger or resentment if they feel that they bear a chunk of
the burden of earning family finances as well as the nonnegotiated responsibilities for household functioning and child care. Even if families
have household help or someone to assist with children, family work
remains intensive. The model proposed in this book assumes that the
burden of responsibility is negotiated and divided among family members
so that no one individual carries an impossible household burden, and that

couples negotiate for responsibilities, which decreases stress, anger, and resentment. Both partners are encouraged to develop their own parenting styles so that they can fully appreciate the rewards of fatherhood or motherhood.

ASSUMPTIONS OF MODEL OF DUAL CAREER COUPLES

The current model makes a number of assumptions. First, families have a variety of responsibilities that must be performed. Details of responsibilities as well as why they are important will vary from couple to couple. Second, the way that these responsibilities can be divided comfortably will vary from couple to couple with their skills, talents, and preferences. Third, attitudes toward responsibilities need to be communicated, conflicts need to be discussed, and, ideally, resolved. Fourth, because many dual career couples know few couples whom they consider role models for equitable balancing of family and career roles, counselors need to be creative in establishing new methods for assisting dual career couples. Groups consisting of dual career couples at different life and career stages are often helpful in expanding couple perspectives concerning functional models. Fifth, approaches to resolving conflicts over responsibilities within the couple as well as the appropriate solutions may change over time. Therefore, communication, negotiation, and problem solving are ongoing processes throughout the couple's life span. Sixth, appropriate solutions to couples' family and career conflicts will vary because of their individual differences, personal needs, gender concerns, and so on. Counselors should be sensitive to finding unique solutions for each couple rather than operating with a preconceived notion of an optimally fair balance for the dual career couple. Seventh, individuals need to balance their own family and work responsibilities with those of their partners. Eighth, dual career couples operate within the framework of the institutions, corporations, universities, and businesses that employ them. Individual solutions to dual career couple issues need to be made within the context of each partner's particular career demands. To help counselors address these various assumptions, a variety of assessment instruments are presented throughout the second part of the book. These include instruments that address family and career priorities, negotiation and communication skills, conflict resolution styles, and goals for success.

Family Responsibilities

Responsibilities will vary across families and among couples in early relationship stages, in formative stages, and in more mature stages. Additionally, the presence of preschool children or school-aged children and the number of children in the home will present different family demands. Whether or not the family is responsible for caring for aging parents will also create a differential impact on the definition of a fair balance between both partners' careers and family.

Couples' disposable income is directly related to their balance of responsibilities. In couples where one or both partners earn a high income, the couple has greater resources available for hiring outside private help for child care, home care, and other home-related responsibilities to ease the burden of family and career conflicts. Even with household help, many issues related to home care typically arise, and couples will still need to establish rules about how they want to balance responsibilities.

Skills, Talents, and Preferences

What constitutes a fair division of responsibilities will vary among families because of partners' abilities and distinct definitions of "fair." For example, discussing of the marital contract (mentioned in chapter 3) can help couples articulate what they are willing to do and what responsibilities they would like their significant others to perform. Marital contracts can be general, or complex, detailed agreements of individual roles, responsibilities, and expectations (cf., Wilk, 1986). The constraints of gender stereotypes with respect to what partners will consider "fair" to do at home is also an important area to address. Discussions of family/couple equity can begin only after the couple has confronted gender issues in career and family demands. Through negotiation each partner will assume responsibilities for some family roles. Negotiation can revolve around dividing responsibilities for "orphan" areas that neither partner wants responsibility for, or planning on sharing responsibilities that both partners want to perform.

Communication

Communication is essential to effective functioning within dual career couples and may include career demands and personal needs, family issues, job demands, politics, or current events. Although some of these topics may sound trivial, some couples have refused to pursue commuter relationships because of the importance of this daily chitchat to the fabric of their lives (Wilk, 1986). Communication is also related to achieving couple equity (see chapter 7). For example, when partners work in the same fields, they may have intricate knowledge about each other's institutional goals. In contrast, partners may remain unaware and ill-informed of the demands and pitfalls of the significant other's work unless this information is communicated clearly and directly. It is easier to develop functional family patterns when partners' career demands are understood and appreciated.

Negotiation is impossible without effective communication. Individuals may need to communicate their relationship expectations to a spouse or significant other, or negotiate regarding a relocation or promotion offer. Counselors can be particularly helpful to dual career couples in assisting them to develop communication, negotiation, and problem-solving skills (Stoltz-Loike, 1990, 1991, 1992a, 1992b). These negotiations often require extensive and open discussion over a long period of time in order to arrive at an equitable solution.

Establishing New Role Models

A major problem dual career couples face is the isolation they feel in trying to balance their multiple roles. In only rare cases have they known adults one generation older who have artfully balanced career roles and family responsibilities. Among their workplace colleagues, issues related to balancing family and career may not be openly discussed, and many of their community neighbors may have a more traditional lifestyle than theirs. Therefore, partners can benefit directly from group discussions with couples facing similar career and family dilemmas. Even when group participants are involved in careers with different prestige, salary, or job demands, it is particularly meaningful to discuss the experience of how couples have made choices or compromises to ensure that the family can function effectively. Groups can also be organized within corporate settings so that couples can share family and career experiences with others facing similar challenges under similar constraints.

Responsibility Through the Life Span

Development, challenge, and choice are parts of a life-span process that begins at the time that the couple is formed and continues throughout its duration. The pressure for one partner to cut back on business responsibilities may be particularly pronounced when there are preschoolers at home, although once children enter school, this pressure abates. Parents may feel increased responsibility to earn more money as children approach college age, and elect to take on additional work or business responsibilities. Within the couple, different choices about business-related travel, time away from family, and relocation may be made at different points in the career history of the couple. Couples also attribute differential values to family and career at different points in their lives. Expectations for career progress can also affect career and family performance. Partners who have plateaued in their careers may be willing to assume different family responsibilities than they would have at earlier points in their careers.

Defining Unique Solutions for the Couple

The optimal balance of family and career responsibilities will differ for every couple because of the partners' self-definitions with respect to their personal roles and their roles as part of a family. In some couples, one individual may elect to change career paths when young children are present, or during the early stages of a relationship. Alternatively, couples may choose to pursue career interests actively and to spend less time on couple or family relationships. Counselors should assist couples in identifying their own optimal solutions for career and family balance rather than imposing a counselor-derived solution, and offer insight to the couple about the strengths and pitfalls of their solutions. For example, one focus may include financial losses and career path damages that accrue from sequencing strategies of family and career needs. Similarly, counselors may highlight for the couple the negative impact of high career involvement on their own relationship. Although the counselor can assist the couple, ultimately the couple must arrive at their own unique solution for balancing their couple, family, and career needs.

Family and Career Balance

Individuals' satisfaction with their balance of family and career responsibilities varies with the stage of the family. Balance means that couples have reached a solution that works for them, but it does not mean that there are no mixed feelings or guilt associated with family and career choices. Perhaps a father is employed full-time, uses the corporate on-site day care, but still misses his child. If the father can do his job effectively and also feel that he has adequate time to form a meaningful bond with his child, this is an effective solution. Similarly, a father may cut back on his very demanding work schedule so that he can spend more time with his children. The father may miss the hectic pace of work but be satisfied with his new, more intimate relationship with his children. This balance of high work involvement and time with family is successful for this father.

An important aspect in the personal balance of family and career revolves around the issue of guilt. Often, parents or counselors may look for quick fixes to resolve guilt over work and family responsibilities. In fact, guilt makes parents come home rather than making one more phone call and reminds them of the value of the children who remain at home. Guilt is a problem only when it is excessive or affects an individual's ability to participate in other roles.

Employer Versus Family Reality

Couples work within the context of their career strictures. Some jobs are 9 to 5 and others have different patterns of flexible hours. More typically, however, careers have longer, more demanding hours and require regular work-related travel. Decisions relating to the couple and individual family-career balance must be made within the context of these employment realities.

For partners these career realities mean that they must plan time together for couple growth and development. For parents other questions arise. Although many businesses and universities make special work schedules available to accommodate family needs, this is not currently the norm, nor are programs comprehensive, meaning that family and career requirements will conflict (see chapter 10). Additionally, questions arise concerning whether parents who use family-friendly programs will be viewed as insufficiently committed to their work and will therefore be passed over for promotions or interesting assignments. Complex questions about what constitutes family and career balance must also be addressed. In a career where 80 to 100 hours of work per week is the norm, part-time employment would involve 40 to 50 hours of work per week. Is this an adequate arrangement for parents who wish to cut back on their work schedules to accommodate family needs, and would part-time work at this employer truly be family-friendly?

Counselors need to help dual career couple clients focus on the realities of the interaction of family roles and work environments. It is easy to be idealistic and expect employers to change to accommodate individual needs. This is unrealistic and often impossible. However, as more workplaces address the needs of dual career couples, creative planners will develop flexible programs that satisfy the business needs of the employer as well as the family and career needs of the employee.

REALITY VERSUS FANTASY IN COUPLE EQUITY

The idea that all responsibilities within the family can be negotiated may be a pleasant fantasy. Reality, however, may be quite different. Gender differences exist, and gender stereotypes are pervasive (see chapter 2). Men and women have different expectations for themselves and their significant others. External social pressure can also affect the viability of the dual career couple lifestyle. It is not uncommon for career-committed individuals to be questioned, somewhat accusingly, about when they find time for their children, or for couples to be the brunt of snide remarks about "Yuppies" who would rather have material wealth than a family with children. Demonstrated competence, however, engenders respect and circumvents accepted social norms. Friends are happy to dine at the home of a couple who serve delicious food, whether it was prepared by a man or a woman. Male corporate executives who leave meetings early to attend little league, or pick up a child from day care, are often of little concern to others within the company when the man is a competent, productive member of the corporate hierarchy. Analogously, women who can fix the plumbing capably and attend to the infrastructures of their homes are often viewed with envy by both men and women who are less competent.

Gender Issues

Although functioning along strict gender boundaries may be difficult and undesirable for many couples, it is particularly problematic for dual career couples. When counselors sense that gender stereotypes are undermining the couple's ability to function, interventions may be appropriate. Counselors can help partners develop self-definitions that are more gender-sensitive and assist them in learning methods for negotiating roles and obligations (cf., Stoltz-Loike, 1991). For example, through individual counseling or within a group setting, counselors who work within corporations can target successful individuals in upper levels of management who may be willing to share details of their own more gender-free balancing of family and career responsibilities.

Counselors can also underscore the importance of incorporating both instrumental (masculine) and expressive (feminine) characteristics in successful performance at work and at home (see chapter 2). For example, managers may need to be aggressive and able to take care of themselves to move up the corporate ladder; however, if they are unable to develop their technical staff by being attuned to their ways of functioning, they may ultimately be unsuccessful as managers. Similarly, at home, individuals must be able to identify and argue for their own needs to negotiate successfully with their partners. Being a supportive partner, however, also requires good listening skills and concern for others.

As counselors work with clients to expand their gender definitions, couples may experience feelings of loss and confusion. For example, a woman might feel that if she shares responsibility for the children or the home she will be confused about her self-definition as a woman. Similarly, a man may feel that sharing household decisions or balancing career priorities might conflict with his ability to achieve. In reality, both concerns are valid. It clearly is special to hold the role of most significant parent for one's children, and to be the first one that the children go to for comforting, or caretaking. It is also special to be viewed as the expert in household functioning by all family members. The problem with becoming an expert at home is that it exacts a price, which is usually the cost of the woman's ability to function optimally in her career. Moreover, the children's father is missing out on a special relationship with his children and the pleasant satisfaction of knowing that he has played a significant role in their development.

Analogously, successfully performing as the decision maker and having the primary role within the career world can be truly satisfying. However, there is a cost involved with respect to personal growth and development both as an individual and as a member of a family. By sharing these family and career responsibilities with one's partner, pressures for financial success may be lessened, the significance of financial setbacks may be mitigated, and opportunities for intelligent feedback may be achieved. Counselors can help couples appreciate the positive and negative impacts of their career and family choices on their experiences as individuals, members of a couple, and employees. Such insight into the functional and dysfunctional aspects of their performance can be truly helpful to dual career couples.

Couple Issues

This book assumes that couples are partnered and wish to remain that way. For example, an individual who comes to see a career counselor is looking for a way to expand his or her career options and perhaps to enhance the couple's life together, or individual roles within the couple. Creative counselors can identify the impact of career choices on each partner's career, personal life, and relationship as a method for helping partners prepare for future choices and crises. For example, the decision of a woman to pursue a career in management within a company that will require relocation every 5 to 7 years will differentially affect her significant other depending on whether he is a tenured professor in a major university or a fourth-year graduate student.

Couples may find it significant and enlightening to verbalize their expectations for themselves and their partners as part of a review of their overt and covert relationship expectations. Once couples recognize their needs and interdependent expectations with regard to personal and financial concerns, it becomes easier to negotiate their respective career needs. Moreover, expectations involving personal, couple, and career development can significantly affect the equitability of negotiated decisions.

Individuals in dual career couples also may need assistance in planning time to develop as a couple. Often the demands of two careers become so exhausting and overwhelming that the couple relationship may stagnate. Successful functioning within the dual career couple involves growth of the couple as well as each individual within a chosen career. Couples who choose to pursue careers and to put couple growth in the background should recognize the relationship dead end toward which they are heading.

CONCLUSIONS

The integrated approach presented in this book represents an innovative method for counseling dual career couples. It is predicated on the assumption that the needs of dual career couples are distinct from those of other couples. Dual career couples have overlapping responsibilities for career, family, and child-care roles. By reducing the overlap and balancing the responsibilities, partners can function more effectively in their multiple roles. Counselors who can incorporate couples' unique relationship parameters into their work with dual career couple clients can assist these couples successfully.

Eight specific assumptions of the model were outlined, highlighting gender differences and life-span issues relevant to couple functioning. Particular aspects of couple responsibilities and the goal of equity can be achieved when dual career couples master relationship skills like communication, negotiation, and conflict resolution. Counselors can train partners in these skills and reinforce their acquisition. Successful dual career couples are characterized by mutual respect for achievement at home and performance in the work force, and a true commitment to personal and partner accomplishments. The sense of equity or fairness associated with both partners' achievements enriches the couple and family relationship as well as enhancing career productivity.

6 Assessing Family and Career Priorities

A PRIMARY STEP IN working with dual career couples is to help each partner articulate his or her personal orientation to work and family. This chapter focuses on how counselors can assist couples in assessing family and career priorities. The first part of the chapter will discuss general concerns in evaluating family and career balance, and the second part of the chapter will detail specific tools for assessment. The key factors for developing appropriate strategies to balance family and career responsibilities among dual career couples are their career development expectations, relationship as a couple, gender beliefs, and life-span perspectives.

Three aspects of family and career balance will be described: (1) personal balance between family and career, (2) balance between careers of partners, and (3) couple balance between family and career. Only when individuals can identify or articulate their own orientation to family and career issues can they communicate this to their significant others effectively.

PERSONAL BALANCE BETWEEN FAMILY AND CAREER

Each partner may want to consider the kinds of balance he or she would like to establish between family and career obligations. Counselors can play a significant role in assisting clients in determining and expressing their commitments to career or family, and in helping couples recognize in which areas the balance is lacking. Equitable choices around family/career balance and decisions may differ between members of a couple.

After they have children, some individuals will continue full-time work schedules; others will elect to take advantage of the many currently available alternate work schedules, such as part-time work, flextime, and telecommuting (see chapter 10). Men typically have not availed themselves of these options, but this may change in the future.

Career Balance

Every couple expresses the balance of family and career commitments differently. In some couples, this balance is reflected by the equal commitment of both partners to their careers. Other couples may decide that one member of the couple will pursue a lead career and the other person's career will be secondary. This means that both partners' career decisions are determined by how they will affect the progress of the partner with the lead career. Attributing a lead career to one partner may depend on a person's skills or talents, particular field of expertise, the presence of a mentor who assists the person's career progress, or the high earning potential of one partner's career. Thus, balance will be achieved differently in the couple with equal career commitments as compared to the couple with one partner in a lead career, and this balance may be expressed in different choices about daily work schedules, responsibility for housework, relocation decisions, or family decision making. (It is important to note here that although dual career couples may place a high value on their family life, career-committed individuals, by definition, are highly involved in their employment-related accomplishments.)

In couples who place equal value on both careers, each partner's career may take priority at different points in the relationship. In this regard, couple communication and negotiation will be critical to balance family and career effectively throughout the couple's life span (see chapter 7).

Gender differences also may be related to career balance within the couple. The relative inclination of men and women to discuss work and family commitments may differ. For example, men may be reluctant to admit that they are frustrated by working hard and would like more time with their families, whereas women may be reluctant to admit that they may want to give their careers priority over family concerns.

Industries and employers vary in their family-friendliness. For example, institutions in health-related areas, which employ many women, generally have family-friendly benefits. Additionally, younger corporations, such as high tech industries and others that may have difficulty recruiting women, also have family-friendly policies. Only when employed by institutions that are truly flexible can workers comfortably negotiate for family and career equity. Otherwise, the couple may be equitable, but career demands may countermand that fair balance.

Balance Between Family and Career

Typically, client couples will first attend career counseling sessions as individuals. To address career dimensions of the dual career couple within the appropriate context, counselors can routinely bring clients and their partners into the counseling process. This can then ensure that the needs of both members of the couple are fairly addressed and their perspectives are accurately represented. Otherwise, counselors may find that career development dimensions are not implemented because of competing career demands of the spouse or significant other. Another approach to counseling dual career couples is to use a group setting focused on family and career balance, where all participants are members of dual career couples.

Too often, dual career issues are viewed as women's issues by couples, employers, and counselors, when, in fact, choices affect the career progress of both members of the couple. When one partner chooses to work part-time, the effect on the dual career couple lifestyle may be less pronounced. Career development theorists have proposed that the career paths of men and women may differ because women typically assume primary responsibility for child rearing (Fitzgerald & Crites, 1980). In dual career couples, however, where responsibilities for family and career are shared and where both partners are employed full-time, the career progress of both men and women may be distinct because of the slowdown in career progress associated with children.

Examples of Conflicts in Dual Career Couples

Three examples will illustrate some of the conflicts dual career couples face and identify some key concerns that can be addressed in counseling.

Long and Min are partners in a dual career couple. They are both managers at different Fortune 500 companies. Both of their companies have career development specialists on staff who have used various assessment instruments to evaluate their employees' career interests. Min would be satisfied with achieving a middle- to upper-level management position, but does not want to put in the time or energy necessary to progress farther. Long wants to reach the top levels of management in the executive suite, and her career goals are strongly supported by Min. Min might be able to stay at his company site without relocating; Long's career plans, however, will require relocating every 5 to 7 years. Moreover, she will need to be involved in an ongoing educational process that involves on-site and university-based courses that will be subsidized by her company but can be taken only on weekends or in the evening.

They both remember how they used to dream about having money to take vacations to exotic places and enjoy one another's company. Now, they both worry about having *any* time together. Additional questions arise about the impact of her career progress on his career path, and the impact of relocation on both of their careers. Long also questions whether, as a woman, she has a chance of making it to the top of her corporation because women currently hold no executive-level positions.

Pam is an investment analyst. Seth is a technician in a Fortune 500 corporation. They have two children, ages 5 and 7. Pam travels extensively on a regular basis. Although she misses her family during her travels, she knows that there are no alternatives if she is to move up in her company. Although Seth supports Pam's career, he often expresses his lack of understanding as to why she needs to travel. He has read about tele-commuting and how it is changing the workplace and can't understand why she needs so much face-to-face interaction with clients at the expense of her family. Pam wonders whether Seth's feelings relate to her career or to the fact that she is a woman. Both Pam and Seth feel stressed by the demands of their children.

Lori and Ben are partners in a dual career couple. She is a social worker with supervisory responsibilities and he is a corporate attorney. They have two teenaged children. Lori takes primary responsibility for the home and children, largely because her husband does not return home from work before 10 o'clock in the evening. Lori has developed an extensive network of friends with whom she speaks and visits regularly. It is not uncommon for Ben to work on weekends, when Lori visits with her friends and members of the extended family. Although both Lori and Ben would like more time together, they realize that given the parameters of Ben's work, this is not possible. Neither Lori nor Ben considers dis-cussing a change in his career. Ben finds his work stimulating, and they both appreciate the luxuries they can afford because of his high income. They find that they are drifting apart, however, and their teenaged daughter has been cutting classes and taking drugs. They have come to counseling ostensibly to address the needs of their daughter (the identified patient). They wonder if they are going through a temporary stage or if their feelings of isolation from one another will pass and whether their daughter will "settle down."

In each of these examples, the career choices of one partner signifi-cantly affect the career choices of the significant other, as well as their status as a couple and their relationship to their families. The ways in which these couples choose to resolve their conflicts will affect work schedules, relocation possibilities, career development, development as a couple, expectations of the relationship, and relationships to children.

SELECTED FACTORS AFFECTING BALANCE

Couple Factors

Couples need to devote time to a relationship if it is to flourish. Therefore, they need to discuss ways to nurture their relationship and reinforce their bond. This may include time alone in the evening, on weekends, or for periodic vacations. Moreover, when children are living at home, the couple will need to consider ways to expand their dyadic relationship to include both time with the family and time as a couple. Individual and couple ease with communication and negotiation can affect the positive attitude of both members of the couple to their relationship (see chapter 7). By clearly presenting personal needs, each individual can ensure that those needs as well as partner needs are addressed.

Discussing the effect of career on the couple relationship also may involve issues related to partners' level of emotional commitment and the pursuit of common and independent interests. Details of how time is to be spent with members of the extended family need to be addressed. Couples also may consider the ability of each partner to pursue personal friendships and relationships independent of the couple relationship, and commitment to other friends may interact with considerations of time available for each other.

Career Factors

Particular careers may be characterized by excessively demanding work schedules. In those instances, couples may be advised to pursue creative planning to ensure that this does not end the growth of their relationship. Long weekends together, vacations to secluded spots or warm, communicative phone calls can have a positive impact on the development of a couple's relationship and can be used as an attempt to counterbalance long hours of work. Nonetheless, certain career paths do conflict with couple goals and are likely to change the couple relationship.

Another common issue for dual career couples is relocation, which many companies consider an essential part of the progressive nature of career development. Planning and discussing issues related to relocation can make the process easier for dual career couples. Attempts at timing transfers so that moves are potentially positive for both members of the couple can make relocation more successful and less stressful. In addition, because so many employees within major companies are part of dual career couples, supervisors and managers may be receptive to creative planning in addressing relocation needs.

Family and Career Factors

Counselors also can educate couples about a life-span perspective that involves integrating the current expectations of each individual for career development and the growth of the couple and family relationships, planning for the interaction of these factors as they evolve, and recognizing how these expectations may change throughout the life span.

For example, in the early stages of a relationship, a couple may comfortably devote many hours to their careers and still have time left for one another. If the couple decide to have children, each partner's career or personal values may need to be reevaluated. Preschool children are extremely demanding and require a good portion of parents' nonwork time. At this stage, parents may feel conflicted in identifying what defines a fair balance among the many demands on their lives. Parents may want to be with young children as well as achieve career success, making it difficult to set priorities during this stage of family life. Furthermore, the lack of sufficient time to develop in career, couple, and family relationships may be frustrating.

Once children enter grade school, conflicts are less prevalent because children are in school during most of the parents' working hours and their needs are more easily addressed. Therefore, opportunities for pursuing career options intensively can be met with fewer mixed emotions. As children mature further and their needs for parents diminish, the parental balance of family and career also will change. When a partner is the noncustodial parent of a child, the needs of that child also must be met and become a factor in establishing career/family balance.

Appreciating the demands and rewards of each stage of family development can help couples plan family and career concerns realistically. Moreover, recognizing the conflicts that may ensue and planning creative ways to address those conflicts can help couples develop a life-span perspective on family and career. The length of a typical workday and financial remuneration are important considerations of dual career couples and affect the kinds of choices partners make about the issues of career-family balance. Partners who work longer hours will not be available to perform household chores, and partners who earn higher incomes will be able to hire outside help for caretaking at home.

Counselors also should evaluate the couple's gender-driven behaviors. Although couples may not wish to nor be able to discuss gender stereotypes, particular behaviors and assumptions may be related to gender-stereotyped beliefs. Often couples are unaware of their own stereotyped beliefs. In particular, the division of household labor often reflects gender stereotypes, so that the woman performs the lion's share of household work even among couples who functioned as coequals before children were born.

Couples or individuals may also express gender-related beliefs about who can work in certain types of careers, or concern about the impact on their relationship of the woman's earning more or having the more prestigious career. These may be crucial points for discussion with the couple because women's earnings have become critical to family lifestyles at all income levels. No longer is a woman's income used solely for pocket change.

ASSESSING FAMILY AND CAREER ISSUES

In order to orchestrate discussions of family and career balance, the counselor may first want to obtain information on important issues with regard to family life including couple status, stage of family, plans to have children or more children, and type of child care used. Next, within the career domain, information about career field, institutional culture, and promotion ladder may be assessed.

Individual and couple balance of family and career concerns will affect each partner's decisions regarding work schedules, long work hours, promotions, travel, and other work-related obligations, as well as parental leaves, care of a sick child, and involvement in child-related activities. Counselors and clients, however, can use this information only when it has been clearly specified. Counselors may obtain this information informally or through a more rigorous intake interview. In either case, such information can be essential in dealing with dual career concerns.

Long and Min are the members of the dual career couple discussed earlier. Up to now, Long has taken primary care of their home. However, the recent progress in Long's career will require that she take on additional supervisory responsibilities. Long feels that it is not fair that she brings in more than half of the family income and must also spend 20 to 30 hours a week on household chores. Min, grudgingly, agrees to explore a more equitable approach to balancing responsibilities. Together with a counselor they explore options that seem fair both to Long and to Min, giving Long greater freedom at work without Min feeling that the complete burden of responsibility at home has been transferred to him.

Questionnaires for Assessing Family and Career Concerns

Tables 6.1, 6.2, 6.3, and 6.4 are examples of questionnaires that can be filled out by the couple, or by the counselor and couple together, to assess work-family orientation. The advantage of filling out this material with the counselor is that responses can be discussed and clients hear their partners' responses. Sometimes a variety of information not previously discussed between the partners may be articulated. However, when working with only one member of a couple or when couples are seen in a group, couples can be requested to fill out the questionnaires at home.

Within the dual career couple counseling session, attempts can be made to include "homework" responsibilities for the clients. Couples may leave sessions with a great deal of information but without a context to discuss the information. Homework provides them with that context. Moreover, homework generates greater enthusiasm between sessions, offers clients something to think about from session to session, maintains continuity from session to session, and helps clients feel that they will be prepared for the next session.

The intake questionnaires presented in Tables 6.1, 6.2, 6.3, and 6.4 are particularly useful for determining specific areas for intervention and concerns to explore with the couple. Counselors may choose to use the questionnaires in these tables or only parts of these questionnaires. Other forms of client interviews may be utilized to derive most of the same information. The parts designated as homework should be used routinely because of the information and insight they provide regarding how the members of the couple view family and career responsibilities.

Examples of Responses to Questionnaires

Examples of excerpts from hypothetical questionnaire responses that can be of particular concern to the counselor are found in Tables 6.5 and 6.6. This information refers to the couples cited as examples in the beginning of the chapter, and are used to illustrate a number of significant points.

The hypothetical responses in Table 6.5 are those of Pam and Seth before counseling began. The first point to be noticed is that family responsibilities break down along gender-stereotyped lines. Pam takes responsibility for shopping, cooking, home activities, and obligations for children, whereas Seth takes responsibility for the car and periodic home maintenance chores.

The counselor may first want to explore their relative time commitments to career and family roles. Exploration may focus on the career demands of Seth's and Pam's jobs to determine whether the different responses reflect different work demands or gender-stereotyped roles. If the difference in work demands is related to gender roles, both partners may be hampered by gender role stereotypes. The counselor may wish to explore whether these roles are constraining Pam's career and Seth's ability to participate fully in family life. Pam has already expressed frustration with her many household responsibilities. Moreover, Seth's feelings about Pam's business travel can, if unresolved, affect either her upward mobility or the success of their relationship.

TABLE 6.1
Assessing Family and Career Status

Names of partners _____

_____

If unmarried, number of years as a couple _____

If married, number of years married _____

Were you previously married? Yes _____ No _____

    If yes, were you divorced _____ widowed _____ separated _____

Age of man _____ Age of woman _____

Children living in household?   Yes _____ No _____

    Number of children _____

    Ages _____

    Grades in school _____

    Number of preschool children in family _____

Children under the age of 18 not living in household?

    Yes _____   No _____

    Number of children _____

    Ages _____

    How often do you see these children? _____

What kind of child care do you use (please check one)?

    day care center _____

    non-relative in own home _____

    non-relative in your home _____

    neighborhood group care _____

    relative in own home _____

    relative in your home _____

    other (please specify) _____

_____

    not applicable _____

Do you use after-school child care? Yes _____ No _____

    Not applicable _____

If yes, please specify site _____

_____

Do you use before-school child care? Yes _____ No _____

Not applicable _____

If yes, please specify site _____

_____

What are your normal work hours?

Man _____

Woman _____

For man:

Please check the response(s) that most accurately describes your work schedule:

employed full-time _____ employed part-time _____

flexible site _____ flexible hours _____

job sharing _____

Do you typically bring child to child care or wait for babysitter at your home?

Yes _____ No _____ Not applicable _____

Do you typically pick up your child from child care or take responsibility for child care after babysitter goes home?

Yes _____ No _____ Not applicable _____

For woman:

Please check the response(s) that most accurately describes your work schedule:

employed full-time _____ employed part-time _____

flexible site _____ flexible hours _____

job sharing _____

Do you typically bring child to child care or wait for babysitter at your home?

Yes _____ No _____ Not applicable _____

Do you typically pick up your child from child care or take responsibility for child care after babysitter goes home?

Yes _____ No _____ Not applicable _____

For both:

When do you typically spend time together with your spouse/significant other?

every evening _____ weekends _____

whenever we can, but not on a regular basis _____

other _____

What kinds of things do you do when you are together?

go out to dinner _____

spend time together at home _____

go to the movies _____

visit friends _____

visit relatives _____

other (please specify) _____

When do you spend time with your children?

Man:

does not apply _____

every evening _____

on weekends _____

whenever I can, but not on a
regular basis _____

other _____

Woman:

does not apply _____

every evening _____

on weekends _____

whenever I can, but not on a
regular basis _____

other _____

What kinds of things do you do with your children (Check all that apply, circle most frequent activity)?

Man:

does not apply _____

read books _____

roughhouse _____

play ball _____

visit relatives _____

visit friends _____

shopping _____

home repairs _____

baking _____

cooking _____

other _____

Woman:

does not apply _____

read books _____

roughhouse _____

play ball _____

visit relatives _____

visit friends _____

shopping _____

home repairs _____

baking _____

cooking _____

other _____

Do you have non-familial household help to perform routine housekeeping chores?

    Yes _____ No _____

    If yes, how often _____

If you have more than one child, what do you do so that you can have private time with each child?

Man:

    does not apply _____

    set different bedtimes _____

    set family rules for private time with each child _____

    go out to dinner with one child at a time _____

    share a special hobby _____

    attend special events together _____

    take one child out to do shopping _____

    other (please specify) _____

    _____

Woman:

    does not apply _____

    set different bedtimes _____

    set family rules for private time with each child _____

    go out to dinner with one child at a time _____

    share a special hobby _____

    attend special events together _____

    take one child out to do shopping _____

    other (please specify) _____

    _____

If your child does not live with you, what do you do so that you can have private time with your child(ren)?

Man:

    does not apply _____

    try to find private time with each child _____

    go out to dinner with children _____

    share a special hobby _____

    attend special events together _____

    take children out to do routine chores _____

    other (please specify) _____

_____

Woman:

    does not apply _____

    try to find private time with each child _____

    go out to dinner with children _____

    share a special hobby _____

    attend special events together _____

    take children out to do routine chores _____

    other (please specify) _____

_____

A second issue to be explored is the difference between Seth's perception of his participation in certain activities and Pam's perception of his involvement in those same activities. Pam considers herself always responsible for household chores, but Seth sees her as having responsibility but not always performing these chores. Evidence from the research literature (reviewed in chapter 1) indicates that men and women view equitable sharing in distinctly different ways. The counselor can highlight this perceived gender difference to the client couple and also focus on achieving effective communication so that Seth and Pam can express appreciation more directly for what the other person does as well as request that the significant other participate in more or different household activities. Relevant concerns involve how Seth behaves when he participates in household chores, how Pam responds when Seth participates in household chores, and what additional changes each would consider necessary

TABLE 6.2

Assessing Career Dimensions

Identical copies of the same questionnaire should be filled out by the man and the woman.

Name _____

What is your highest educational degree? _____

    In what field did you receive this degree? _____

    When did you receive this degree? _____

    From what institution? _____

What is your field of employment? _____

_____

What is your current position? _____

_____

How long have you been with your current company? _____

_____

How long have you been in your current position? _____

_____

What are your typical work hours? _____

_____

Is this considered (please check all that apply):

    full-time _____

    part-time _____

    flextime _____

    job sharing _____

    other (please specify) _____

_____

Do you use any other family-friendly work options?

    telecommuting _____

    flexible workplace _____

    other (please specify) _____

_____

Do you work on weekends?   Never _____

   Sometimes _____   Regularly _____

Are you expected to punch a time clock? Yes _____   No _____

What is the career history for moving up in your company?

_____

_____

Do you expect to keep moving up in your company?

   Yes _____   No _____

Or do you feel that you have plateaued? Yes _____   No _____

Would you like to move up further? Yes _____   No _____

Are you considering a job or career change in the near future?

   Yes _____   No _____

   If yes, please specify _____

_____

For upward mobility in your career, will you have to relocate?

   Yes _____   No _____

   If yes, how often? _____

_____

Do you travel for business? Yes _____   No _____

   If yes, please mark one of the following responses:

   every week _____   every month _____

   periodically _____   not more than a couple of times a year _____

Do you like your present employment position?

   Yes _____   No _____

Are you satisfied with your chosen career?

   Yes _____   No _____

TABLE 6.3

Assessing Perceived Balance

Homework

(Separate copies are to be filled in by each partner.)

Please indicate who performs the following household responsibilities by placing an x in the appropriate box.

	Always woman	Mostly woman	Half man, half woman	Mostly man	Always man
Shopping					
Cooking					
Household organizing					
Children's bedtimes					
Children's baths					
Paying bills					
Caring for car					
Home maintenance (e.g., electrical)					
Scheduling family activities					
Gardening					
Carpooling children					

TABLE 6.4

Assessing Personal Balance Between Family and Career

(Each member of the couple should fill in a separate copy.)

Please indicate the approximate percentage of your time at home that you spend in each of the following activities:

activities with significant other (e.g., dinner, movies) _____

leisure time alone _____

time with children (non-caretaking) _____

caretaking time with children _____

housework (e.g., cooking, cleaning) _____

home maintenance (e.g., repairs, painting, decorating) _____

time with friends _____

time with relatives _____

religious activities _____

civic/community service _____

other volunteer organizations _____

other (please specify) _____

1. On a separate page, please describe how you balance your family and work responsibilities.

2. On a separate page, please describe how you and your significant other divide family and work responsibilties.

Copyrighted by Marian Stoltz-Loike, 1991. Reprinted by permission.

to achieve balance. Discussion about hiring household help as well as a new division of household responsibilities would be appropriate. Couples may benefit by a clear statement about perceptions, pressure, and career and family goals.

Table 6.6 is another hypothetical profile and reflects other issues that the counselor may wish to explore with Lori and Ben, the couple mentioned at the beginning of this chapter.

A number of points are worth noting about this profile. Assume that Lori and Ben have come to a marriage and family therapist because of the problems with their daughter's behavior. Besides the need for the therapist to address this critical issue, other concerns related to Lori and

TABLE 6.5

Examples of Responses to Sample Questionnaires

Seth's Responses:

	Always woman	Mostly woman	Half man, half woman	Mostly man	Always man
Shopping	x				
Cooking	x				
Household organizing		x			
Children's bedtimes			x		
Children's baths		x			
Paying bills			x		
Caring for car					x
Home maintenance (e.g., electrical)					x
Scheduling family activities	x				
Gardening					x
Carpooling children		x			

Pam's responses:

	Always woman	Mostly woman	Half man, half woman	Mostly man	Always man
Shopping	x				
Cooking	x				
Household organizing	x				
Children's bedtimes		x			
Children's baths	x				
Paying bills			x		
Caring for car				x	
Home maintenance (e.g., electrical)					x
Scheduling family activities	x				
Gardening				x	
Carpooling children	x				

TABLE 6.6

Examples of Responses to Sample Questionnaires

Ben's Responses:

Please indicate the approximate percentage of your time at home that you
  spend in each of the following activities:

activities with significant other (e.g., dinner, movies) _____5%_____

leisure time alone _____15%_____

time with children (non-caretaking) _____5%_____

caretaking time with children _____5%_____

housework (e.g., cooking, cleaning) _____5%_____

home maintenance (e.g., repairs, painting, decorating) _____15%_____

time with friends _____10%_____

time with relatives _____10%_____

religious activities _____10%_____

civic/community service _____15%_____

other volunteer organizations _____5%_____

other (please specify) Most of my time is spent on business-related activities.
These are approximate percentages of very little time.

Lori's Responses:

Please indicate the approximate percentage of your time at home that you
  spend in each of the following activities:

activities with significant other (e.g., dinner, movies) _____8%_____

leisure time alone _____5%_____

time with children (non-caretaking) _____10%_____

caretaking time with children _____15%_____

housework (e.g., cooking, cleaning) _____25%_____

home maintenance (e.g., repairs, painting, decorating) _____

time with friends _____10%_____

time with relatives _____10%_____

religious activities _____12%_____

civic/community service _____5%_____

other volunteer organizations _____

other (please specify) _____

Ben's dual career lifestyle demands are noteworthy. First, both Lori and Ben consistently indicate that they spend a fair amount of time with relatives and friends and on other activities that take them away from home, but spend little time alone with their nuclear family. A goal of the couple is to determine a way to create closeness between partners and to separate themselves from others (family and friends) (see chapter 3). Ben and Lori do not seem successful at maintaining these boundaries. The counselor may wish to explore this information within the context of other family issues. Ben's work demands take him away from his family. However, the counselor may want to explore whether the job parameters of his work actually require him to be away from his family so regularly. Additionally, the counselor may want to explore the uneven distribution of household responsibilities between Ben and Lori to analyze how gender stereotypes might be affecting Ben's work involvement, Lori's household involvement, and their lack of involvement with each other and their family.

Because Ben and Lori have teenage children and teenagers often prefer the company of their peers to the company of their family, it is not surprising that there is limited time spent with them. Nonetheless, all members of the family may benefit by planning couple and family time. The counselor may also explore whether the family has particular communication problems and could focus on more effective modes of communication so that they could take full advantage of the limited time available for relationship building.

Questionnaire for Setting Priorities for Family and Career Concerns

The last element of assessing family and career issues is identifying the relative priorities for couples regarding their career, couple, and family concerns. Couples may have expressed a variety of information concerning their attitudes toward family, career, and couple roles during intake interviews or on questionnaire responses. Counselors may wish to explore this further through other questionnaires, or published material such as the Career Salience Inventory (Nevill & Super, 1986), or oral discussion. Table 6.7 presents 13 statements with which clients can agree or disagree. This questionnaire can be used to engage a particular couple in a discussion of the relative priority of family and career concerns. The questionnaire in Table 6.7 is meant to be used as an adjunct to a discussion between the counselor and the client couple. Comparing the responses of couples concerning family and career priorities with their earlier responses to time balance issues can offer insight into family and career perspectives.

TABLE 6.7
Assessing Family and Career Priorities

Each partner should fill out a copy independently.

Please place a number between 1 and 5 next to each statement using the
  following criteria:

1 = strongly agree   2 = agree   3 = neither agree nor disagree
    4 = disagree   5 = strongly disagree

_____ 1. I would like to be home when my children are young.

_____ 2. Only I can really tell what my young children need.

_____ 3. Spending time with my family is a great source of pleasure
             to me.

_____ 4. After a day at work I look forward to quiet time with my
             children.

_____ 5. My children are well cared for and stimulated by their
             caretaker/day care provider.

_____ 6. My work is a great source of satisfaction to me.

_____ 7. I am devoted to spending as much time as necessary to
             complete a work-related project.

_____ 8. My work role is one of a variety of roles that gives me
             self-esteem.

_____ 9. My work is not as challenging or rewarding as I would like.

_____ 10. I look forward to spending time with my partner
              at the end of the day.

_____ 11. Our schedules are so busy that my partner and
              I rarely have time together.

_____ 12. My partner and I regularly spend time with our many
              friends.

_____ 13. My partner and I routinely schedule special time to
              ensure that we have the opportunity to be together.

Copyrighted by Marian Stoltz-Loike, 1991. Reprinted by permission.

Counselors may also suggest that couples write a marital contract (see
chapter 3), listing their expectations for themselves and their significant
other, as a convenient way of articulating the parameters of their relationship. The advantage of such a contract is that it forces couples to identify
and express their expectations. The drawback is that couples may find it
confining and use it as a checklist to be sure that commitments are fulfilled.

CONCLUSIONS

A first step in the dual career couple counseling process involves having couples articulate the relative priorities of family and career in their lives. Often societal norms affect the way individuals function. By asking couples to articulate their priorities during the course of counseling, counselors can obtain raw data for addressing family and career concerns. For example, a man who places a high priority on family needs and works in a company without any family-friendly policies may experience significant conflicts. Alternatively, a woman who places a low priority on family issues but is responsible for primary child care because of her more flexible schedule may also experience stress. Counselors can use information on family and career priorities to assist clients in achieving relationship equity and success at home and at work. For each couple, these definitions will be different.

Career achievement and the couple/family relationship are considered to be of great significance to dual career couples, irrespective of how they balance family and career issues. Career success requires the investment of many hours in a career, as contrasted with the few hours available to develop couple and family relationships. Therefore, hours spent at the place of employment as contrasted with time spent with family or partner cannot be considered to reflect the relative value an individual places on a particular role. Instead, work hours are defined by the demands of success in a particular career or institutional environment. Utilizing other measures of the relative priority of family and career parameters is critical to counseling dual career couples effectively.

7 Developing Communication and Negotiation Skills Within the Couple

---

COMMUNICATION

Some time ago, I led a group called "Decision Making as a Couple" for corporate employees of a Fortune 500 company and their significant others who were about to face a plant shutdown. Because relocation affects the career goals of both partners, I urged the couples to set aside a good deal of undisturbed time to communicate with one another. Couples listened and nodded as I suggested that they take walks together, have candlelit dinners, or simply take the phone off the hook during these discussions. After the session was over, one young couple came up to thank me for these insights. They understood why it was necessary to have private time without interruptions for their discussion, and they were planning to follow my advice and set aside time together—in Hawaii.

Mastering effective communication skills enhances the couple's relationship, motivates the speaker and listener to discuss a variety of issues that form the basis for relational growth, and is necessary for effective negotiation and conflict resolution. Poor communication, however, can

TABLE 7.1
Couple Communication Checklist

Whom do you speak with when (please check one):

1. you have received news of a work-related success?

_____ significant other   _____ family member
_____ business associate   _____ friend
_____ other   _____ no one

2. you are having difficulties at work?

_____ significant other   _____ family member
_____ business associate   _____ friend
_____ other   _____ no one

3. you are having financial setbacks?

_____ significant other   _____ family member
_____ business associate   _____ friend
_____ other   _____ no one

4. you are having problems with your children?

_____ significant other   _____ family member
_____ business associate   _____ friend
_____ other   _____ no one

5. you are overwhelmed by all that you have to do?

_____ significant other   _____ family member
_____ business associate   _____ friend
_____ other   _____ no one

6. you want to shoot the breeze?

_____ significant other   _____ family member
_____ business associate   _____ friend
_____ other   _____ no one

7. you want to brag about your children?

_____ significant other   _____ family member
_____ business associate   _____ friend
_____ other   _____ no one

8. you want someone to make you feel good?

_____ significant other   _____ family member
_____ business associate   _____ friend
_____ other   _____ no one

9. you want someone to stimulate your creative problem solving?

_____ significant other	_____ family member
_____ business associate	_____ friend
_____ other	_____ no one

10. you need encouragement to face a new client/associate?

_____ significant other	_____ family member
_____ business associate	_____ friend
_____ other	_____ no one

the information conveyed is clearly understood. These factors are: (1) setting, (2) intelligent listening, (3) feedback, and (4) nonverbal cues.

Setting

Both speakers and listeners will benefit when they set up an appropriate environment for communication. This may involve removing extraneous distractions by doing such things as putting on an answering machine, going out for a walk, or scheduling an intimate, relaxing dinner. Some settings (e.g., a noisy party) are inappropriate for serious discussion. When important issues need to be addressed, partners may indicate their readiness to speak and listen by creating a setting to minimize conflict and maximize mutually positive feelings.

Bonnie has just been offered a promotion that will involve relocation. Because she recognizes that this is an important decision, she has invited Larry, her significant other, to dinner at their favorite restaurant, so she can speak with him undisturbed. Because Larry tends to get anxious when they discuss relocation, Bonnie feels that the ambience of the restaurant will reduce Larry's anxiety level. Home is not an appropriate place for such a conversation because they would be involved in preparing and serving dinner and taking care of the children, which would affect their ability to have a "serious talk" and would surely increase tension between them.

Another aspect of the setting involves the awareness of both the speaker and the listener that the atmosphere they create can encourage or discourage the communication process. For speakers, different language is appropriate for different audiences. Sometimes this language is intimate, involving endearments, and sometimes this language reflects respect for and interest in the listener's opinions. It is important that listeners make speakers feel that they are worth listening to, especially if the discussion relates to a difficult topic. For example, Earvin works as a manager in a computer company, and his wife, Althea, is a high school teacher in the public school system. Earvin has been having difficulty motivating his staff and feels that Althea might have some good ideas about staff motivation. If Earvin begins the discussion by presenting various complex ideas related to his high tech company, Althea might be put off. On the other hand, if he brings up motivation and group management by expressing his respect for the fine job Althea does in her classroom, Earvin will have encouraged Althea to listen and share her ideas. Here, Earvin is using Althea's experience in group management to create a sense of mutual respect that will enable him to communicate effectively.

Intelligent Listening

Effective listening is not a passive process. Instead, it involves thinking about and integrating the information the speaker communicates. At times, listening might also involve questioning the speaker for clarification and elaboration. Sometimes it is appropriate to ask the speaker to wait while the listener thinks about what has been said. Within a couple, intelligent listening encourages the speaker. This promotes a positive relationship and motivates the members of the couple to find time to speak with one another.

Active Listening

This technique keeps the discussion focused on the issue at hand rather than letting other issues interfere with the couple's discussion. This technique is most appropriate when conversations are emotion-laden or when the other person disagrees, factors that render conversations extremely stilted or stop them completely.

Active listening has four components:

1. The listener tries to place him- or herself in the speaker's position and then reiterates the facts from the speaker's perspective;
2. The listener attempts to describe the speaker's emotions and restates the speaker's most significant thoughts and feelings;
3. The listener uses a variety of nonverbal behaviors, including voice tone, facial expression, gestures, posture, and eye contact to show understanding of and acceptance of the speaker's position; and
4. The listener focuses attention on the speaker, not interrupting, offering advice, or giving suggestions.

Feedback

Both speakers and listeners use feedback to maintain communication. Feedback in a couple may involve asking questions, offering advice, problem solving, or just listening intelligently. Engaged listeners provide a variety of responses to the speaker that indicate that they have understood what the speaker has said. These variables may involve verbalizations like yes or uh-huh, or a variety of nonverbal cues. Feedback might also involve discussion or follow-up of particular points mentioned by the speaker. Speakers provide feedback to listeners by responding to their questions and addressing issues of particular concern to the listeners.

Nonverbal Cues

Nonverbal cues of the speaker can affect how listeners attend to conversations, whereas nonverbal cues of the listener can affect the way the speaker says things. Eye movement, head movement, hand movement, and body stance are all nonverbal parts of the interaction that the listener notices. The tone, pitch, and volume of a speaker's voice can also affect the understanding of a communication. A masterful speaker looks directly at the listener, and integrates hand and body movements with the message being communicated, lending strength and credibility to what is said.

Nonverbal elements of listening include gaze (e.g., looking at the speaker), postural adjustments, use of gestures, body movements, and facial expressions. The interaction of the listener and the speaker through these various nonverbal methods affects the length and quality of communication. In contrast, doing something else during a conversation, such as looking at one's watch or answering phone calls, discourages the speaker.

When Paulette and Arthur converse, they unconsciously mimic one another's postural adjustments. As the listener, Paulette may lean toward Arthur, who is attempting to engage her attention, as a reflection of her comprehension of what he has said. Paulette likes to smile at appropriate points and hold Arthur's hand during their discussion to reflect her focus on Arthur.

Communication Blocks

Specific individual behaviors, whether conscious or unconscious, can make communication more difficult. Communication blocks include acting superior, interrupting, or putting a person down. When couples routinely exhibit these behaviors, both conversation and their relationship will stagnate. These behaviors may be effective for making one person feel empowered, but undoubtedly compromise the self-esteem of the other person. In addition, when speakers seem overly sure of what they say, communication can be impeded because this perception gives listeners the sense that their input is of little relevance. When speakers communicate using loaded words that elicit strong emotional or defensive responses from listeners, the conversation may focus on the emotions and not the content or the issue being discussed.

Counselors can teach communication techniques. Couples often need to learn both how to avoid communication blocks in conversation and how to develop effective ways to transform conversations from angry, critical interchanges to more productive ways of communicating. Communication is facilitated when partners support one another's goals and the relationship is characterized by reciprocal concern and respect. Counselors can videotape couple interactions to show them how harmful communication blocks are and to illustrate the details of how they communicate. When using a videotape, counselors can point out how communication blocks hampered conversation, and by stopping the videotape at appropriate places, they can help the couple to devise more effective means of interrelating.

Evaluating the Couple's Perception of Communication

Clients often recognize when their significant other is not communicating effectively, and can see how the other person could say things better. As a step to fostering more effective communication, counselors might use Table 7.2 to explore couple communication.

Partners can benefit by recognizing how their statements are perceived by their significant other. Gender differences may also affect how people say things and how they feel about what the other person says (see chapter 2). Counselors may need to be attentive to these gender differences in client responses to the questionnaire in Table 7.2.

Using "You" Messages Versus "I" Messages in Communication

"I" messages allow feelings, needs, concerns, and thoughts to be expressed without blame. In contrast, "you" messages involve blaming or judging the listener, which causes listeners to defend themselves rather than focus on what the speakers are saying. Couples may argue using a variety of critical "you" messages, like "You never listen to me" or "You're so inconsiderate." These "you" messages are so overgeneralized and nonspecific that their impact is minimized and they become hurtful barbs. Individuals accused of never listening or of being inconsiderate can undoubtedly bring up a variety of instances where they *were* considerate and listened carefully.

In contrast, "I" messages are direct, specific, and effectively communicate speakers' feelings. A typical "I" message might be "When you don't look at me when I speak, I feel that you are not listening to me." Here the speaker has clearly identified an action (without attributing meaning to the action) causing the problem situation, and how he or she feels. Using "I" messages in couple communication is positive and integral to successful negotiation (this chapter) and conflict resolution (chapter 8). When counselors train couples to negotiate, teaching them the use of "I"

TABLE 7.2

Evaluating Couples' Perception of Communication

Please answer the following questions:

How does your significant other make you feel when you discuss finances? (Please circle one):

a. empowered   b. indifferent   c. stupid

d. stimulated   e. other (please specify) _____

    What does he/she say? _____

    _____

    How could he/she say it differently? _____

    _____

How does your significant other make you feel when you discuss family achievement? (Please circle one):

a. empowered   b. indifferent   c. stupid

d. stimulated   e. other (please specify) _____

    What does he/she say? _____

    _____

    How could he/she say it differently? _____

    _____

How does your significant other make you feel when you discuss work-family balance? (Please circle one):

a. empowered   b. indifferent   c. stupid

d. stimulated   e. other (please specify) _____

    What does he/she say? _____

    _____

    How could he/she say it differently? _____

    _____

How does your significant other make you feel when you discuss career achievement? (Please circle one):

a. empowered   b. indifferent   c. stupid

d. stimulated   e. other (please specify) _____

What does he/she say? _____

_____

How could he/she say it differently? _____

_____

How does your significant other make you feel when you discuss success? (Please circle one):

a. empowered   b. indifferent   c. stupid

d. stimulated   e. other (please specify) _____

What does he/she say? _____

_____

How could he/she say it differently? _____

_____

How does your significant other make you feel when you discuss your relationship? (Please circle one):

a. empowered   b. indifferent   c. stupid

d. stimulated   e. other (please specify) _____

What does he/she say? _____

_____

How could he/she say it differently? _____

_____

messages can be effective in addressing and resolving both verbal and nonverbal conversation stoppers.

As an example of the appropriate use of an "I" message, consider Karl, a husband who feels that his relationship to his wife, Laura, has stagnated because they are both so involved with their careers and their children. Karl would like to discuss making some changes in their lifestyle so that more time would be available for relationship building. He feels that every time that he broaches the topic, Laura remembers something that must be done immediately. Karl might address the issue directly by saying something like, "When you find something else to do every time

I try to discuss our life together, I feel very frustrated.'' Laura cannot feel blamed because Karl has not accused her of anything, and the initial discussion can focus both on ways to communicate that will be satisfying to both parties, and times for communicating when both members of the couple can focus on the discussion at hand. The question of why Laura has been avoiding these conversations may be addressed at a later point.

Other Special Communication Issues for Dual Career Couples

Telephone Communication

Telephone communication and voice messages present special problems for couple communication. ''Persons who use the telephone on a regular basis should be sensitive to the importance of the voice and the impression the voice makes . . . Without the benefit of gestures, facial expression and so on we must rely on the voice to indicate pleasantness'' (Capps, Dodd, & Winn, 1981, p. 266). Voice communicates information via words, rate, pitch, volume, quality, and articulation, but can use no other nonverbal cues to transmit information. Because nonverbal cues affect how couples understand what is being said, and few nonverbal cues are available by phone, it is possible for many misunderstandings to result from these communications. Therefore, couples should pay attention to ensuring that there is harmony between the words they are saying and the information that they are communicating with their voices.

Counselors may want to practice telephone and answering machine communication by having clients record messages for their significant others. For example, someone might say something like, ''Hi, this is Bob, I just called to say hello,'' and then add a personal message. Individuals are often surprised by the level of tension and anxiety revealed in these messages. By recording each partner's voice, counselors can help couples improve their phone or voice message communications.

Techniques for Improving Communication and Listening Skills

Sometimes practice in the counselor's office can be of great assistance for couples in developing effective listening skills. For example, couples may evaluate their listening skills by taking turns listening to one another speak. In this exercise, speakers present topics of their choice for 2 to 3 minutes, listeners only ask questions but may not criticize, disagree, or in any other way respond to the presentation. After the time is up, listeners are asked to paraphrase the speakers' presentations. After both members of the couple have done this task, counselors help couples evaluate their interaction. Was it difficult to just listen? Was it difficult to be the center of attention as the speaker? Was it difficult to paraphrase the information back to the speaker?

The topics that each person selects to speak about also provide insight into couple communication. Did one member of the couple select an esoteric topic that would have been impossible for anyone to understand or paraphrase? What kind of message were speakers trying to convey about themselves and their significant others? Couples can greatly benefit by counselor-directed training in techniques of active listening.

Rarely do poor listening or communication skills improve without direct intervention. Without help, poor communication problems will be carried forward through the dual career couple's life span. Counselors play critical roles in aiding couples to develop supportive communication skills that may affect other crucial issues like role balance within the couple's relationship.

Gender Differences in Communication

Recently, sociolinguists have begun to discuss the specific differences between men's and women's methods of communicating that are related to their different worldviews and different perspectives on human behavior. Young boys view their developmental goal as achieving independence, whereas girls view their developmental goal as achieving interdependence (Gilligan, 1982). As they mature further, boys master the interdependence associated with a "couple" relationship and girls master the independence associated with personal success and achievement. Unfortunately, neither boys nor girls may completely master these other methods of interrelating. Even in coeducational schools, young children function in a gender-based environment. Past the ages of 5 or 6, boys tend to play exclusively with boys and girls tend to play with girls. Moreover, boys and girls (as well as parents and teachers) reinforce some gender-typed behaviors of children so that by adolescence, children have embodied their own gender's rules, and it is hard to master alternate ways of behaving successfully. Speech is one area that reflects these gender differences. Boys and girls speak differently and their motivations for speaking are distinct. This presents few problems when boys and girls spend their time in same-sex groups. However, in mixed-sex groups, boys and girls and men and women speak differently and speak about subjects differently, as if they were using different "genderlects" (Tannen, 1990).

Problems can arise because men view communication as a way to assert their independence, whereas women view it as a way to assert their interdependence (Tannen, 1990). This is exemplified by Joe who will not ask for directions when he is lost in an unfamiliar place. Joe is in the car with his wife Sylvia, and he insists that he will find their destination any minute by looking at the map, although he has already been lost for well over 30 minutes. She sits beside him, furious, wondering why he always feels threatened by asking for directions. Sociolinguists, like Tannen (1990), explain these behaviors as reflecting the different styles of men and women. Joe is asserting his independence by not asking for directions. Sylvia assumes people help one another and is demonstrating her respect for human interdependence by expecting Joe to ask for directions.

The motivation to speak differs between men and women. Women are involved in rapport-talk and men participate in report-talk (Tannen, 1990). Female communication represents connectedness so that details of situations and people's behaviors are analyzed at great length, making rapport-talk an ongoing process that can be renewed daily. In contrast, men's report-talk involves presenting important details of events, if they occur. That is why men may come home and say that nothing happened at work. Men may also refer to other men as close friends even if they have not spoken to each other for many years. If something important were to occur they could always call these close friends.

Another difference in talk between men and women apparently derives from practice in early interactions. Men speak as a way of achieving a "one-up" status, but women speak to reinforce their sameness (Tannen, 1990). Therefore, men will comfortably speak of their achievements, whereas women may match stories with one another even when they are discussing troubles. This difference, when not understood, can engender conflict in the couple, because the wife may feel that the husband is trying to dominate or control her, whereas he may feel that he can't tell her how he feels because she becomes overly sympathetic and sounds like his mother.

Within dual career couples, gender communication can create partic-ular difficulties related to career goals. If couples need to agree on issues of work and family balance and they do, in fact, speak different "gender-lects," how can they understand one another? A woman may be severely blocked in discussing the importance of her partner's doing more around the house so that she can spend more time at work, because then she will be challenging her interdependence. He cannot easily offer to do more or he will challenge his own sense of independence and therefore waits for her to ask. Nonetheless, each may judge the other by his or her own gender's standards and be disappointed. She may look at him, expecting him to exhibit his interdependence by simply volunteering to share family responsibilities. He may assume that if she felt things were not equitable, she would discuss it with him. The couple is left at an impasse.

One solution to addressing these communication differences is for the counselor to enlighten couples about specific issues related to gender differences in communication. Individuals do not usually want to change the way they speak, preferring to try to alter the way their partners speak.

Counselors might attempt to use role playing with dual career couples to increase their understanding of the differences in communication between the two partners. Counselors who work with dual career couples may also be interested in examining their own perspectives on gender roles (see Table 7.3).

NEGOTIATION

One of the applications of effective communication is to negotiate change within the couple. Although negotiation is a complex process, it can be taught and mastered. For dual career couples it is an important relationship strategy that is a stepping stone to couple equity. The goal of negotiation as addressed in this chapter is to create a win-win solution that is acceptable to both partners and makes both members of the couple feel like winners. By definition, it takes account of the needs and goals of each partner. Therefore, when successful solutions have been agreed to, both negotiators win and will be more committed to the negotiated solutions (see, for example, Reck & Long, 1987).

Five steps are related to mastering effective negotiation skills:

1. Identify the problem that requires negotiation;
2. Set goals and targets for negotiation;
3. Plan a strategy for negotiation;
4. Generate solutions; and
5. Establish a life-span negotiation process.

Identify the Problem That Requires Negotiation

The first step in the negotiation process is to identify target areas for negotiation. These areas may be employer-related, such as a relocation or a promotion offer, or personal factors such as stress, conflict, an inability to sleep, or a sense of not knowing one's children. Both members of the couple may agree on the target area, or one partner may request that the significant other negotiate regarding change in a particular area. Negotiated change involves an alteration in behavior in both partners to reach target goals. It does not mean that one partner changes to accommodate the goals of the other.

Both Howard and Mercedes are members of a dual career couple with children in grade school. They are both technicians in a large corporation. Howard feels that he needs more time with Mercedes and identifies this as the target goal. Mercedes would also like to spend more time with Howard, but sees the problem as finding a way to have fewer household responsibilities, or devoting less time to those responsibilities, so that they

---

TABLE 7.3

Perspectives of Counselors on Gender Roles

Answer each of the following questions to gain insight on your perspectives
on gender roles:

1. Are there a variety of "shoulds" and "shouldn'ts" that you differentially
    attribute to men and women?

    Yes _____   No _____

2. Do you believe that children suffer when both parents are employed, even
    though this expectation does not receive reliable empirical support?

    Yes _____   No _____

3. Do you think that men suffer when their wives work?

    Yes _____   No _____

4. Do you think that couples are less happy when their wives work?

    Yes _____   No _____

5. Do you believe that all women should work?

    Yes _____   No _____

6. Do you think that husbands of women not employed outside of the home
    are sexist?

    Yes _____   No _____

7. Do you think that men routinely do less than their fair share at home?

    Yes _____   No _____

8. Do you think that men are insensitive to women's needs and feelings?

    Yes _____   No _____

9. Do you think that women who are homemakers spend most of their time
    playing tennis and shopping?

    Yes _____   No _____

If you answered yes to any of these questions you may want to consider how
  your gender beliefs may affect your counseling practice.

---

can have more time together. Howard and Mercedes agree to explore the
problem of time together as defined by Mercedes.

    Because she performs all the housework, Mercedes's solutions include
considering the possibility of finding more time for Howard by performing

fewer household chores, spending less time with their children, or staying up later to complete her household chores. Each of these strategies would affect her home life negatively. Alternatively, Mercedes could negotiate with Howard regarding the issue of his changing his family role so that she could accommodate to his desire for more time with her. For example, if Howard would give up his bowling league twice a week, he would have more time to perform household chores.

Each partner may understand the meaning of negotiated change differently. Unless both partners win in the negotiated agreement, however, it is difficult to imagine that the negotiation will be viewed as a success. For many dual career couples, this poses a particular problem around the area of housework. Women in approximately 80% of dual career couples perform 70% to 80% of household chores (Hochschild, 1989). If they would like their significant other to be more equitable, they should adopt a win-win strategy for negotiation. Counselors should explore the critical questions of what those women who shoulder the burden of responsibility at home can do to negotiate a win-win solution.

Counselors may be able to change the ground rules for negotiation about household chores within the dual career couple by reconstituting the couple's negotiation process and focusing on particular issues important to both partners. For example, the money that the woman earns may be substantial, so that solutions to the problem of balancing household responsibilities and other demands may revolve around her cutting back on the hours she is employed and the money she earns if her partner can't do more household work, continuing on the fast track if he participates more at home, or hiring outside household help. Although she may be committed to her career, data indicate that married women routinely work fewer hours than married men and change positions and the number of hours they work after they are married (Philliber & Hiller, 1983).

Counselors may also propose that couples who wish to have an equitable relationship renegotiate household, family, and career responsibilities using a plan where partners negotiate for household tasks, rather than women negotiating away their household responsibilities. In this negotiation, each partner would first have an opportunity to request responsibility for particular chores. Couples would then negotiate around the chores and responsibilities neither partner has selected. Equitable negotiation is predicated on the willingness of both members of the couple to problem solve or to compromise. Moreover, it requires that the identification of the problem to be solved addresses the needs of both partners. Howard, who wants more of his wife's time, may need to take on more household responsibility, or shift his schedule to accommodate to Mercedes's household chores so that Mercedes can have more time with him.

Counselors can provide critical help to couples in arriving at win-win solutions. First, counselors can offer insight concerning the problem to be solved. Second, counselors may offer solutions that couples had not previously identified. Third, with the counselor's assistance, couples may articulate issues that partners were reluctant to verbalize. These critical concerns may become part of a negotiated agreement couples can use to develop win-win plans for negotiation.

Set Goals and Targets

The next step in negotiation involves setting goals. Both partners may accept that there is a problem that needs to be addressed. Their goals, however, for solving that problem may be quite different. Before the negotiation process begins, it is important for each partner to determine independent goals for negotiation. When one partner initiates the negotiation process, some initial discussion by the couple about the "problem" may be appropriate. Then each person should prepare his or her own set of goals. If one partner feels that change is necessary, the other partner may willingly discuss that change; however, real evolution in the dynamics of the relationship is not possible unless change occurs within each partner. The partner who would like to instigate relationship change should prepare for negotiation, paying particular attention to encouraging a win-win negotiation by anticipating the needs of the significant other.

Change may involve long-term or short-term effects. Jane may need to travel more extensively for business for the next month and therefore would like to negotiate a change in the family structure with Bob for that period of time. In another couple, Isaiah would like to accept a promotion but it means that he will no longer be able to make dinner or pick up the children from day care. In both these cases, a significant other is being asked to change to accommodate Jane's or Isaiah's needs. Unless Jane and Isaiah can address with their respective partners how their significant others will win in this change of relationship, there is sure to be resentment, frustration, or lack of compliance with any negotiated agreement.

Win-win negotiation for Jane and Bob might involve alternating demands, so that this month Jane will work harder and Bob will take greater responsibility for family chores, and next month she will take on more family responsibilities so that Bob can be more highly work-involved. Alternatively, extensive travel for the next month may mean that Jane will not need to travel for the rest of the year, which both partners may perceive as a win-win solution. For Isaiah and his significant other, his promotion might mean a higher income and standard of living for the family, allowing them to hire more household help, which might be a win-win solution. Another win-win possibility is that his promotion might offer greater career flexibility, which could accommodate a relocation for his significant other's career.

Whenever possible, negotiation should revolve around a specific goal rather than a general goal. Specific goals include taking out the trash, picking up the children from day care, preparing dinner, changing work schedules, or traveling more frequently for business. General goals include doing more at home, working less, or being more involved with the family. Sometimes it is very difficult for couples to set goals, or for individuals to anticipate the goals of a significant other. Unspoken marital contracts may also affect the points on which couples will negotiate. For example, a wife who would like her husband to take out the trash may feel that her unwritten contract with her husband specifies that she do all of the housework. She may be concerned that violating that contract will have a serious negative impact on her relationship to her husband. Counselors can play an essential role in cases like this by helping to expose unspecified marital expectations and training couples to negotiate change within their relationships.

In reality, it is much easier to negotiate around a specific topic or topics than in generalities. A wife may say to her husband that she would like him to do more around the house so she will have more time for their relationship. He offers as a solution to take responsibility for picking up the dry cleaning on his way home, when she had really wanted him to take out the trash every evening. If she either accepts his offer or rejects it, she cannot easily make a counterrequest. On the other hand, if she would like him to take out the trash she may say something like, "You have expressed an interest in spending more time together. Perhaps if you did some of the small chores around the house, we would have more time available for each other. Do you think that you could take out the trash every evening?" Then the issue of negotiation becomes what household chores he is willing to do. (This can form the basis of a win-win solution. He gets more of her time, and she has to do fewer chores.)

Counselors can point out issues related to marital contracts, and also raise the discussion of gender-based expectations as a way to give the couple insight into their behaviors. In a dual career couple where the husband believes that his wife is earning money only for extras, he will be less likely to find time to perform or take responsibility for household chores. On the other hand if he believes that they jointly share the responsibilities of earning money to support their family, he may also be more willing to take responsibility for other activities that help her to progress in her career.

Find an Equitable Balance for Solutions

Three possible combinations of demands among dual career couples can be specified: (1) Career-committed men do all the housework, while the women more actively pursue a fast-track career. (2) Career-committed women do housework while the men more actively pursue a fast-track career. (3) A variety of different combinations in-between are pursued. When these decisions relating to career and family balance have been fairly negotiated based on win-win strategies, an attempt to have personal needs and preferences satisfied, and the recognition that constraint by stereotyped gender roles can derail careers, then the negotiated decision is by definition equitable. (As mentioned elsewhere, sometimes the demands of an employer can block the implementation of the negotiated decision.)

Within the dual career couple, personal commitment to the relationship will affect the success of negotiation. The more committed partners are to the success of the relationship, the more motivated they are to negotiate a decision. Views of the negotiation process can also affect outcome. Partners who believe that they can both win will enter the negotiation process more optimistically and with a flexible attitude. When an individual feels that the negotiation process will favor only one member of the couple, the negotiation is less likely to be successful without counseling intervention.

I have heard the same issue time and again in various women's support groups I have facilitated: Women feel guilty because they never have time to take care of their personal needs, or don't have the opportunity to attend relevant conferences or business meetings. Yet, they recognize that they would also feel guilty if they took care of these needs because it would mean denying time and support for the needs of everyone else. Therefore, they live in limbo, never winning, and feeling that if they win and take care of their own needs, they ultimately lose. Successful negotiation is predicated not only on negotiating for a win-win solution but commitment to the idea that it is acceptable to win. For clients to acknowledge that winning is okay requires understanding that balance is necessary between family and career roles and between the privileges to which either a man or a woman is entitled. This understanding is a necessary element of successful negotiation. Perhaps neither partner can attend every conference or meeting; however, a fair compromise may be reached if partners negotiate from a position where both may come out winners and it is expected that the needs of both can be taken care of.

Plan a Strategy for Negotiation

Planning for negotiation involves a step-by-step process each partner pursues prior to discussing change. The better prepared partners are, the more likely they are to reach a win-win solution with the least emotional residue. Partners can plan for the negotiation independently by anticipating areas of agreement and disagreement and beginning to plan solutions for their expected disagreements. During the actual negotiation process, partners may use communication skills (e.g., active listening) to verify agreement over particular concerns.

Planning for the negotiation has four substeps (based on Reck & Long, 1989):

1. identifying personal goals;
2. identifying the goals of the significant other;
3. anticipating areas of agreement; and
4. anticipating areas of disagreement and preparing for resolution of those disagreements.

Anticipating a partner's goals is related to individual knowledge of the significant other with respect to a variety of different couple needs. Presumably, when couples have developed good communication skills, and set aside opportunities for relationship building through communication, they are familiar with one another's goals and expectations and have already laid the groundwork for negotiation. Once individuals have identified their goals in the negotiation process they can begin to think about the goals of the spouse or significant other. What are their goals for success? For upward mobility? For family life? For the couple relationship? What kind of lifestyle does the significant other want? What are their financial goals?

Questions addressing the area of agreement or disagreement and the impact of negotiated change may be posed. Would the negotiated decision mean a change in financial arrangements? A change in work schedule? A change in household responsibility? A change in one's value system? How will the other person respond to any of these changes? Does the negotiated solution make each partner feel empowered within the relationship?

If there are anticipated areas of disagreement, the individual can begin to think of solutions. Can other resolutions be offered? Can individuals offer their significant other a concession that would resolve the area of disagreement? As partners prepare to negotiate, they should remember that if the needs of both partners can be considered during negotiation, the greater the probability that the negotiation can be concluded fairly and effectively, and that the agreed-upon solution will be implemented.

Counselors also can offer insight into areas of agreement and disagreement by identifying partners' distinct perspectives. As counselors help clients recognize their independent and interdependent needs, the couple relationship is enhanced and the communication process is improved.

Master Negotiation Skills

Counselors can also assist client couples in developing their negotiation skills in preparation of planning a negotiation strategy. Within the couple, effective negotiation is dependent on mastering and implementing a variety of skills. A primary skill is communication, discussed earlier in this chapter. Other skills may include taking turns, compromising, sharing, postponing, avoiding, apologizing, using humor, and learning to problem solve. Counselors may also remind couples of the impact of nonverbal skills on effective negotiation. These skills can be mastered relatively easily.

Brainstorming is another important part of the negotiation process. It involves accepting all ideas generated as valid and allowing no positive or negative evaluation of the other person's ideas, which could constrict the number of ideas proposed. Partners encourage one another to verbalize whatever comes to mind and to express as many ideas as possible. When partners ultimately discuss the efficacy of ideas generated, they can use their discussion as a springboard for new approaches to the negotiation. Positive and negative consequences of each solution might be discussed as well as ways to minimize consequences of any particular decision (see Table 7.4).

Be Assertive in Negotiations

Negotiators can adopt three attitudes. First, they may be aggressive, which means that they push forward with their own needs without considering the other person's needs. Second, they may be passive, which involves concealing personal wants and needs for any reason, including not wishing to offend another person, and allowing negotiation to proceed only according to the needs of the other negotiator. Third, negotiators may be assertive, which involves communicating personal goals and needs effectively while listening to what the other negotiator expresses. Any person who wishes to negotiate successfully should master assertiveness skills. Counselors can assist clients in learning to be assertive and to "talk straight" by direct training and by modeling assertive communication.

Gender issues may constrain the woman's ability to articulate personal needs and may affect expectations, attitudes, and entitlement. Responsibility for household chores may rest on the woman not because she is satisfied with the arrangement but because she feels she cannot ask for any other. Men may not do household chores because they feel that they are entitled not to do housework by virtue of being men (Gilbert, 1985). Additionally, from the perspective of gender communication, women may not be comfortable verbalizing their needs for independence. Counselors can discuss gender issues with the couple and help them use techniques such as role playing to practice negotiating gender-fair family relations. Counselors can also help couples achieve insight into developing win-win negotiation strategies. Furthermore, counselors can play an important role in encouraging couples to identify the positive gains of fair negotiations for both partners.

TABLE 7.4

Planning for Negotiation

What is the general area of concern for negotiation? (Please check one)

_____   finance

_____   career

_____   family relations

_____   couple relations

_____   household tasks

_____   other (please specify) _____

Area for negotiation (specified above) _____

List five goals your significant other has in this area:

1. _____

_____

2. _____

_____

3. _____

_____

4. _____

_____

5. _____

_____

What are your goals for negotiation in this area?

1. _____

_____

2. _____

_____

3. _____

_____

4. _____

_____

5. _____

_____

What are the areas of agreement between you and your significant other?

1. _____

_____

2. _____

_____

3. _____

_____

4. _____

_____

5. _____

_____

What are the areas of disagreement?

1. _____

_____

2. _____

_____

3. _____

_____

4. _____

_____

5. _____

_____

What solutions or approaches do you have to resolve the disagreements?

1. _____

_____

2. _____

_____

3. _____

_____

4. _____

_____

5. _____

_____

Generate Solutions

Once the negotiation process has been undertaken and couples have expressed their goals and plans, agreed on certain goals and areas of change, and acknowledged areas of disagreement, solutions can be proposed. The endpoint of negotiation involves generating a solution, or a variety of solutions, that each member of the couple feels is fair.

Solutions may involve a decision to change, or the agreement that change at the present time would be difficult for the couple. When change is agreed upon, solutions that involve constructive change for both partners are likely to be the most successful. Couples may find it particularly helpful to specify in detail the various changes solutions will entail. When consequences are discussed, individuals may gain a clear understanding of the implications of change, and if the decision was reached through a win-win solution, both partners should be motivated to keep their end of the agreement. Couples and counselors should plan a "check-up" into the negotiation process. By agreeing, at the end of the negotiation, to reevaluate the agreement after a certain period of time, the motivation to conform to the agreement is increased.

For example, Lee has been offered a tenure-track position for the coming academic year at another university, which will require that he and Jan, his partner, relocate. Jan is a manager at a local phone company and will have to change companies if she is to move with him. After negotiation, Jan and Lee generate three alternative possibilities: (1) They will not relocate for now, but Jan will begin to make more contacts in other companies, through conferences and other business-related activities, so that she can have more relocation options in the future. (2) They will pursue a commuter marriage for the present time, while Jan considers her own relocation options. (3) Both Jan and Lee will move at the beginning of the academic year. Lee will take on more home management responsibilities over the next 6 months so that Jan can visit the new city and have more time to pursue business contacts that might lead to employment options. Even if she has no job offer, they will move. The couple decides to pursue option number 1, feeling that it will prove most satisfactory for their present couple and career needs.

Establish a Life-Span Negotiation Process

Life-span issues can also affect the negotiation process. When partners in a couple feel that they both win over time, decisions can feel fair even when an individual does not come out ahead in a particular negotiation. In one women's support group at a major company, a manager explained how she had come to the present location because of her significant other's career opportunities. Currently, they were preparing to relocate to a new corporate site to benefit her career progress.

Counselors also play critical roles in highlighting the meaning of life-span development within the life of the couple. For example, if Lee and Jan negotiate a certain household balance, either of them may be concerned that an agreed-upon change cannot be altered. They may fear that if couple or career needs change, they will be unable to rebalance roles and responsibilities because they have already negotiated the "ideal" balance. A counselor can explain to Lee and Jan the need for regular discussion regarding a variety of couple and career issues, and the possibility that renegotiation of balance may be appropriate (and necessary) at a variety of points throughout their life span as a couple.

Counselors may caution couples about renegotiation pitfalls. When a decision is fairly negotiated after an extended period of time, a partner cannot casually ask for a reconsideration. However, exceptions to negotiated decisions are fair, as is the expectation of renegotiation after an extended period of time.

Implement Preventive Negotiation Strategies

Because negotiation is a difficult process, and it takes practice to negotiate well, couples may want to use negotiation on an ongoing basis. Counselors might offer couples a variety of hypothetical situations involving couple and career issues and have the couple practice negotiating to devise solutions. This would provide couples with opportunities to hone their negotiation skills and understand some factors that will enter into their significant other's future decisions. Moreover, by practicing negotiation, couples will be able to handle unexpected crises more effectively.

For this next step it is necessary to practice the negotiation process mentally, trying to see the other's perspectives and anticipating areas of disagreement by raising some objections expected from the other person. This gives the negotiator greater perspective and understanding of both sides. The final step is to progress through the negotiation with one's significant other, believing in one's power in the negotiation and the fact that the other person also wants a solution that's fair for both people.

Elizabeth and Matthew are a young dual career couple with one child. Elizabeth is a corporate manager and Matthew is a graduate student in physics. They have a close relationship characterized by a true commitment to their mutual success. They frequently use preventive negotiation to discuss how they will handle future career and couple issues. Elizabeth understands that Matthew's career will require them to relocate (at least after he receives his first academic appointment). Therefore, she has made contacts at various company plants in large cities so that she can create options for herself near academic institutions that may offer Matthew a position. When Matthew decides to look for an academic positions at some large midwestern university, it will be near one of the corporate plants where Elizabeth has developed her contacts.

After their first child was born, Elizabeth initially took on most of the responsibility, but found that her career was beginning to suffer. Elizabeth and Matthew negotiated around this issue and came up with the solution that Matthew would take on more of the daily responsibilities of child care because of his more flexible graduate school demands, and Elizabeth would be responsible for other aspects of child care, like doctor's visits and clothes shopping. In this way, both partners benefited. They now use the day care center at Matthew's university, rather than at Elizabeth's company, so he can have responsibility for drop-off and pick-up and any child-care emergencies. Elizabeth was able to continue at her high-paying job while Matthew was able to continue his graduate studies. Family needs were equitably divided according to the parameters of this dual career couple's family and career demands. Matthew and Elizabeth plan to re-negotiate child-care arrangements after Matthew begins looking for a postgraduate academic appointment.

CONCLUSIONS

Communication and negotiation skills are the hallmarks of a healthy couple relationship. Communication involves mastering both listening and speaking skills so that partners can understand each other clearly. Nego-tiation depends on mastering a variety of skills so that couples can develop win-win solutions that benefit both partners.

Counselors play significant roles in the negotiation and communication process. By training and educating partners in different methods of com-municating, counselors can expand the couple's interactive repertoire. By providing insight into particular concerns, counselors can help partners understand independent viewpoints. Furthermore, by offering creative ap-proaches to couple concerns, counselors can assist couples in developing win-win solutions to their problems. Negotiation and communication skills are important to couples at all stages of development. Mastering and implementing these skills forms the basis of a life-span approach to eq-uitable couple relationships.

8 Living With Conflict

THE DUAL CAREER COUPLE lifestyle is extremely demanding. Dual career couples have the responsibility to perform well in careers, as partners, and for some, as parents. Other roles may include caretaker for elderly parents, home manager, volunteer, and friend. Establishing balance among these diverse roles is difficult and conflict can easily arise as couples juggle each of these very important life roles. By mastering effective conflict resolution skills, problems can be more easily addressed. Otherwise, the daily struggle of balancing many roles can become overwhelming.

Conflict within the couple can be viewed from two opposite perspectives. On the one hand, conflict may be considered as counterproductive for a couple, leading to problems and tensions, and eventual relationship stagnation. Alternatively, conflict can be an opportunity for couple growth and development through using creative problem-solving approaches to address differences between partners. The heightened emotions associated with conflict can also motivate couples to resolve their conflicts. Rather than avoiding a conflict to maintain peace, successful conflict resolution allows the couple to reach a level of greater mutual understanding and interdependent and independent functioning so that there is a new depth to the relationship and a greater sympathy toward one another's needs.

Effective conflict resolution is dependent upon each partner's having good communication skills and the confidence to "talk straight" about individual needs and goals. Not only can good communication and negotiation skills (see chapter 7) reduce conflict, but poor communication skills may actually create or increase conflict.

TYPES OF CONFLICT

Three types of conflicts exist: conflicts over resources, conflicts over needs, and conflicts over values (Kreidler, 1984). *Conflicts over resources*

171

involve disagreements over how resources are to be spent and allocated. *Conflicts over needs* involve both how needs are to be met and how personal needs are to be defined. Some essential needs include primary needs like effectiveness at meeting goals and feeling competent, self-esteem needs such as feeling good about oneself, authority needs involving being in control of oneself and situations, and positive interaction needs related to being liked by others. *Conflicts over values* involve differences in personal attitude toward the world and what is important to have or to achieve. Conflicts over values also may relate to how success is defined either individually or as a couple. It is significantly easier to resolve conflicts over needs or resources than to resolve conflicts over values, especially if both partners are personally invested in their values. When values are challenged, individuals may view it as a threat to their sense of self or their upbringing. Gender differences may be evident in how conflict is defined (see chapter 2). Men and women may identify conflict over the same issue differently. For example, asking for help might be a conflict of values for a man, whereas women experience no conflict around the issue of asking for help. Analogously, deciding whether to read the morning newspaper or talk to a significant other may represent a conflict of values for a woman and no comprehensible problem for a man, because she must decide whether reading when her partner is around conflicts with her interdependent definition of relationship. The impact of gender differences on defining and resolving conflicts should be acknowledged by the couple and the counselor.

Conflicts over values can pose particular problems for dual career couples when the issues under consideration relate to balancing family and career needs. These conflicts can exist within the individual and between partners. Most adult men and women were socialized with "the motherhood mandate," which specifies that a woman's primary role is that of mother and she should always be available for her children. This may cause a gender conflict among career-oriented women over the positive valuations of both child care and career achievement. Conflict may arise for traditional men with career-oriented wives regarding the issues of participating at home. Moreover, for women and men, infants and children have high interest value, and there is an inborn motivation to form an attachment bond (e.g., Bowlby, 1969), further increasing the conflict between family and career concerns. Counselors may address these conflicts in two ways. First, counselors may underscore that these conflicts may not be resolvable. Being with children is important, and parents who are employed full-time and find work satisfying may still wonder about whether or not they have made the right choice. This is not a conflict that can be resolved because parental feelings reflect the parents' strong positive attachment to the child. Second, and alternatively, counselors may explore possible resolutions involving flexible work schedules or work slowdowns so that parents will have more available time for child care.

Both men and women may experience conflict between respecting personal career goals and feeling that as parents they should be home with young children. When the conflict between parenting and career roles is between partners, counselors can help couples by expanding their definitions of men's and women's roles. When parents share child-care tasks, both parents and children benefit. Moreover, counselors can assist couples to explore their goals for family relationships and to plan family activities. When parents feel that they are involved in constructive relationship building when they play with their children, not just "wasting time," both parents and children benefit. By helping couples master conflict resolution skills, dual career couples may be able to address difficult conflicts between family and career demands more effectively and arrive at workable solutions.

HOW DO COUPLES RESOLVE CONFLICTS?

Conflict resolution depends on the couple's ability to define clearly the nature of their conflict. This might involve a statement about the source of the conflict, an attempt at distinguishing whether it is a conflict of needs, values, or resources, or a description of problems engendered by the conflict. Next, couples will use the conflict resolutions skills with which they are familiar to initiate either a long-term conflict resolution, or a short-term cessation of overt conflict. This section will review five conflict resolution approaches, and then focus on the significance of the collaboration (or problem-solving) approach for achieving long-term relationship change.

Five responses are most typically used to resolve conflicts: (1) avoidance, (2) accommodation, (3) confrontation, (4) compromise, and (5) collaboration (problem solving). With the exception of confrontation, each of these responses represents a productive way of dealing with conflict at different times and for different situations. However, when only one conflict resolution technique is used consistently without obtaining long-term solutions, conflict may become a source of problems within the relationship rather than an opportunity for couple growth and development. Counselors can help partners to identify the type of responses they use in conflict resolution and how these might affect the couple's family and career balance. Additionally, when each partner uses different conflict resolution techniques, counselors can help partners appreciate one another's style.

Despite the fact that problem solving is the most effective means of conflict resolution, dual career couples may experience particular areas of unresolvable conflict and find that other approaches to conflict resolution may, at times, be appropriate. These conflicts may include personal conflicts over time with a child as opposed to time at work, or career-career conflict regarding the needs of each partner to work long hours and have less time than desired for relationship building. Although many of these conflicts cannot be resolved without major revisions of career choices, sometimes short-term conflict resolutions can involve avoidance or accommodation. As the couple matures, partners can renegotiate these formerly unresolvable conflicts and eventually arrive at a lasting conflict resolution. Therefore, the dual career couple can benefit by mastering multiple techniques of conflict resolution.

Avoidance

Avoidance involves denying the possibility that conflicts can be resolved. This approach is based on the belief that conflicts are rarely resolved, and that any attempts to solve them merely result in unproductive arguments and stress. Avoidance can be a neutral way of dealing with a potential conflict with few ramifications on the couple's relationship. However, couples may also use avoidance in responding to conflicts concerning significant areas of concern. They may decide not to discuss family finances because they always disagree about issues related to earning and spending. Similarly they may avoid an argument about one partner's business travel even though the other partner is unhappy with the schedule. When discussions are avoided, problems and frustrations may continue to increase. Denying underlying problems in the relationship obviates the possibility of ever resolving these issues effectively. Avoidance, however, may be employed to address easily resolved issues.

Accommodation

Accommodation involves accepting conflict and deciding not to address it directly. As they accommodate, individuals may agree to abide by the other person's perspective, give up a personal viewpoint, or agree to change their own ideas just to keep the peace. Like in the issue of avoidance, the problem area is neglected rather than addressed. The difference is that when couples use avoidance, they deny that there is a problem. When couples use accommodation, they may accept that the conflict exists but agree not to deal with it now to avoid direct confrontation. Ostensibly, the couple's relationship may seem congenial, but by not addressing significant differences, an underlying, unresolved sense of frustration in the couple may develop, resulting in a progressive distancing between partners.

Avoidance or accommodation can be used effectively to address career-family conflicts that are presently unresolvable. For example, Ardith may be unsatisfied with the job demands of Tyrone's career, although she recognizes that presently there is no possibility of change within his career parameters. Tyrone and Ardith may negotiate around the issue of Tyrone's chosen career; however, as long as Tyrone works at his particular company, Ardith's only choice may be to avoid discussion of or to accommodate to the demands of his career.

Confrontation

Confrontation occurs when one or both partners attack each other verbally. Even if confrontation can win battles, it will lose the war by leading to a relationship typified by poor communication and a lack of respect between partners. Moreover, confrontation is associated with an attack mode of interaction that leads to an escalation of conflict.

Compromise

Compromise involves reaching a solution that both individuals feel is acceptable, rather than expecting to reach a solution where both partners feel that they have won. Within the couple, compromise can be an effective strategy when there is a limited amount of time available for conflict resolution, or when the issues involved are not of critical importance to either member of the couple. Compromise is an effective method for deciding on a movie to rent at the video store. However, compromise may also be used to help couples address major decisions like corporate relocation, a critical area with significant implication for each partner's career, their relationship, and their lifestyle. By settling for only an acceptable solution, partners may be left with lingering resentment and frustration over the resolution process.

Collaboration or Problem Solving

This process involves expressing the conflict from each person's perspective so that an effective solution can be derived. It is called collaboration because both partners have to work together for this approach to succeed and feel that the solution lets each of them win. It is called problem solving because the conflict is viewed as a problem that can be solved if the couple is creative and respectful of one another's goals and needs.

By focusing on ways to resolve conflicts through a collaborative approach, counselors can also enhance couple growth. In the collaborative technique, counselors' first goal with clients is to reach a resolution to restructure the conflict into a problem to be solved. Partners must address their commitment to arrive at a win-win solution (see also, win-win negotiation, chapter 7). The next step is for each partner to express his or her feelings constructively and to define the point of conflict effectively by using good communication skills. Couples generate solutions to the conflict that satisfy the needs of each individual, and then can negotiate about the benefits and losses of each solution. The final stage involves generating solutions, which are then evaluated for fairness to each partner and for appropriateness. Couples may decide to accept the proposed solution or decide that it does not work, then redefine the problem and repeat these steps until a solution is acceptable to both partners (see Table 8.1). To resolve conflicts effectively, couples should be motivated to be cooperative, to tolerate diversity, to develop a variety of solutions, and to be committed to acting on a solution.

EXAMPLES OF PRACTICAL APPLICATIONS OF CONFLICT RESOLUTION TECHNIQUES

The following example illustrates how each of the five conflict resolution methods would result in a different approach to a conflict. In a dual career couple, Roberto is a bank manager and Carla is a physician. Roberto feels that when they are among other career professionals Carla belittles his work and doesn't give him an opportunity to talk about his career and professional aspirations. Roberto has approached Carla to discuss this issue. If Carla uses an *avoidance* response she might say something like, "I don't understand why you get so upset about this. Everyone knows that you are committed to your career and do a good job. This discussion will just get both of us angry and won't change the way you feel." In an *accommodation approach*, Carla might say, "You know people are interested in what you have to say, they're just worried that they don't understand finances. If what I do bothers you, I'll just try to stay in the background when we go to a party together." If Carla uses a *confrontational approach*, she might say, "Look, you know that I make lots more money than you do. You might progress up the career ladder, but you know that we really don't need the money. Anyway, my job *is* much more interesting and important than yours, so folks do want to talk more to me about what I do." If she uses a *compromise approach*, she might say, "Look, I hear what you're saying. How about if I try not to interrupt when you talk and you try to believe in me and not think that I am always trying to put you down." In the *collaboration approach*, she might say, "I hear what you're saying and it troubles me. I really wasn't aware that I was doing anything to make you feel that way. Can we spend some time

TABLE 8.1

Diagram of Conflict Resolution Using a Collaboration Approach

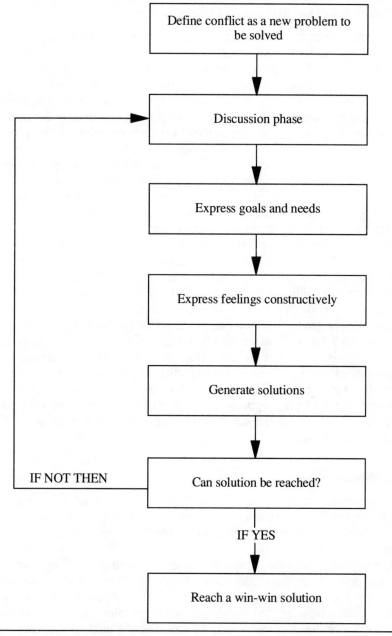

talking about this and then think of some different solutions that both of us could implement that would make you feel I support you more?''

Problem Solving and Conflict Resolution

When couples are able to generate a variety of possible solutions, they increase their skills at conflict resolution. Moreover, the recognition that the couple's needs may override individual needs is directly related to couple well-functioning. (This point was also mentioned earlier in chapter 3 as integral to the basic philosophy of work-family therapists.) Although each of the five conflict resolution approaches can be effective for resolving different conflicts, only the collaboration approach will have a long-range impact on the quality of the couple's relationship. As part of the conflict resolution process, it is essential that couples represent their various perspectives even if they have discussed this information previously in another context. Clear presentation of the relevant viewpoints ensures that couples do not operate under erroneous assumptions.

Barbara and Tom, a middle-aged couple, were preparing for a job transfer from one city to another almost 1,500 miles away. Although the move would be difficult, Tom was willing to relocate. Barbara, however, seemed reluctant to move, and Tom assumed that her reluctance was based on her concern with her inability to find a job in the new city and the impact this would have on their finances. In fact, in the course of a dual career couples group, Barbara expressed tearfully that her daughter was to be married approximately 6 to 8 months after their move. Although she would miss all of her children, Barbara was especially distraught by the idea of not being actively involved in planning her daughter's wedding. Once she expressed this, the couple pursued a problem-solving approach, focusing on developing opportunities for Barbara to be involved in her daughter's wedding preparations, including delaying her move to the couple's new domicile.

Counselors' Role

Counselors can foster effective couple conflict resolution by training couples in conflict resolution techniques and by positively reinforcing the use of effective problem-solving skills. Moreover, counselors can help clients develop the sophisticated communication skills necessary for conflict resolution, including speaking clearly, listening carefully, making sure that perceptions are accurate, avoiding comprehension blocks to communication, and making the partner feel comfortable during conflict resolution discussions. In this way, dual career couples can adopt conflict resolution techniques meaningfully as a means of functioning effectively in their many roles.

Counselors may wish to explore alternate methods of dealing with conflict. Both the accommodation and avoidance approaches may be effective ways of having an apparently peaceful household, although unresolved "old" conflicts may be frustrating both members of the couple, and there is no opportunity for positive growth from effective conflict resolution. Both accommodation and avoidance are effective ways of dealing with conflict when others are around. For example, if a couple hosts a party they might agree to avoid or accommodate in a particular area of conflict rather than problem solve or confront one another publicly.

Pragmatic considerations can relate to couples' selection of a conflict resolution approach. Couples may decide to compromise in their solutions because the issues are relatively simple and clear-cut, or because they want to reach a solution quickly. This strategy also may be adopted if the goals of the conflict are not that important to the couple, or if there has been no success at conflict resolution using problem-solving approaches.

TECHNIQUES FOR CONFLICT RESOLUTION USING A PROBLEM-SOLVING APPROACH

It is helpful for the couple and the counselor to assess the conflict resolution style of each member of the couple. Table 8.2 is a simple exercise (adapted from Kreidler, 1984) to help provide some insight into conflict resolution style. Although couples may use different conflict resolution styles at different times, this exercise highlights their preferred mode of conflict resolution.

Assessing Conflict Resolution Style

Once the prevalent pattern of conflict resolution has been established, counselors can help each partner become cognizant of the other person's style. As part of a counseling exercise, underlying issues related to each conflict resolution approach and occasions when each method is appropriate could be explored. Although counselors may not wish to change partners' conflict resolution styles, they can help to empower the couple by demonstrating and modeling other techniques for conflict resolution.

Counselors can explore the relationship between gender issues or life-span perspectives and conflict resolution style. For example, if a man adopts a confrontational approach, counselors may explore whether this is associated with particular gender issues and stereotypes that he holds. Perhaps this man and his partner could benefit by exploring some gender role expansion. In a couple who uses the accommodation approach, questions arise concerning whether this strategy will work throughout the life

TABLE 8.2

Assessing Conflict Resolution Style

(Have each member of the couple respond to the following.)

Name _____

If you and your significant other have a conflict, which of the following responses do you typically use? Use the following response criteria to answer the question:

1 = rarely used,   2 = often used,   3 = usually used

1. I tell my spouse or significant other that this is just the way things are.
2. I try to relax and get my spouse or significant other to relax.
3. I try to understand my spouse or significant other's points of view.
4. I find something else to do until we both cool down.
5. I talk to a friend about our problem.
6. I decide who was wrong.
7. I try to assess the source of the problem.
8. I attempt to reach a compromise.
9. I try to make a joke.
10. I tell my spouse or significant other that it is no big deal and we should just forget it.
11. I apologize if I am wrong and my spouse or significant other should apologize if he or she is wrong.
12. I brainstorm with my spouse or significant other so we can come up with new solutions.
13. I try to reach an agreement with my significant other about how we can each give in a little.
14. I do something to shift attention from the conflict.
15. I just try to ignore it.
16. I threaten to leave the house.
17. I decide how we can use different solutions to our conflict.
18. I try to make both of us feel comfortable with our decisions.
19. I find something else to talk about.
20. I tell my spouse or significant other that it's not really important.

I	II	III	IV	V
1 _____	2 _____	3 _____	4 _____	5 _____
6 _____	7 _____	8 _____	9 _____	10 _____
11 _____	12 _____	13 _____	14 _____	15 _____
16 _____	17 _____	18 _____	19 _____	20 _____

TOTALS _____

Now add the numbers in each column:

I   =   The confrontation approach
II   =   The collaboration approach
III =   The compromise approach
IV   =   The accommodation approach
V   =   The avoidance approach

The highest total indicates the preferred approach to conflict.

span of the couple. Perhaps the strategy is effective in a couple without children; when the couple has children, however, will this conflict resolution strategy lead to stress and relationship problems, or function as an effective technique?

Practical Application of the Collaboration Approach

Because the collaboration approach has the greatest promise for conflict resolution and promotes growth in the couple, the remainder of this chapter will focus on this technique. John and Yolanda are in conflict because Yolanda travels a great deal for business and John feels that she should spend more time with the children. Here, there is a conflict of the needs (for career roles and success) and values (doing well at her job) of Yolanda and the values (mother should spend time with the children) of John. If this couple has mastered the techniques of negotiation, communication, and active listening and can avoid communication blocks, they can begin to solve this conflict. The initial formulation of the problem to be solved becomes how to find both time for Yolanda to pursue business travel and yet (from John's perspective) have more time with the children. John and Yolanda can begin conflict resolution by defining the problem to be solved using the approach outlined in the flowchart in Table 8.1. Next, reasons for working or wanting to change schedules and their feelings about the problem can be uncritically discussed. This means that both partners express all points and listen to and accept them as valid perspectives. Understanding whether John feels that the children need more parental time or that he harbors a gender-related dissatisfaction with Yolanda's work schedule is important to the effective negotiation of this problem.

Next, this couple may attempt to brainstorm a variety of solutions. One solution might involve seeing if it is possible for Yolanda to plan to take the children out for dinner or to go to work late on the day after her business travel so that she can spend some special time with the children. Another solution might be for Yolanda to cut down on some of her traveling. Yet another may include recasting the original problem. The problem to be solved might then become deciding how each parent can pursue his or her career more effectively while the children have more time with their parents. Another solution might be that John take over primary care of the children and provide "quality" time because his schedule may be more flexible than his wife's. Or they might decide to hire additional help for child care. Once these solutions have been generated, the couple evaluates the pros and cons and the anticipated effectiveness of each solution in solving the problem. Finally, John and Yolanda will need to agree upon one solution, decide on a method for implementing the solution, and commit themselves to follow that method.

Problem-solving approaches involve a great degree of collaboration on the part of both partners and are appropriate when the issues involved are complex and will require detailed discussion to reach a solution acceptable to both partners. Because problem solving is quite slow, both partners must be willing to take the time needed to express and deal with mutual needs and concerns. Before entering into a collaboration conflict resolution, both partners should feel that their concerns are important enough to justify the time that will be needed for the conflict resolution process. For problem solving to be successful, both partners must approach the resolution process with an open mind and the willingness to listen to the other person's concerns, and both partners should feel that they are seeking a permanent solution, rather than a short-term, temporary solution that is merely acceptable to both members of the couple.

Eight important characteristics of the discussion phase of conflict resolution using the problem-solving approach can be identified (based on Scott, 1990):

1. Get emotions under control: Make your partner feel as comfortable as possible.
2. Agree on ground rules: Agree to listen carefully, not to interrupt, not to express hostility even if there's disagreement, to show respect, and to try to see the other's perspective.
3. Clarify positions: Use the other's perspective. Avoid judgments about the other's thoughts or beliefs. Discuss differences in perceptions, assumptions, and beliefs. Involve the other person in the negotiation process and show that his or her ideas have been heard. Keep bargaining position reasonable and realistic.
4. Explore underlying needs and interests: Identify why the other person has selected his or her position. Understand why different positions were not chosen.
5. Discuss personal needs and interests.
6. Generate a quantity of possible alternatives: Focus on future, remain open to different alternatives, and avoid closing off possibilities too quickly.

7. Agree on best win-win options: Discuss benefits of options for both members of the couple. Help the other to feel comfortable in making concessions.

8. Try not to take the other person's behavior personally: Sometimes expressing emotions can be useful. Use creative listening techniques to let the other person express emotions. Each person should distance him- or herself from the other person so that emotions are not "picked up."

Once couples have expressed their responses to the problem, they can generate solutions, accept one resolution, or decide to redefine the problem and repeat the discussion phase. If conflicts cannot be resolved, couples may decide on a cooling-off period and then approach the problem again. Alternatively, they may decide to turn to outside assistance, in the form of a friend or counselor, to help them find novel approaches to the problem. Or, they may agree to use another problem-solving approach to address the conflict. Examples of unresolvable conflicts are when partners hold contradictory feelings about having children, or about relative time commitments to their relationships and careers.

Planning for Success

Although dual career couples may implement conflict resolution techniques to address a variety of situations, these techniques are of critical relevance to defining goals for success. Success goals may relate to career success, couple success, family success, and personal success. These goals may be long-term (e.g., to retire with X number of dollars in the bank), or short-term (to complete a report before schedule) (see chapter 9). An exercise related to this topic offers couples an excellent opportunity to practice collaborative conflict resolution skills (see Table 8.3a and Table 8.3b). Couples can use these exercises to explore personal and couple success goals.

Counselors can devise a variety of exercises to assist couples in planning success goals. As an example, counselors can prepare charts like those listed in Tables 8.3a and 8.3b, and have each member of a couple select 10 success goals from these charts, or list their own goals. Partners can try to reduce these separate goals into 5 goals that they can work together to reach. These goals may involve coordinating relocation schedules so that both partners will be able to find an optimal work environment, or both partners' working at high-paying jobs so the couple can amass a great deal of money. Counselors can use these same exercises differently to look at ways that partners can help significant others reach independent success goals. This may involve taking a greater role in child care so that a partner can be more career-involved, or willingness to be involved in a

TABLE 8.3a

Dual Career Couple Success (Career)

Being successful means that I have a job with _____

Please circle all that apply. Then put a number from 1 to 5 in the space to the
  left of the items that you circled, using the following rating criteria:

1	2	3	4	5
somewhat important		moderately important		extremely important

_____ supervisory responsibility

_____ high stability

_____ great variety of tasks

_____ coworkers I can feel
close to

_____ high prestige

_____ need to use my creativity

_____ opportunity to exercise
competence

_____ opportunity to be part
of a team

_____ ability to influence people

_____ good benefits

_____ high salary

_____ leadership responsibilities

_____ security

_____ intellectual stimulation

_____ opportunity to design and
test new equipment

_____ great independence

_____ ability to become expert in
field

_____ opportunity to develop new
technical methods

_____ opportunity to use
problem-solving skills

_____ ability to control work
behavior of others

_____ decision-making
responsibilities

_____ ability to act as
troubleshooter in problem
situation

_____ flexible work schedule

_____ high profit gain

_____ many opportunities for
upward mobility

_____ fast pace of activities

_____ a supportive environment

_____ lack of pressure

_____ supportive company policies

_____ variety of responsibilities

_____ expectation of high   _____ coworkers who are similar in
achievement   values and beliefs

_____ opportunity to travel   _____ opportunity to invent
                                                        valuable product

_____ opportunity to work   _____ ability to plan team/company
on products that benefit   goals
society

_____ rewards for high-quality work

---

partner's extracurricular pursuits, if that's essential to a partner's vision of success. As couples discuss the significance of various goals, their mutual understanding will be enhanced. When areas of conflict arise, they can use effective negotiation and communication skills for successful resolution.

This exercise provides mutual insight into individual needs and offers couples an opportunity to identify the differences between individual and couple goals. Discussing whose goals take precedence and whether individual or couple goals are more significant is important.

DUAL CAREER COUPLES' SUCCESS NEEDS

Another exercise may assist couples in further understanding mutual needs. Each member of the couple selects 10 success goals at random and rates the partner's goals on a scale of 1 to 5 (adapted from Kreidler, 1984), where

1 = extremely important goal, "I would not give this up";
2 = very important goal, "It would be difficult for me to give this up";
3 = moderately important goal, "I could pursue this or give it up";
4 = unimportant goal, "I really don't feel this is very important"; and
5 = worthless goal, "Achieving this goal would not represent an important achievement, it's a waste of time."

Counselors can then initiate a discussion between the members of the couple about why each of the goals listed is significant or unimportant to the individual. Particular areas that cause conflict may be identified. Counselors can ask couples a variety of questions including: Are any of the unimportant or worthless goal areas sources of conflict? How well did

TABLE 8.3b

Dual Career Couple Success (Family and Friends)

Being successful means that I _____

Please circle all that apply. Then put a number from 1 to 5 in the space to the
left of the items that you circled, using the following rating criteria:

1	2	3	4	5
somewhat important		moderately important		extremely important

_____	can handle myself in any crisis	_____	have close relations with friends
_____	am well known in community	_____	have a college degree
_____	am an outstanding athlete	_____	have traveled abroad
_____	have mastered non-work-related skills	_____	have mastered a foreign language
_____	am socially active	_____	have a vacation home
_____	play essential role in volunteer organization	_____	am at my ideal weight
_____	am popular	_____	have a graduate degree
_____	am politically involved	_____	have a substantial savings account
_____	am a prominent member of community/civic organization	_____	live in a place that complements my lifestyle
_____	have friends who are important people	_____	am prominent member of religious group
_____	have friends who are good athletes	_____	have friends who are moral/religious people
_____	have close relationship with spouse or significant others	_____	have close relationship with my children
_____	provide well for family	_____	ensure well-being of family
_____	have beautiful home	_____	ensure family security
_____	have close relationship with extended family	_____	have opportunity to pursue non-worked-related interests

partners know the goals of their significant other? Could the couple deal with these issues differently and more effectively in the future by using their expanded conflict resolution techniques? Has improved couple communication affected their perception of the partner's goals? How can partners resolve different perspectives on the same goal?

The success of conflict resolution techniques interacts with the realities of the employment environment and the nature of individual and couple goals. Within the framework of career development, particular career issues can be related to the couple's conflict resolution ability and flexibility. For example, more senior members of a company will have greater flexibility in their work schedule, facilitating a variety of conflict resolution schemes. However, individuals who are at earlier career stages, beginning a job at a new institution, or considering a career change, even if it is a lateral move within the same company, may have fewer career and work scheduling options. This will limit the applicability of problem-solving approaches to conflict resolutions involving career issues. Conflict resolution can also be relevant as couples plan their moves within their work environment. Planning for unexpected events, such as promotion offers, will make couples more flexible in addressing career-related change and more capable of understanding functional work-family strategies.

Long-range goals or short-term goals will have profoundly different implications for the nature of conflict resolution for the couple (see chapter 9). For example, Kareem and Aretha are part of a dual career couple. Aretha is a corporate attorney. Kareem is a high-level manager at a cosmetics manufacturing concern. If Kareem's goal is to secure an anticipated promotion within the next 6 months, the negotiability of any particular conflict around success goals may be hampered. Only an intensive productivity schedule could facilitate Kareem's upcoming promotion. However, if Aretha's goal is to become a partner in a law firm within the next 6 years, a variety of different problem solutions can be proposed that may facilitate this goal and also resolve a particular couple conflict. Planning for unexpected events, such as both partners' being offered promotion opportunities at the same time, will make them flexible in addressing career-related changes.

The corporate culture within any company should also be considered as an important element in solutions to particular career-related conflicts. For example, Aretha, the corporate attorney mentioned above, is employed by a large metropolitan law firm, where she is expected to work a minimum of approximately 60 to 70 hours per week. There is only minimal flexibility with respect to her career decisions if she expects to be successful and eventually become a partner in the firm. Therefore, (re)solutions with respect to conflict between Aretha's family and career issues cannot realistically involve changes in her work schedule, unless, of course, there is a possibility of part-time work at the firm, or if leaving corporate law is a realistic option. Instead, solutions to this conflict may involve mastering more effective communication behaviors when Aretha is with her family, or encouraging Aretha to make a greater effort to be involved in activities of the nuclear family when she is at home. Alternatively, Aretha's family may choose to adopt other conflict resolution techniques like compromise or accommodation regarding the issue of career-family conflicts.

As part of this chapter's focus on living with conflict, it is important to note that sometimes conflicts cannot be resolved because of external constraints, so that living with conflicts may be the only option available. Among dual career couples, the most significant conflict is between family/couple and career. As workplace cultures change, the needs of parent-employees may become more flexibly accommodated (see chapter 10). Nonetheless, some of these conflicts may never be eliminated. Even part-time workers may experience a sense of sadness when they are not with their children, whereas at home these same workers may question their own ability to perform successfully at work. Couples, also, may feel conflicted over the competing demands of job productivity and finding the time necessary for their relationships to flourish. Even those couples who are successfully involved in their careers and family functioning may not have the time to build close relationships with friends.

BONDING AND CONFLICT RESOLUTION

Dual career couples benefit through involvement in tasks that lead to greater self-perception and by learning how to deal with anger and frustration. Some individuals may find it difficult to let go of anger associated with conflicts. To minimize feelings of anger, counselors can help couples learn good communication skills (see chapter 7) so that they can express their negative feelings appropriately. Also, if couples come to view conflict resolution as an opportunity for personal growth and development, they will approach conflict resolution with a more positive attitude and express less residual frustration.

After a conflict has been resolved, there may still be some emotional residue. Especially if a collaboration approach was used, the resolution process may have been physically exhausting and protracted. Sometimes physical activity like running or walking can help to relieve tension. Furthermore, after conflicts are resolved, it may be helpful for couples to engage in ''bonding'' types of activities (quiet dinner, a night out) to reinforce their special relationship and to relieve the tension associated with conflict resolution.

It is important for both members of the couple to talk about any residue of feeling they may still be experiencing with regard to the conflict.

Individuals may feel guilty about the solution for a variety of reasons. Partners may feel guilty for having asked for special consideration of their needs, or because they feel that the resolution benefits them more than their significant other. If this is the case, further discussion of gender issues and gender equity may be appropriate as well as analysis of life-span issues in couple equity. Counselors can play a particularly crucial role in these ''after-stages'' of conflict resolution by providing insights for the couple and encouraging them to freely express both appreciation and resentment over the conflict resolution process or result.

CONCLUSIONS

A couple may use a variety of conflict resolution approaches. Each approach has different implications for the transience or permanence of a solution, the time necessary in reaching a solution, and the sense that individuals will have about themselves and their relationships after the resolution process is completed. Only the collaboration approach leads to effective, long-range solutions that result in personal growth and empowerment. However, this approach is effective only with couples who have mastered good communication and negotiation skills and those who are willing to commit the time necessary to achieve a successful resolution. Among couples who express a positive regard for their spouses or significant others, there is great opportunity for finding a solution that is fair to both parties. Counselors can train clients in conflict resolution techniques. Additionally, by offering insight into a variety of dual career couple issues, counselors can help clients live productively with conflict.

9 Success in a Life-Span Perspective: Building Blocks to Success

WHAT DOES A LIFE-SPAN perspective for a dual career couple mean and how is it different from that of other couples? Suppose there are two couples: Sam and Nancy and Arthur and JoAnn. Both couples have two children. Sam and Nancy are a "traditional" couple. Sam works full-time, and Nancy is primarily involved with their home and family life. Sam's career takes precedence over most other aspects of his life, although he is quite involved with his children, and he and Nancy try to set aside time to talk every evening. Nonetheless, schedules will be rearranged even at short notice if Sam has an unexpected meeting. Moreover, the family has and will continue to relocate so that Sam can keep moving up the corporate ladder. Nancy provides a warm home atmosphere and is involved in a variety of volunteer and child-related organizations. Although Sam tries to spend time with their children, Nancy is the primary family caregiver who is responsible for building relationships with their extended families, friends, and children.

Arthur and JoAnn are a dual career couple whose lives and lifestyles are distinctly different than those of Sam and Nancy. Both Arthur and JoAnn are committed to their careers and to their family. They both would like to achieve positions of prominence within their companies and are working toward those goals. Decisions about work schedules and business travel are routinely discussed and negotiated. Arthur and JoAnn try to be flexible and support one another's careers. Often, however, real-life considerations, such as picking up their two preschoolers at day care and arranging for someone to care for the children if they are both out of town on the same evening, compete with their goals for success. Both Arthur and JoAnn will have to relocate in the near future if they are to keep moving up within their companies, and they recognize that this will represent another decision requiring extensive discussion and negotiation. They feel that they have not set clear goals for themselves as a couple and a family. They recognize that if "family time" is not planned into their hectic schedules, there will be no time available for family relationship building as their children grow. They understand the implication of their choices and try to live with their conflicts.

FLEXIBILITY IN A LIFE-SPAN PERSPECTIVE

As can be seen from these two examples, there are distinct differences in the demands and flexibility necessary within a dual career and single career couple. Roles are clearly defined within single career couples, whereas for the dual career couple, roles and responsibilities are more complex and must be discussed and negotiated.

Dual career couple flexibility has three components. First, it implies that each partner will assume new roles and responsibilities in support of the career aspirations of a significant other. Flexible support for a partner does not just involve providing extra time, but also signifies verbal support and expressed interest in the career goals of the significant other in an equitable manner. Even when one person has a lead career, the other partner will want to feel that his or her career is important and supported, rather than only of secondary importance.

Second, flexibility represents a willingness to take a creative approach to routine home responsibilities and career demands so that both career and family/couple relationships can flourish. Flexibility should enable each partner to achieve his or her success goals within the couple relationship. With regard to family obligations, either partner may need to absorb normal family responsibilities because of the increased career demands or travel demands of the other partner. Or, if the housekeeper unexpectedly quits, both partners may pick up extra household chores.

Decisions about child-related responsibilities also necessitate flexibility. For example, it makes sense for the partner who has a shorter workday to pick up a child from day care and begin preparing dinner, irrespective of the gender of that person. Furthermore, caring for a sick child requires flexibility with respect to the work schedules of both partners and their business demands.

Third, flexibility means that couples should take a "preventive maintenance" approach through routine communication and negotiation in preparation for unexpected future events or crises. Couples can develop a flexible approach to their relationship by discussing a strategy for flexibility and preparing for unexpected crises by discussing hypothetical situations. Unexpected promotion or relocation offers can create new career opportunities but will also multiply family stress. Thus, well-functioning couples utilize frequent discussions to establish and maintain flexible modes of interaction and to become aware of both partners' attitudes toward family and career issues.

For example, in a family with two young children, parents may pose one another hypothetical questions regarding routine child-care responsibilities or caring for a sick child. As possible solutions, the couple might consider a variety of flexible plans including dividing responsibilities between the parents, hiring a friend or relative, or investigating whether there are local child-care providers who will care for a sick child or provide other emergency child-care services. The parents can investigate and discuss each possibility so that they are prepared when an unexpected child-care crisis occurs.

It is important to note here that although a couple may be equitable, the employers of the couple may be less fair. A supervisor may view employee concern with family as a threat to the well-functioning of a department, rather than as the worker's method for balancing personal achievement with the achievement of a significant other. This may be especially relevant early in an employee's career when he or she has not yet established a performance track record within a company.

Women may recognize how their career achievement suffers when they marry and have children, a finding well documented in the literature. What is typically not discussed or assessed is how men's careers are affected when they are part of a dual career couple. If women are postulated to follow a more complex career path than men because of their family concerns (Betz & Fitzgerald, 1987; Ornstein & Isabella, 1990), then in dual career couples, where the man and woman share provider, housekeeper, and caretaker roles, both men's and women's careers are likely to follow a different or slower path than that described in traditional theories of career development like those of Super (e.g., 1983, 1986) and Levinson (1986; Levinson, Darrow, Klein, Levinson, & McKee, 1978). Both partners may have to leave work early, refuse business travel because of child-care issues, or turn down relocation options because of their partners' careers.

Gender differences may affect the interaction of parental roles and career progress differently. Men may face more subtle discrimination if they take extended parental leave to be with a newborn child as a manager wonders about the new father's commitment to the company. In a traditional company, a woman, in contrast, might be expected to take time off to be with a newborn child, and supervisors might look askance if she does not take this leave or is away from the company for too short a time.

Dual career couples require greater flexibility in reaching their goals than other couples in order to ensure that both partners can eventually achieve their goals. For example, if an individual's goal is to be a tenured professor at a major teaching university, he or she may need some flexibility about where that university is located or when that position will be achieved. Compromise and consideration in career decisions will help both partners to reach career milestones.

A counselor can help couples build life-span flexibility into their career and family goals. Achieving life-span goals can be compared to following a road map. There are many different ways to get from one city to another. Once a particular path is chosen, it is possible to change to another road only with some backtracking and loss of time. Similarly, a variety of career paths can be implemented to reach ultimate success goals, but only one major career choice can be made at any one point. Current decisions will affect the career direction of the couple and their family life. Career directions can be changed at later points with some loss of time and the necessity of additional effort to reach ultimate career goals. It is this ability to change directions that defines career flexibility and explains the different choices couples make at different points in time.

SUCCESS: A LIFE-SPAN ACHIEVEMENT

From a life-span perspective, success can be measured only over long spans of time, rather than being a function of day-to-day achievements. On a daily basis it is difficult to see the accumulation of skills and talents related to success. For dual career couples, this is particularly true because the daily stresses of balancing multiple roles may obscure ongoing couple, family, and career achievements.

Although the parameters of relationships among dual career couples can show great diversity, each successful relationship must be nurtured. Arranging couple time may require strategic planning; without such time, the couple relationship will stagnate. Couple time may involve hours, days, weekends, or weeks spent together. Time together should represent the building blocks of the couple's relationship across the life span. The value of time together among dual career couples can be measured only over the life span because other, competing demands may take precedence over the relationship on a day-to-day basis.

Within the career domain, success is also a function of life-span achievements. Daily frustrations and challenges can make it difficult to have perspective on how one is doing. Prospectively, plans can be made to reach career goals, but only retrospectively can career achievement be evaluated. For both partners, the ability to achieve particular goals and subgoals is also affected by family stage. Attainable goals may be different when there are young children at home and when children are in school or have already left home. For example, writing a series of articles or editing a book might be a success subgoal a professor who is the parent of an infant may pursue easily; however, regular traveling to conferences and speaking engagements might be particularly difficult at this time for this same parent.

Success is a function of an integrated lifestyle involving couple, family, and career issues. Couples plan and work toward achieving the balance of life roles that seems appropriate to them. This balance is different for each couple and should be periodically reequilibrated and reevaluated. Moreover, as couple or family dynamics or career levels evolve, fair balance of life roles will also need to evolve. Success throughout the life span will be contingent on planning opportunities for couple/family growth and nurturance and career development.

Success as a Dual Career Couple

It may be difficult for couples to identify how individual goal achievement can be integrated into couple success. The three couples described exemplify this difficulty and highlight some approaches to reaching this integration.

For Hubert and Tiffany, success is defined as combining a significant couple and family relationship with productive careers. For this couple, the life-span strength of the couple and its success is more important than the day-to-day achievement of each partner. Each partner may at times forego personal goals in favor of couple or family goals. Hubert and Tiffany believe that success involves playing active roles in their children's lives and having ongoing relationships with their children's teachers. They are in the process of assessing how these active roles will affect career success and who will assume primary responsibility for the parent-teacher relationship.

For Gabriel and Ardith, success involves both members of the couple being high performers in their careers and spending less time together. Often their individual goals take precedence over couple goals. If they have children, they have decided that they will require household help so that they can manage career and family responsibilities. Because of their high career involvement, individual goals can be facilitated or thwarted by the career and family choices of the significant other.

For Paulette and Robert, success means Paulette's being at the top of her career while Robert performs well in his chosen profession, but is satisfied with not being at the top and is more concerned with balancing success in career and other domains. Because each partner has a different philosophy about success, extensive discussion and sophisticated communication may be necessary to achieve respect and understanding within the couple. For Paulette and Robert, the different career goals of each individual need to be attended to and understood.

Even among couples like Paulette and Robert, where one person has a lead career, the other person's career also plays a role in the decision-making process. When competing demands are addressed, the couple may favor the lead career; however, on a day-to-day basis, both careers need to be attended to and nurtured. The equilibrium within the various domains of couple and career will vary as individuals work toward ultimate success goals. Career achievement may be associated with a more prolonged career path for each member of a dual career couple. Because specific skills necessary for promotion may take longer to master, dual career couples may show major achievements at later points in life. Nonetheless, success can be achieved if individuals and couples remain clear-sighted about their ultimate goals, plan related subgoals, and try to reach those subgoals by using creative planning.

SHORT-TERM AND LONG-TERM GOALS

When couples plan for success, two types of goals can be identified. *Short-term goals* constitute achievement over a few months up to a year or two. *Long-term goals* can be achieved only over many years. Short-term goals involve both minor themes, or goals one wants to achieve but that may not directly result in long-term benefits, and major themes, or goals that one wants to achieve as stepping-stones to long-term goals.

Couples may wish to distinguish between major and minor themes for success (see Table 8.3a and 8.3b). Major themes are generally immutable, whereas minor themes are often negotiable and may change even over a short time span. Within the context of negotiation around the area of couple success, minor themes are the goals that can most easily be given up to help partners achieve their own major success themes. However, short-term goals that directly affect long-term achievement are not easily negotiable, and may often be given priority over other family or partner goals.

For example, Daryl likes to keep busy, so he has decided to take classes in Japanese. The classes meet at 7 PM twice a week. Sonya, his wife, loves the fact that Daryl is always involved in something interesting, but finds that the timing of Daryl's classes interferes with their family life and her ability to work late. Given their busy schedules, Sonya questions whether it is currently important to pursue the minor goal of learning Japanese. Daryl's short-range goal is admirable but negotiable. Perhaps

Daryl could take classes later in the evening, or postpone learning Japanese for a few years, so that both Sonya and Daryl could pursue other short-term goals more effectively.

Success in a life-span perspective assumes that long-term goals are attained through the step-by-step achievement of various subgoals over the course of many years. For example, the goal of a couple may be to retire with three million dollars in the bank and close relationships with their children. Subgoals may involve pursuing high-income careers with stock options, profit sharing, and good retirement benefits, as well as planning family vacations and special weekly or biweekly family outings. As another example, quite a number of the major American corporations still require that employees relocate approximately every 5 to 7 years as they move up the corporate ladder. Couples may be able to plan (subgoal) transitions in both of their careers around the necessary relocation of one member of the couple. Creative planning and sensitive discussions with corporate managers can facilitate these transitions.

TYPES OF COUPLE CAREER GOALS

Couple goals comprise personal goals and family goals, which may be subclassed as distinct goals, complementary goals, or competing goals (Table 9.1).

Some examples will illustrate the difference between distinct, complementary, and competitive goals. Alan and Jane have different goals for success. Alan would like to develop his medical private practice so that he has a couple of partners and can devote some volunteer time to working in a clinic. Jane is a university professor who appreciates the flexibility of her schedule, which affords her time to attend to her children's needs. Alan and Jane have *distinct* goals, and are able to pursue them effectively.

Roy and Lola would like to purchase a summer home and earn enough money to travel frequently and have many luxuries. Both Roy and Lola are graduating from law school and are both in the top 10% of their classes. Their goals are *complementary*, reflected in their plans for the future. Roy and Lola plan to have one partner take the lead career in corporate law and the other to work either in a small firm or the DA's office. That way one partner can earn the money to furnish them with the luxuries that they want, and the other person can be more involved in home-care responsibilities and child care, if they decide to have children.

Tony and Odelia are both managers at Fortune 500 companies and have *competing* career goals. Each of them is devoted to reaching the top of their corporate ladder, which requires frequent business travel and relocation every 5 to 7 years. Up to this point they have managed to relocate to cities within commuting distance of each of their corporate

TABLE 9.1
Definitions of Different Types of Dual Career Couple Goals

	Distinct Goals	Complementary Goals	Competing Goals
Partners' definitions of success	Different	Different	Similar
Career goals for success	Low ach't (1) High ach't (1)	Moderate ach't (both) or High ach't (1) Low ach't (1)	High ach't (1) High ach't (1)
Family vs. career	Family (1) Career (1) or Both same	Family (1) Career (1)	Both career
Pressure of career achievement on couple's relationship	Moderate	Low	High
Response to crises	Accommodated by planning and negotiation	Most easily accommodated by discussion and negotiation	Most difficult to accommodate without significant degree of strategic planning

Copyrighted by Marian Stoltz-Loike, 1991. Reprinted by permission.

plants. Eventually, Tony and Odelia may want to move to corporate headquarters within their respective companies, which are located hundreds of miles apart. They recognize that this will mean that they will live apart and have a commuter marriage for a number of years, or that one of them might consider employment at another company, or that they might each reorient their long-term goals.

For counselors, assessing whether couples have distinct, complementary, or competing goals can affect the counseling and decision-making process. Couples with complementary goals may most easily accommodate unexpected changes or crises within their career paths. Couples with distinct goals may have more difficulty accommodating crises, and would benefit by strategic planning. For couples with competing goals, however, it will take sophisticated planning to maintain the integrity of their couple relationship and career goals. As the examples above demonstrate, Roy and Lola can most easily accommodate change, even if it involves job loss or relocation. Alan and Jane have distinct goals, so that the career achievements of each partner do not enhance or detract from one another's careers. However, when there is a crisis, the couple will have to negotiate the issue of responsibility for crisis management, and both partners will be affected. Tony and Odelia will have the most difficult time handling crises relating to couple or career concerns, and these will have a major impact on both of their career paths.

In a complementary relationship both partners will maximize the possibility that they will succeed, although it may be difficult for each to achieve success at a young age. Thus, time necessary to achieve success in dual career couples may be longer because of the importance given to couple and other family success goals. Even among couples with competing career demands, couples who are committed to having both members achieve success may find it necessary to slow down the rate at which they can achieve their goals. Flexibility within a life-span perspective provides the key to balance within each of the three different types of couple relationships. Identifying long-term goals and then determining specific short-term steps to these goals can help couples develop within career and couple dimensions.

With regard to family and career balance, flexible planning provides the best possibility of having a meaningful career as well as a meaningful relationship with one's partner and family. However, because of job demands, optimal balance cannot always be achieved and career and family conflict may, at times, be unavoidable. Certain careers simply do not lend themselves to the flexibility that is most desirable for parents and partners. Similarly, it is difficult to imagine a parent who is securely attached to a preschooler leaving home for work without some degree of conflict. Thus, parents may have to plan special time with children in the evening and on weekends and recognize that meaningful relationships can be developed in a variety of ways other than solely by full-time parenting.

HOW CAN COUNSELORS HELP CLIENTS PLAN FOR SUCCESS?

As mentioned above, the consideration of success is dependent on two separate areas: defining what couple success actually means, and recognizing success as a life-span developmental phenomenon. Counselors can help their clients recognize that each person has a variety of different aspirations. These aspirations may involve having a rewarding career, earning a high income, being recognized as an expert in a particular field, being a significant contributor to one's community, and having a meaningful relationship/family life. The individual may achieve a number of these goals simultaneously, or may choose primarily to pursue only one goal. Goal pursuits of both partners must be blended into couple goals. There is no unique path to achieve a goal. Rather, achieving long-term goals involves the accumulation of various skills as one reaches different short-term milestones. Using short-term achievements to reach long-term goals defines life-span development.

One helpful tool for identifying both long-range goals and short-term building blocks is for couples to use a goal stepladder (see Table 9.2). The stepladder consists of five steps. Each step specifies a short-term goal with the final step specifying the long-term goal. Individuals and couples can use this for identifying their goals. To use the stepladder, long-term goals are first specified on the last, long step. Next, the five intermediate, attainable short-term goals are identified that will culminate in the achievement of the long-term goal. Some clients require more than five short-term goals. Each short-term step should utilize skills, knowledge, and abilities that are critical and related to the final, long-term goal. These stepladders offer clients a way to reassess periodically whether the proposed path is realistic based on current family and career issues, and whether it can be achieved within the institutions where the members of the couple are employed. Stepladders also can be used for planning ways to achieve family goals, career goals, or integrated goals of family and career. Individuals can use the stepladder alone or with a significant other to plan together for their future. Family goals may involve planning for vacations or time together, involvement in community activities, or childbirth.

EXAMPLES OF CAREER STEPLADDERS

Tables 9.3 a, b, and c are examples of stepladders designed to help individuals and couples reach long-term goals. These ladders were de-

TABLE 9.2
Career Stepladder

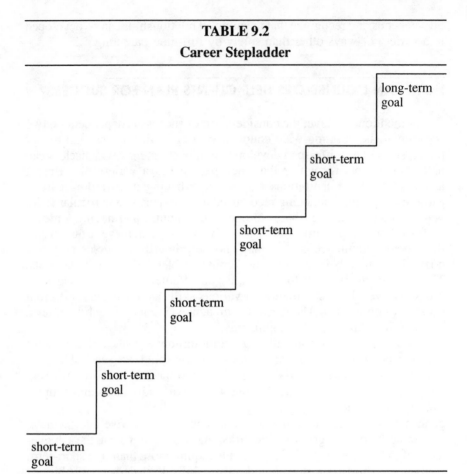

Copyrighted by Marian Stoltz-Loike, 1991. Reprinted by permission.

signed for the hypothetical couples in the cases mentioned earlier in the chapter.

DEFINING SUCCESS GOALS

Couples who have clearly articulated success goals probably developed these goals within the career domain (because workers are continually reminded that planning is the key to achievement). Currently, career development programs within corporations are including programs that encourage employees at all levels to plan career goals. Some of the more forward-thinking of these programs are also open to spouses and signif-

TABLE 9.3a
Example of Career Stepladder for Alan and Jane

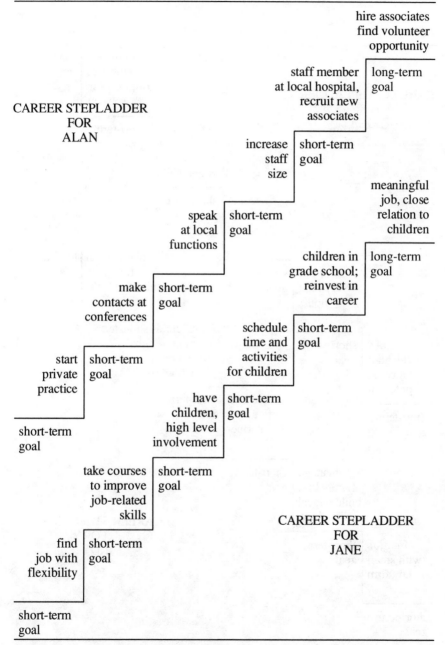

CAREER STEPLADDER
FOR
ALAN

CAREER STEPLADDER
FOR
JANE

hire associates
find volunteer
opportunity

staff member
at local hospital,
recruit new
associates | long-term
goal

increase
staff
size | short-term
goal

speak
at local
functions | short-term
goal

meaningful
job, close
relation to
children

make
contacts at
conferences | short-term
goal

children in
grade school;
reinvest in
career | long-term
goal

start
private
practice | short-term
goal

schedule
time and
activities
for children | short-term
goal

short-term
goal

have
children,
high level
involvement | short-term
goal

take courses
to improve
job-related
skills | short-term
goal

find
job with
flexibility | short-term
goal

short-term
goal

TABLE 9.3b
Example of Career Stepladder for Lola and Roy

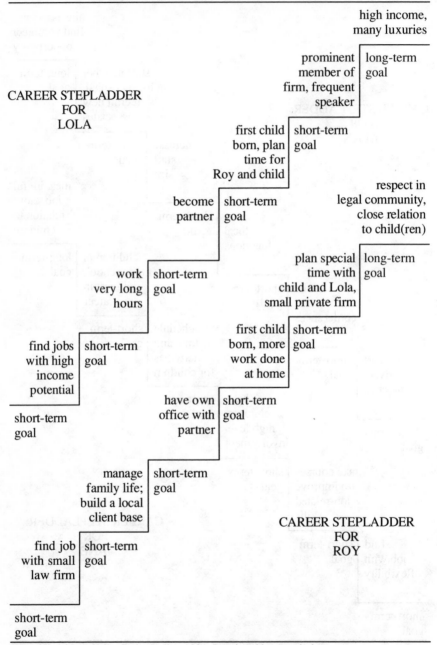

TABLE 9.3c
Example of Career Stepladder for Tony and Odelia

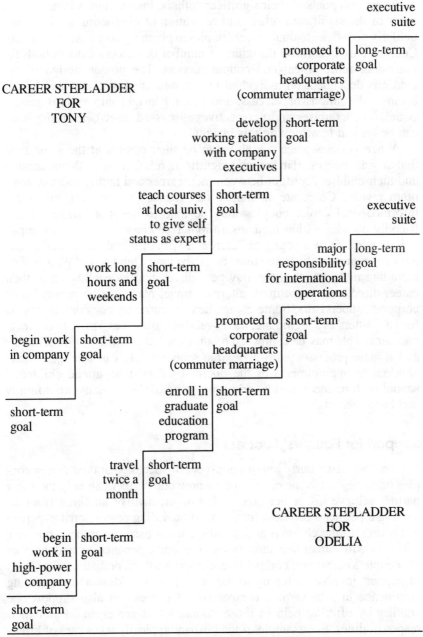

icant others, reflecting company recognition of the impact of dual career couple development on corporate success (cf., McCook, Folzer, Charlesworth, & Scholl, 1991). However, members of couples are often unaware of the success goals of their significant others. Insight into personal goals, goals of the significant other, and resolution of conflicting goals is particularly beneficial to dual career couples in planning couple success goals. Couples may benefit by designing a number of success ladders both for individual achievement and couple success. The unique design of the ladder is dependent on individual knowledge of ideal career and family balance, definitions of success, and general insight into various gender issues. The exercises and perspectives discussed elsewhere in the book can be critical to achieving this insight.

When couples place a high value on their careers at the same time that they are interested in having a significant relationship with one another and their children, conflict between their career and family success goals often results. Corporate flexibility can reduce this conflict, and well-informed dual career couples may be able to negotiate some family-friendly policies within their institutions (see chapter 10). For example, if a couple has two young children and if both members of the couple are sales representatives and must be on the road Monday and Wednesday, including night travel, there may be a direct conflict each week in their career directions. Sometimes, alternate travel plans can be pursued with corporate supervisors. Some companies are currently considering paying for babysitters as a legitimate, travel-related business expense. In contrast, another couple may be composed of a female lawyer with a rigid schedule and a male professor with a flexible schedule. He can arrange to take children to appointments at the doctor or dentist, to attend childrens' school performances, and be primarily responsible for many other family and home activities.

Support for Partners' Success

Another particularly important aspect of success that dual career couples often neglect is the discussion of how one partner can help the other partner achieve his or her goals. This might involve anything from attending a partner's business functions to providing professional expertise to picking up the children at day care. How a partner can be supportive will vary with career demands, family demands, personality, and whether the couple's careers are competitive, complementary, or distinct. One level of support involves listening to the other person's ideas and expressing confidence in achievement perspectives. Couples can also support one another by offering help in those domains that are normally not their responsibilities. For example, if the husband typically takes care of bringing the children to the library and arranging doctor's appointments, the wife may offer to take over some of these responsibilities during her husband's work crunch period. Couples can also be supportive of one another by using the expertise of their career experience to enhance their partners' career development.

Using Career Stepladders to Help the Significant Other

A final, extremely difficult step is for couples to identify couple success goals. These do not supersede individual goals, but rather should complement individual goals and represent the goals that the couple can most realistically achieve by working together. Some intense discussion involving negotiation, communication, and conflict resolution skills may be required to balance individual and couple goals. (It is important to note that couple goals are not necessarily items like having a satisfied family. Couple goals can also include items like both individuals being very successful at their careers.) For many families integrating individual goals into a family success model is quite productive. In Table 8.3a and Table 8.3b, a number of success goals were specified. As an exercise, counselors may ask couples to elaborate on how they can help their significant other to achieve these goals. Using a career stepladder, couples can specify short-term goals and how the significant other can help to facilitate these goals.

Academicians, for example, may read one another's papers or grant proposals, or business people may analyze particular business strategies. Even when members of the couple are in different career domains, personal expertise may enhance the partner's career success. A psychologist, for example, may offer his lawyer-partner insight into some of the interpersonal interactions of her firm or ways to achieve a psychological edge over someone during cross-examination. An office manager-wife may, similarly, share her management expertise with her husband who is part of the management team at a computer company.

CONCLUSIONS

Developing success goals as a couple is dependent on the commitment of both members to their own achievement as well as the achievement of their partners. Life-span success is reached when both members of the couple can benefit according to their own standards, rather than when one person's self-defined success overshadows and perhaps obviates the other's ability to achieve. Identifying couple goals in addition to personal goals is relevant to the success of the dual career couple. Thus, the blending of personal, couple, and career achievements defines the unique parameters of the life-span goals of each dual career couple.

Life-span success can be achieved by pursuing a series of short-term goals that represent distinct achievements and lead to long-term objectives. The skills mastered as these goals are pursued are invaluable tools for the successful dual career couple. However, it is critical to recognize that each of these goals can be reached in multiple ways. Therefore, life-span success can be achieved even when members of couples have taken time-outs or work slowdowns for family care and when overall achievement occurs at a slower pace as partners negotiate personal success and facilitate the achievement of their significant others.

Part III

10 Corporate Response to Dual Career Couples

FOR DUAL CAREER COUPLES to function effectively in the workplace, they must be able to negotiate a balance between their various family and career concerns. However, equitable balance within the couple is affected by the parameters for success in the corporations in which they are employed. Each demand required for upward mobility, such as relocation, business travel, long work hours, or weekend work affects the lifestyle of the significant other and the dual career couple relationship. "In some instances it's a no-win situation. If parents work overtime their children suffer, if they leave work early to pick up their children from daycare, their work suffers and they stand to harm their chances for advancement" (BNA, 1989b, p. 3). This chapter offers counselors a comprehensive perspective on work-family programs currently available within corporations and describes some anticipated future directions corporations may adopt regarding family policies.

Family issues within corporations have long been considered a women's issue. Now, however, companies are beginning to view family issues as a major concern of employees of both sexes. As more younger male workers become part of dual career couples, family issues will continue to move into the mainstream of the corporate agenda. Dual career couple programs are currently subsumed under the set of family policies (variously referred to as work and family programs or work/life programs) within corporations. Despite the fact that in many corporations 60% to 70% of all employees are part of dual earner couples, few programs specifically address the unique needs of dual career couples. No separate statistics are available concerning the proportion of dual earner couples who are dual career couples because major businesses have only recently begun to build demographic profiles of their employees. Anecdotal evidence suggests that among managers under 40 who are partnered, the percent who are part of a dual career couple may be above 60% or 70%. Because corporate relocation is one of the few areas where dual career couple issues are specifically addressed, a special section in this chapter will be devoted to reviewing corporate relocation efforts.

GENERAL ATTITUDE OF CORPORATIONS

Ten years ago, there were no corporate programs for dual career couples. Five years ago, work-family programs were beginning to appear. Today, virtually every major corporation has some work-family program. Why the dramatic change in such a short time? What are the motivations for this change? Do family-friendly programs reflect the altruism of the corporation, or are they based on sound business decisions?

Most family-friendly policies are instituted because they make good business sense. They address corporate goals like diversity and gender equity, and reflect corporate concerns about recruitment, retention, productivity, and absenteeism. Although there is often a dearth of data on the impact of family-friendly programs, anecdotal evidence indicates that even among employees who do not use the family-friendly programs, employee attitude toward the corporation changes when these programs are available. For example, when adoption assistance is offered it provides a powerfully positive message to corporate employees about the company's concern with employee needs.

One dramatic impetus for change within corporations was the publication of *Workforce 2000* by the Hudson Institute (Johnston & Packer, 1987), which presented a new and unexpected picture of the future work force indicating that women would be a significant part of the future, shrinking labor pool. Because all major companies recruit, train, and plan to retain the *best* employees, it became obvious with the publication of *Workforce 2000* that many of these best employees would be women. This means that needs that women and dual earner couples bring to the work force, such as family issues, must become a priority on the corporate agenda if the top women are to be recruited and retained. Moreover, as women become a larger part of the work force, it is more likely that men will have a spouse or significant other who is also employed, making family issues important for men as well.

In the past, women's achievement concerns and their family issues may have conflicted, as reflected by the fact that among women in executive positions, only 30% are parents, compared with 95% of executive men (cited in Schele, 1991). Among younger members of today's work force, however, both men and women are concerned with dual career couple issues because these issues affect partners of both sexes who have serious concerns about both family and career roles. Thus, a commitment to women's employment is associated with exploring issues of gender equity, which extends to more comprehensive programs for all employees.

Even younger workers who plan to have families reflect a greater sophistication about their future family and career needs, recognizing the importance of working in a family-friendly environment so they can continue their employment throughout their life spans. For example, at the university level, students have begun to ask campus recruiters about the details of work-family policies at potential corporate employers, emphasizing that satisfying the anticipated needs of future parent-employees is an important recruitment consideration.

Many major American corporations promote from within. Employees who find that their companies are not sensitive to family issues may leave their jobs because of the stress of balancing multiple roles, thus diminishing the available talent within those corporations. This is especially relevant for career-committed couples who have children some time later in their career lives than do other couples, or approximately 10 to 15 years after they have begun working for a corporation (Wilk, 1986). The estimated cost to the corporation of retraining and replacing an employee is approximately $20,000 (Seliger, 1991), but it can be considerably more in terms of cost and productivity to replace an employee who has been with the company longer. When that employee decides to return to work, he or she may find another, more family-friendly corporate competitor. Thus, corporations not only lose money when they are not family-friendly, but can also lose their competitive edge.

Another reason why companies began considering family-friendly policies was a greater concern with the impact of employee health on corporate productivity. During the 1980s there was an increase in on-site fitness centers to encourage physical health among employees and the appearance of employee assistance programs (EAPs) to promote employee mental health. Other aspects of employee mental health also are of interest to employers. Married mothers with young children and married fathers with employed spouses both reported that they suffered from work-family stress and strain (BNA, 1989b). Moreover, among corporate employees in one study, 71% of men and 54% of women reported that they thought family responsibilities affected their career advancement negatively (BNA, 1989b). It made sense for companies to address work-family issues in an attempt to reduce this major source of stress among employees.

A final reason that companies have begun instituting family-friendly policies is that dual earner couples are expected to represent 80% of all married couples by the year 2000 (Johnson, 1990). Therefore, family issues and couple issues will continue to represent a major concern of employees in the foreseeable future and will remain the concern of both corporate men and women. Companies that do not offer competitive family benefits packages may be unable to recruit or retain the best workers from this talent pool.

CORPORATE POLICIES

Instituting some kind of work-family policy has become part of the corporate philosophy at many major American corporations. For example, the Johnson and Johnson Credo advocates the company's commitment first to health professionals and product users, second to employees, third to the community, and fourth to the stockholders. As part of its commitment to its employees, the credo states, "We must be mindful of ways to help our employees fulfill their family responsibilities." Other companies may be less dramatic in their statements but still are highly committed to their employees' family needs. Many companies have clearly articulated corporate policy statements and advertise these programs to employees in glossy brochures discussing the company's family programs.

Corporate commitment to work-family issues is reflected by the presence of the work-family team or the work-family director, who manages corporate work-family programs at most major corporations. Despite the downsizing and layoffs that have characterized the corporate climate during the current recession, no company has eliminated its work-family group (Amy Segal, Catalyst, personal communication, July 18, 1991). Although there is often no stated policy on work-family issues in smaller companies, many smaller companies are family-friendly, and through coordinated efforts of company employees and supervisors, they have developed a variety of individually tailored programs that address work-family needs.

AVAILABLE PROGRAMS

For dual career couples, family-friendly programs are of critical importance to functioning in their work and family roles. Flexible options can relieve part of the strain on dual career couples in their multiple roles. For a couple without children, flexibility can provide valuable couple time within the strictures of demanding work schedules. More significantly for parents, flexible options, especially if they are used by both men and women, offer parents a meaningful way to negotiate their multiple roles. Career-minded parents want to work, perform well, and move up. They also want to be involved in their children's lives and must also take care of various child-related obligations such as medical and dental care and school-related activities. Workplace flexibility gives parents the option of being high performers at work and involved parents at home. Moreover, when both partners share family care equitably, both men and women can progress in their careers and reduce the negative impact of family concerns on their couple and career roles.

The range of programs in corporations shows great variability, including child care and eldercare, flexible employment, flexible hours, telecommuting, parental leave, relocation assistance, and employee assistance programs. The common feature among the programs is that when programs are well developed, both the corporation and employees benefit.

Child Care and Eldercare

Many companies have resource and referral services for local and out-of-town child care and eldercare services because quality care is a major concern of employed parents. Some corporations also offer some kind of employer-sponsored child care. This may be on-site, corporate-sponsored child care, a local child care center supported by the company, or a subsidy for off-site child care. Anecdotal evidence indicates that on-site child care is an important tool for employee retention.

Flexible Benefits

Flexibility in the workplace is an important profamily policy. Flexible programs represent a set of family-friendly policies that are distinct from child and eldercare programs and address different employee needs.

Flextime

An important family-friendly policy is nontraditional work hours. If it is assumed that standard work hours are 9 to 5, then one form of flexibility may be to allow employees to work from 8 to 4 or from 10 to 6. Flexibility, in fact, may be interpreted in even more novel ways. Some companies offer a compressed workweek of fewer workdays and longer hours, where a 4-day compressed workweek would be equal to 40 hours of work divided across four 10-hour workdays per week.

One retail chain encourages employees to master skills from stockroom clerk to cash register operator. Employees who prefer to work full-time can work around their children's schedules, working at the cash register from 9 to 2, and working a few extra hours in stock in the evening when children are in bed (Marcy Swerdlin, Editor, National Report on Work and Family, personal communication, August 8, 1991).

Part-Time Work

This refers to an arrangement whereby employees work an average of fewer than 35 hours per week throughout the year. This may involve reduced weekly employment, reduced seasonal employment, or project-based employment.

Job Sharing

Job sharing involves two individuals' sharing the responsibilities of a single job. Each employee will typically work 2½ days. Because communication between both employees is important, the job sharers may overlap for a few hours each week in the office so that they can discuss their work plans together, and supplement these discussions with frequent phone conversations to evaluate work issues. Workers in many different companies, including the State of New York, successfully use job sharing as a flexible option (Marcy Swerdlin, Editor, National Report on Work and Family, personal communication, August 8, 1991).

Flexible Workplace

Some companies also offer the option of a flexible workplace, which means that employees can work at home rather than at the workplace. This may involve either an ongoing agreement whereby an employee regularly works a number of days every week at home, or an occasional arrangement to address a personal crisis. With the advent of the personal computer, utilizing flexible work sites has become a more feasible option.

Telecommuting

Telecommuting involves dividing work hours between home and work. Employees can conduct business at home by telephone, receiving and making routine business phone calls. Moreover, work done by computer can be instantly available in the employee's home office via MODEM, a dual-line hookup network, or via FAX. Because telecommuting employees cannot be involved in the daily face-to-face interactions of the office, special planning on the part of the employee and manager may be necessary to include the employee in the ongoing office life.

A vice president at a Fortune 500 company had a child in the hospital. Although the father wanted to be with the child, he still planned to continue working on his current project. The solution, supported by this family-forward company, was for him to visit the hospital, conduct business by phone from the hospital during his son's hospitalization, and to receive full pay. In this way the father could be with his son and continue to work rather than taking a week of personal leave, which would have set him and his staff behind in their work schedules and not allowed him to be with his son.

Flexible Benefits

Another important flexible option available in some corporations and of special significance to dual career couples is flexible benefits. Instead of every employee having the same benefits package, employees can select, cafeteria-style, the benefits they need most. Among dual career couples, this reduces the redundancy of benefits, allowing the family to cover basic health, education, and child-care needs more effectively.

Examples of Corporate Flexibility

In a dual career couple study of over 500 employees of NCR corporation and two other major corporations, parent-employees identified flexibility as a key to their balancing various roles (Elaine Hicks, NCR, personal communication, August 8, 1991). Both hours and workplace were also specified by parents as prime elements of flexibility, which positively affected their ability to balance their work and family demands. Flexibility, according to corporate philosophy, is directed to managing for quality results, rather than managing for hours. The role of the manager in "flexible" corporations is that of a facilitator who encourages each employee to grow and develop within his or her job, rather than tell employees how things should be done (Nancy Arnosti, Personnel Director with Johnson & Johnson, personal communication, May 15, 1991).

When supervisors recognize the importance of flexibility to parents, they can use it to address both parental and corporate goals. In one company, a parent-employee was forced to request that she be excused from a meeting that was running way over time. It was already 6 o'clock and this parent was responsible for picking up her child at the day care center. The male supervisor told the mother to pick up the child and return to the meeting. It is clear that this supervisor considered himself flexible and open-minded in his offer. In reality, this option did not meet the needs of the employee and placed her in an uncomfortable position where her needs as an employee and parent were in conflict. Even if the child did not disrupt the meeting, the supervisor exhibited a lack of understanding of the inappropriateness of his demand because parents do not want to bring their infants into their workplaces.

In other forward-thinking companies, a variety of ongoing flexible options are offered so that parent-employees can maintain their involvement in work and their children's lives. Citibank's approach is one example of how management at a forward-thinking company plans to implement flexibility (Bruce Donatuti, Citibank, personal communication, July 31, 1991). Instead of wages being calculated on a weekly basis, they will be calculated on an hourly basis. An employee who needs to take time off for a school play or for another reason can choose to take 2 hours of vacation time rather than losing a half day or a full day of wages. Furthermore, if on a particular week an employee requires an altered schedule to take care of personal business, managers will work with the employee to find a work schedule for that week that meets both corporate needs and the employee's needs.

Leave Policies

Parental Leave

Currently a variety of parental leave programs are available. Parental leave is usually available for 6 weeks to 3 months after the birth or adoption of a child. This leave is with pay at some corporations and without pay at others, and can sometimes be extended either to 6 months or to a year without pay, with guarantees of returning to the same or a comparable position. Parental leave is often available to both mothers and fathers. Fathers, however, do not generally avail themselves of this option, instead utilizing some combination of available leave days, and taking off approximately 7 to 10 days postpartum. Even in companies that have family-friendly policies, fathers are apparently cuing into a message about how those men who take parental leave will be viewed by the company. Plans at several companies include new ways of managing benefits packages that encourage both men and women to use parental leave comfortably.

Personal Time

Many corporations have also developed leave policies where employees can take personal days for child-care needs. That way if a child is sick, parents can use personal days, rather than pretending to be sick, so that they can remain home with a sick child and do not have to come to work when they are actually ill, because they have no more sick leave remaining. Additionally, some companies allow employees to take hours of personal leave (see above), not full days, so that parent-employees can use personal time more easily for short but important family maintenance tasks, like children's visits to the doctor or dentist.

Employee Assistance Program (EAP)

Although EAPs were initially designed to deal with workplace alcoholic problems, today corporate EAPs deal with a range of problems from substance abuse to family and work concerns. EAPs are primarily problem-oriented and respond to crisis situations rather than taking a preventive role in addressing employee concerns. EAPs generally offer one-on-one counseling as well as seminars and fairs geared to different employee needs.

Evaluation

A major concern of parent-employees is whether using nontraditional work patterns will affect their career development. When companies manage for quality and results, promotions are based on quality of performance and not only on hours employed. Even employees on flexible work schedules will be promoted regularly (Amy Segal, Catalyst, personal communication, July 18, 1991). To document the impact of flexibility on workplace issues, Catalyst, a national research and advisory group that works to encourage the development of women's career and leadership roles, is currently involved in a major study of the relationship of flexibility to career development (Amy Segal, personal communication, July 18, 1991).

RELOCATION

According to Arlene Johnson at the Conference Board, relocation is at the heart of the career-family conflict for dual career couples and serves as a metaphor for dual career couple issues. Relocation forces couples to confront the issue of whether the man's or woman's career takes priority and poses a particularly difficult dilemma for dual career couples. If only one partner is expected to relocate at infrequent intervals, both partners might remain on their career tracks. However, when one partner relocates frequently, the significant other's career will suffer. If both partners work at companies requiring regular relocations, dual career couples may face significant difficulties. Assume that a couple decided to be absolutely balanced and both partners were expected to relocate every 5 to 7 years. Realistically, the couple would move approximately every 3 years, and neither partner could take full advantage of the learning opportunities available at his or her new site or be expected to perform well. Thus, a more sensible strategy for a dual career couple would be to work with managers in planning relocation decisions so that both partners could relocate less frequently and at approximately the same time to a city convenient for the work needs of both partners. Perhaps balance would then involve alternating which partner selected the relocation site. (Partners who plan career moves within a life-span perspective may want to discuss how each new relocation decision may affect future career paths.)

By definition, career development is a progressive series of events associated, in many corporations, with relocation as one moves up the corporate ladder. In some companies, relocation is as frequent as every 2 years; in other companies, it is expected every 5 to 7 years and is considered necessary for employees to understand diverse management and manufacturing issues. For two career couples, the difficulty of balancing career needs after a partner's relocation is particularly difficult. Family issues related to eldercare and child care can also affect relocation for the dual career couple. Availability of these services for family dependents is related to the success of the couple's relocation. Thus, appropriate in-house programs for school-age and older children can facilitate the couple's successful relocation.

Through anecdotal stories, needs analysis, and focus groups, companies are becoming more aware of the changing philosophy of dual career couples and the need for the corporation to be sensitive to couple needs around the issue of relocation. Furthermore, commitment to a significant other's career does not solely represent a philosophical issue for the couple, it also represents an economic issue. The typical income of the relocating family is $50,000–$75,000 (Johnson, 1990). It is likely that there is a fairly balanced split in the income of the partners. Therefore, the temporary loss of one salary (in a move to a new location) would represent a substantial change in the family income and lifestyle. When one partner is a professional with a private practice, relocation will not only mean a loss of income but also necessitate a large investment of time and resources to reestablish the practice in the new site. As more employees turn down relocation possibilities because of their significant other's career concerns, however, companies are beginning to rethink their relocation philosophies. Three particular corporate changes have been considered:

1. change in expectations about relocation;
2. change in career development plans; and
3. new ways of planning for relocation.

Each of these options represents a substantial difference from the way relocation has been viewed in the past. It is difficult to gauge accurately the number of relocations that have been turned down in the past because of family issues. First, employees may be reluctant to admit that they could not move because of their spouse or significant other. Second, employees who anticipate being offered a relocation option may change companies before they are offered (and have to turn down) that option. Third, managers who offer the relocation option may not communicate the offer, the response, or the reason for relocation refusal to human resource professionals or senior management, so that they are unaware of the responses or the employees' perspective.

Companies provide a variety of benefits for relocating workers. These may include some form of training to prepare the employee for a new work role, and paid visits to the new employment site. Additionally, the company will often pay the cost of moving and will also buy employees' homes if they cannot sell them and pay for the replacement cost of items like rugs and electric lights, which cannot be moved. Employee satisfaction with formal and informal relocation assistance is related to its relevance to other corporate goals. When programs are designed in response to needs assessment, positioned alongside other corporate programs and well publicized so that they can affect couple relocation decisions, they are successful in encouraging employees to accept relocation offers (Johnson, 1990).

More recently, a variety of benefits for employees' partners have also been instituted. For example, companies will offer to pay the cost of one or two visits by the significant other to a relocation site. Of particular relevance, companies have acknowledged that the career needs of the partner in dual career couples affect their employees' career performance, and have developed a variety of programs to address these needs. Currently three types of spousal relocation programs exist (Johnson, 1990). (Please note that I use the terminology spousal relocation, which is the title of corporate relocation programs available to both spouses and significant others.) First, there are programs that offer significant others information for marketing themselves to new potential employers. These may involve printed information, employment databases, resumé preparation, and career workbooks. Second, significant others are offered access to the local job market by informal networking and through employer consortia. Third, significant others are given individual support and counseling, which may involve either in-house counseling or referral and subsidies for an external counselor.

The issue of relocation is critical for the dual career couple because couples cannot sustain multiple relocations for one person's career without the sacrifice of the other's career. If couples foresee making multiple relocations for an individual career, the couples will need to engage in extensive negotiation about the relative significance of each person's career, the meaning of family and career balance, and the definition of their dual career couple relationship. Planning for career relocation within a corporation can help employees and their significant others prepare for relocation by addressing these various critical concerns.

Particular sensitivity should be directed to the noncorporate significant other who relocates. The terminology used for the relocating significant other is "the trailing spouse," reflecting the secondary status of that person (Libby Keating, spousal relocation consultant with REA, personal communication, August 7, 1991). Realistically, corporate relocation is primarily directed toward the employee and assistance for the significant other is secondary, which can result in trauma and marital stress for the couple. Effective dual career adjustment relates to both partners feeling that they play significant roles in relocation decisions and that both of their career needs can be met in their new location.

Examples of New Corporate Attitudes Toward Relocation

Dow Chemical's (cited in Johnson, 1990) philosophy reflects a change in expectation about relocation that is administered "as part of a long-term strategy for management development." Using an on-line human resource system, Dow tags dual earner couples and notes their mobility status. It is understood that dual career couples can and will transfer only when the relocation benefits both partners, a significant change in corporate relocation philosophy.

At NCR (Elaine Hicks, personal communication, August 8, 1991), planning for relocation has also become part of the career development philosophy of the company. During employee career development seminars at NCR, employees discuss dual career issues that arise in relocation and career development. Spouse relocation assistance programs are provided to spouses and in some instances to the couple to assist in recognition of the roles and issues in career and relocation decisions.

Mobil Oil (cited in Johnson, 1990) has altered the company philosophy and consolidated parts of the company offices into four hub locations in its family-friendly approach to relocation. One study of their dual career couples revealed that couples were not relocating, or were leaving the company before they were offered a relocation option. Now, rather than requiring employees to move every few years, which had been considered a prerequisite to gaining a broad base of experience, the company has reorganized into four hub locations, reducing the number of relocations necessary. Moreover, the company offers short-term commuter options for mastering specials skills, rather than requiring a long-term move for a short-term learning experience.

Innovative Ideas for Corporations

The stress on dual career couples is related to the issue of balancing work and family life and to concern with taking care of the myriad responsibilities associated with home management and couple/family quality of life. Therefore, some companies have implemented creative ideas to address these concerns, such as on-site health professionals, hair-cutting salons, and dry cleaners. Additionally, some corporate cafeterias will now prepare birthday cakes for children, and others sell prepackaged take-out meals for dinner (Seliger, 1991). These programs represent a new corporate sensitivity to what it means to be part of a dual career couple. When daily chores and obligations can be attended to easily during the day, rather than in a rush on the way home, parental stress is reduced, quality of life is improved, and parents are capable of being more productive at work and find time to enjoy their partners and children at home.

Research

A most valuable support for new program development is the research on the employee response to already-existing programs. Traditionally, few corporations have used contemporary social science techniques to evaluate existing programs because of cost and company focus. Instead, anecdotal evidence and a sense of satisfaction among employees have been utilized to evaluate the effectiveness of a program. Although important for company development, this form of evidence makes it difficult to pinpoint how specific corporate programs affect particular corporate problems across many companies.

An example of the importance of documenting the positive effect of family-friendly policies is a recent research study by Catalyst, which analyzed the responses of the managers and human resource professionals who work with over 150 employees who use flexible work arrangements. Nearly 70% of respondents reported that flexible work arrangements affected retention positively, and 58% reported a similarly positive impact on recruitment. Almost two thirds of the respondents felt that workers who utilized flexible work arrangements exhibited higher productivity, and 70% of human resource professionals identified a positive impact on the morale of employees who used flexible work arrangements (Catalyst, 1991). These data can convince human resource professionals and managers who are reluctant to implement work-family programs of the direct positive gains of family-friendly programs.

CORPORATE CHANGE AND RECEPTIVITY TOWARD FAMILY-FRIENDLY POLICIES

Corporate attitudes toward dual career couples are changing. Perhaps the primary impetus for this development was the recognition of the impact that women will have on the future work force. Further change in corporate attitude has been the result of corporate understanding that addressing the needs and perspectives of dual career couples is a positive business goal. The recognition that both members of dual career couples want to remain in the work force and that it is good business to retain productive employees has motivated corporations to change their philosophy about programs and opportunities for dual career couples and other parent-employees. Moreover, managers who are educated about the needs of dual career couples and the positive impact on workplace productivity of family-friendly programs can engender change in corporate philosophies regarding accommodation to family needs. Furthermore, as dual career couples become the corporate norm, more managers will themselves be part of dual career couples. In fact, managers who are part of dual career couples are the most committed to instituting family-friendly policies and are the most likely to ensure that those programs are successful.

Within individual corporations, the attitudes of CEOs and senior management toward dual career couples greatly influence policies throughout the company. An articulate senior spokesperson legitimizes and encourages positive attitudes toward dual career couple needs throughout the corporation.

The hallmark of a company receptive to family policy is one that respects individual integrity (Nancy Arnosti, Johnson & Johnson, personal communication, May 15, 1991). This means that corporate leaders assume that employees are committed to their careers, want to get their jobs done, and want to perform their jobs well. It is easy to see how this environment would be receptive to family concerns. A company that respects personal integrity would not be concerned when someone is a few minutes late to work because of child-care issues. Moreover, personal autonomy and participatory management might already be catchwords of this corporate environment.

The support of the CEO is important for changing corporate policy, but often the CEO is cut off from daily operations of the company. Therefore, it is possible to find corporations with family-friendly policies that show marked variation in policy implementation from one site to another. For example, in one large Fortune 500 company, the corporate policy clearly states that workers' family and career issues should be a company focus. In one division of the company, 40% of employees are women, half of those women have children, and many use the corporate day care center and flexible work schedules. In another division, 40% of the employees are women, but only two of these women are parents. Despite the articulated family policy in this company, the corporate environment in each of these divisions is different.

When policymakers consider ways to develop an integrated approach to family and career concerns, developing appropriate programs and ensuring that family-friendly policies are well used are relevant. Needs analysis and focus groups can highlight ways for programs to address employee needs more directly. Corporate employees may report that they were unaware of the family-friendly programs or felt uncomfortable using the programs because of concern that they would not be considered serious employees if they chose to utilize them. Likewise, employees may express concern over the impact on their career development of these options. Career-committed individuals clearly want to have more time with their children, but not at the expense of their careers. These employee responses can be addressed effectively by instituting corporatewide education around the company's positive attitude toward family and career balance, and addressing worker concerns directly.

IMPETUS FOR CORPORATE CHANGE

In companies with successful family and work programs, there is often a group of individuals from different parts of the company who can understand the diverse needs of employees, communicate those feelings to corporate decision makers, and encourage program development and implementation (Friedman & Johnson, 1991). A successful group usually includes someone in upper management as the corporate champion, individuals from other corporate levels within the company, and human resource professionals. Their initial motivation for systemic change may relate to shortages in particular areas of expertise, commitment of the CEO, the loss of a key employee, or the expressed interest of employees.

Needs analysis, research on employees' reactions to company programs, and focus groups are critical to the success of any corporate family and career goals. This information pinpoints the programs that employees feel will have the greatest impact on their roles as workers and members of a family/couple. For example, over the last year, NCR used the findings of its work-family and dual career couple surveys before implementing its various programs related to parental leave, spouse relocation, employment assistance, career development, and child-care referral service (Elaine Hicks, NCR, personal communication, August 8, 1991).

If the family-career policy advocates try to bring the work-family company policies further forward, research documenting the past positive impact of family-friendly policies can be useful for stimulating further policy development. Additionally, data from in-house evaluations and focus groups as well as data from other corporations and from independent research detailing the success of other programs should be well publicized. In this way, the family-career policy advocates can develop a broad base of support and understanding regarding the benefit of family-friendly programs to company goals.

Phases of Corporate Change

Three phases can be identified in the development of corporate response to family concerns (Galinsky, cited in BNA, 1989a; Friedman, cited in Seliger, 1991).

Phase I. In the first phase, companies begin talking to employees about their child-care needs, and may implement a single family-related program. Because of the interest and good business sense of instituting family-friendly policies, many large businesses have already entered Phase I. Even companies that have no articulated family policy recognize that their competition probably does, lending impetus to their considering some sort of family-friendly program.

Phase I is typically a low-cost, low-energy investment in employee family and career concerns. According to Galinsky (cited in BNA, 1989a), approximately 3,500 companies were in this stage in 1989.

Phase II. Employees begin to recognize that no single program can satisfy all employee work and family needs and that family policy does not just mean child care. Therefore, companies increase and diversify the programs available to employees. New programs include leave policies, plans for dependent care, flexible schedules, EAPs, and some parenting workshops.

In this stage, companies exhibit qualitative differences in their company's approach to parental needs. New statements may appear in corporate brochures reflecting the company's concern with parental needs and support of a family-friendly workplace as integral to corporate well-functioning. CEOs may issue statements advocating family policies, or corporate credos may change to reflect profamily policies (e.g., see the Johnson & Johnson credo). Phase II requires a greater input of time, energy, and effort. However, when programs are implemented in response to findings of needs assessments and focus groups, resources can be allocated to address the most pressing employee concerns.

Galinsky (cited in BNA, 1989a) estimated that 35 companies had moved into this second phase by 1989. Although Phase II is characterized by novel, forward-thinking planning, it still primarily consists of a variety of independent programs.

Phase III. The hallmark of this phase is a commitment to systemic change in corporate attitudes toward family and career issues. Family and career programs are integrated into a coordinated work-family policy, which plays a clear role in corporate strategic planning. In this phase, corporate decision makers exhibit a commitment to policy implementation, not solely to a policy statement. When companies first develop policies to reflect family needs, many employees are uninformed about the policies, and many supervisors may be reluctant to implement family-friendly policies that require extensive adjustment in group functioning. Therefore, in Phase III there is a corporate investment in educating workers and supervisors about family issues, the needs of dual career couples, and the programs available at the corporation. A key change in the corporate environment in Phase III is the investment in training managers in the benefits of family-career initiatives. Managing employees in flexible schedules can be difficult, but represents a low cost to the company if employee productivity remains high. Nonetheless, managers and supervisors may initially be resistant to changing company policy formally, even when employees have used flexible policies on a case-by-case basis. Training will increase their comfort with and ability to implement these new policies. When managers who have a staff that works under flexible hours are given the encouragement, incentive, and training to attempt to implement a family-friendly policy, it can be highly successful. Furthermore, when managers are trained in proper delegation skills, can adopt advanced planning strategies, and have cross-trained workers in various skills, the flexible workplace can operate with maximum effectiveness (BNA, 1989a). For example, Citibank is a family-friendly company. With their supervisors' support, many employees have been able to arrange flexible work hours. Management training will shortly begin to ensure that family-friendly policies are implemented, and in the future managers will be asked to justify why they cannot implement a family-friendly program (Bruce Donatuti, Citibank, personal communication, July 31, 1991).

The CEO also plays an active role in setting the tone for employee attitude toward family and career programs. When CEOs model family-friendly policies by having members of their staff utilize the program, it sends a beacon to employees throughout the corporate hierarchy (Libby Keating, REA, personal communication, August 7, 1991).

The impetus for moving from Phase I to Phase III varies widely. It may involve forward thinking in the executive suite, employee interest, findings from needs assessments, or agreements based on labor negotiations. Very few companies have moved into Phase III, and no estimates are available concerning the number of companies in this phase. When dual career couple issues are tied to the corporate agenda, it enhances the motivation for developing and implementing corporate change.

COUNSELING ISSUES

Counselors have opportunities to influence workers' attitudes toward their employers and corporations' attitude toward their workers. By understanding the needs of dual career couples, counselors can most effectively enhance the partnership between employee and company, encouraging the well-functioning of both.

Career Counselors

Currently, more corporations are focusing on career development issues, hiring specialists and consultants to work with employees to plan their career futures. For career counselors who work with corporate employees, dual career couple issues are a common-sense link to other career development concerns. Employees are encouraged to take various in-house and external courses to improve their career-related skills. Furthermore, both lateral and horizontal moves are reviewed within the overall picture of potential career strategy. Some companies provide these same career services to the spouses and partners of their employees, reflecting the recognition of the interdependence of performance in dual career couples.

Within counseling, a new aspect of the client decision-making process is presented when the needs of the significant other and the climate of the corporation are considered. As counselors work with clients in planning couple equity, the realistic dimensions of the corporate environment should also be assessed. Among developmental career counselors the concern with family issues may be especially relevant. As these counselors work with clients throughout the life span, changes in issues relevant to the worker, couple, family, and individual take on particular significance. Current corporate culture and the development of corporate philosophy are also significant correlates of life-span development.

Couple Counselors/Marriage and Family Therapists

The traditional corporate philosophy regarding the worker's obligation is antagonistic to that of family therapists. From the employer's perspective, the company is the central priority of the worker. At the executive level, in particular, companies envision a successful business person accompanied by a supportive spouse or significant other both willing to put the needs of the company first (Libby Keating, personal communication, August 7, 1991). In contrast, therapists view the family as having first and central priority in the couple's life.

For dual career couples, the interrelationship of work and family factors may be complex. Among dual career couples, both couple life and career life are important foci. The flexibility of the corporation can create or relieve a significant part of the role stress on dual career couples. Although EAPs are widely available at many corporations, they often represent the company's reactive response to stress rather than an attempt to anticipate or prevent stress. Couples who come to a marital therapist also may have problems with absenteeism or productivity at work. These may be spillover effects from primary couple problems, or a greater degree of worker absenteeism and lower productivity may be associated with very structured corporations. Stress at work may lead to problems at home, which creates increased work problems in a spiraling process of poor client performance at home and at work. Although marriage and family/couple counselors cannot change corporations, they can assess the corporate climate of the employer and its impact on their dual career couple clients. Counselors may wish to explore a variety of options with couples in response to work-family stress, including the possibility of developing new family-friendly policies at work, considering working in more flexible corporations, or learning new methods of coping with stress and pursuing equality at home.

Counselors in Business and Industry

Counselors in business and industry may have the opportunity to develop and implement family-friendly programs. These counselors may also have an opportunity to develop and implement programs that address specific needs of dual career couples. They can respond to specific problems that employees, managers, and others have mentioned as challenges dual career couples face and conduct focus groups and needs analysis to develop creative approaches to these issues. New programs will be successful if they are also sensitive to corporate strategic goals and are consistent with the corporate culture.

CORPORATE CLIMATE

This section will review some corporate concerns addressed by work-family policies. Additionally, particular areas are identified as strategic goals of the corporation that interrelate with dual career couple goals. Only with the support of top management, however, can these initiatives become more than isolated examples of innovative programming.

Policymakers at companies that consider instituting new corporate policies to accommodate the needs of dual career couples are often concerned with how those programs will affect the bottom line. Identifying areas where work and family interact is critical for developing appropriate new programs as well as expanding old programs to meet the needs of each company. Often, a needs analysis combined with focus groups can identify these topics. For example, one common topic relates to the stress that dual career couples experience at work and at home resulting from difficulties of day-to-day life as well as unanticipated crises. In particular, there has been interest in the impact of these programs on retention and recruitment, productivity, turnover, absenteeism, and tardiness.

Retention and Recruitment

As the labor pool shrinks because of a declining birth rate, and women and dual career couples represent a greater proportion of the marketplace, family issues will become of greater concern to corporations. If companies plan to recruit and retain the best talent from a complete labor pool of men and women, family issues must take a more prominent position on the corporate agenda. Many employees report that they have remained at a particular company primarily because of their family benefits. Otherwise, they might have looked for employment at another company that met their work and family needs more effectively.

Productivity

This refers to the worker's ability to be effective at work. A great part of the research on families and work assesses the negative impact of family problems on performance at work. Both women and men view family problems as diminishing workplace performance (Friedman, 1991). Few studies, to date, have assessed the positive impact of family-friendly policies. It seems logical to expect that workers who are less stressed by competing demands of family and career will be more productive.

Turnover

When an employee leaves, a company faces problems of disruption in work, loss of employee talent, and monetary losses associated both with past investment in the departing employee's training and with the current need to recruit and train a new employee. For example, as of 1984, 42% of full-time working women reported that they had previously interrupted their careers for 6 months or longer and 30% of these women attributed the cause to family reasons (U.S. Bureau of the Census, reported in Friedman, 1991). Moreover, 25% of mothers admitted to leaving their jobs because of family reasons (National Child Care Survey, cited in Friedman, 1991).

Absenteeism

All companies expect some employee absenteeism, reflected in sick leave and vacation leave policies. "Research data suggest that job satisfaction and loyalty are related to absence, and that employer-provided family supports may increase job satisfaction. While the company may blame the family for the absence, the employer's lack of accommodation may be the underlying reason" (Friedman, 1991, p. 13).

Tardiness

Tardiness is another concern of employers. When children are brought to school or day care prior to work, there will be occasional lateness. This does not mean that the employee is not conscientious or would complete a project late because there is a difference between lateness to work because of child-care issues and lateness in completing a project. There-fore, when companies focus on the employee's conscientiousness, pro-ductivity, and project performance, concern with lateness due to child issues may be irrelevant.

EXAMPLES OF THE NEXUS OF CORPORATE WORK AND FAMILY CONCERNS

Friedman (1991) identified five areas where there is a "natural linkage between the work-family agenda, and other strategic issues of the orga-nization." These issues include total quality, corporate diversity, gender equity, retention, and career development. This section will offer examples of four hypothetical companies that have linked dual career concerns to corporate strategic goals. These hypothetical companies are Quality In-ternational, Company Diverse, Company Fair, and Career Forward.

Quality Management

Quality International is a Fortune 500 company that focuses on total quality management by linking the goal of satisfying the needs of the customer to the needs of corporate employees. Management continually reassesses and reevaluates corporate values in an attempt to achieve con-tinuous improvement. Top management believes that when workers are satisfied, and the company products are continually improving, the cor-poration is successful.

Recently, Julio, the human resource director, has suggested that senior management consider addressing family needs within the company be-cause members of dual career couples have been regularly coming to his office to discuss their frustration in balancing their multiple roles. Con-sidering the company's focus on satisfying the "internal consumer," each of these employees has looked to him for creative solutions to their dual career couple conflicts. In his discussions with senior management, Julio has pointed out the parallels between corporate quality and dual career couple needs. Addressing family needs is a process requiring flexibility and diversity with changing employee needs, just like the pursuit of total quality. Moreover, Julio has argued that company performance is depen-dent on individual performance; the company cannot perform well if individual needs are not met. These needs include the family and career needs of dual career couples.

Managing Diversity

The philosophy of Company Diverse Inc. involves recognizing that managers should not be doing the same thing for all employees, but rather doing something for each employee. The goal of diversity is to help each employee to maximize his or her potential and make the best contribution to the corporation. Terry, the director of human resources, puts it this way, "We have a great mix of people at Company Diverse Inc. not just with regard to backgrounds but with regard to skills, talents, and experience. Our corporate training department encourages this diversity because we view it as developing the multiplicity of talent and enriching the approaches that workers use to get their jobs done."

Over the last few years, Terry has recognized that a significant proportion of their diverse work force consists of dual career couples and dual earner couples. She recognizes that the company will not be meeting its objective of managing diversity unless the special needs of dual career couples are met. She has recently hired an outside consultant to work with her corporate staff to develop a needs analysis survey and to conduct focus groups to identify the kinds of child-care and flexible programs that parent-employees feel would most effectively address their family and carer needs and help them to continue as productive workers.

Gender Equity

Company Fair Inc. began its pursuit of gender equity in response to the fact that nearly half their applicant pool was female. When they read *Workforce 2000* and recognized that women would represent a significant part of the future work force, top management realized that the only way to recruit and retain the best employees was to be sensitive to the needs of women. Company Fair Inc. has on-site child care, flexible work options, and parenting seminars. Employees are educated about the availability of programs, and efforts are made to maintain employees on an upward track even when they utilize flexible work arrangements.

Recently, top management has realized another benefit of their family-friendly programs. Ronnie is an up-and-coming corporate star. He happened to mention to one of the company's senior officers that his wife had been offered an opportunity to relocate to a far-off city. Before the senior manager had had enough time to wonder what counteroffer he could give Ronnie to induce him to stay, Ronnie said, "But we wouldn't even consider the offer. Company Fair Inc. has great family policies. My wife and I plan to have children within the next few years and we know that we will be able to flourish in our careers and family lives because of the company's generous family benefits." Dual career programs instituted to address the needs of women had also become significant in retaining the best men, reflecting the fact that currently dual career concerns are potentially relevant to *all* employees.

Career Development

Human resource professionals at Career Forward, a Fortune 500 company, have begun to recognize that their career development programs may need to be fine-tuned. Their programs were considered revolutionary back in the late 1970s and early 1980s, with their focus on quality management and their encouragement of both lateral and vertical moves to expand the career options for all employees. Now Barbara, who administers the career development programs, has recognized that the programs may be behind the times because an essential element of the career development program is the assumption that workers are part of couples and that only one partner in the couple is employed.

Currently, 65% of employees of Company Forward consist of dual career and dual earner couples. Therefore, Career Forward has begun to diversify its career development offerings, making programs available to both corporate employees and their significant others. New programs include such topics as "Decision making as a couple," "Planning for success as a couple," "Thinking about relocation," "Family and career balance," and "Couple equity." The response to these programs has been positive and enthusiastic. The comments of Alexis, a member of a dual career couple, are typical. "For the 15 years that I've worked at Career Forward, I've appreciated its many innovative programs on issues related to the work force. The new set of programs for dual career couples has changed my life. It's given me a way of balancing my needs and those of Pat, my husband. I feel that I am in control of my life and my career. Also, I really have the sense that Pat and I are building our career futures as a team. I like that."

CONCLUSIONS

A vast array of corporate programs has been developed to address the needs of dual career couples. These programs affect such corporate concerns as productivity, recruitment and retention, employee turnover, absenteeism, and tardiness. In the most progressive companies, these programs are an integral element of corporate strategic planning. Further development in work-family policies will occur because these policies are essential to the well-functioning of all workers. As companies develop new and innovative programs to address dual career couple needs, three identifiable effects are anticipated.

1. There will be a greater availability of dual career couple workshops and seminars, not just parenting workshops, reflecting the needs of the many dual career and dual earner couples in the work force. These programs will enable couples to make decisions and plan for success as dual career couples.

2. To most effectively address both couple and corporate needs, creative planning for anticipated relocations will be encouraged. Ongoing corporate workshops and seminars that discuss couple issues like decision making may significantly affect couples' ability to plan for and accept relocations as each partner remains on an upward career path.

3. As companies recognize the relevance of family issues, programs may be advertised in novel ways that attract both men and women. Clear statements of corporate policy regarding the impact of flexible scheduling on upward mobility may encourage more employees to explore these flexible arrangements. Also, having a respected corporate mentor discuss his or her experiences as part of a dual career couple can affect and legitimize utilization of specific programs, especially by younger male or female employees.

As worker-friendly programs become more prevalent, corporate policies toward dual career couples will change. This evolution will benefit the goals of both the company and the employee.

11 Future Directions: Achieving Equity

THIS BOOK OFFERS COUNSELORS a multidisciplinary approach to counseling dual career couples that integrates information from studies of dual career couples, human development, career counseling, gender psychology, and couple/marriage and family counseling to develop an innovative life-span strategy for counseling dual career couples. Each counselor will want to custom-tailor the information in accordance with individual counseling style and specific couple needs.

APPLYING THE INTEGRATED APPROACH

An example of the application of this approach is provided by Akisha and Jonathan, a dual career couple. Akisha works as an office manager for a small business in a large city. She considers it a perfect job because her schedule is flexible and her employer appreciates her work and regularly gives her raises and additional responsibility for new projects and staff management. Jonathan is a technician with a large Fortune 500 company. He is known and respected in the company plant and has taken advantage of the company's many training opportunities for moving up. He is well paid and receives excellent benefits. Because of their career commitments they decided not to have children and now, at ages 40+, they are enjoying their occupational accomplishments. Additionally, they have a large home, many friends, and travel and entertain often. Akisha and Jonathan have come to the counselor because Jonathan's plant is closing and he has to relocate, and they must decide what to do with respect to both of their careers.

In their first session with the counselor, they discuss ways to identify their relative family and career priorities (chapter 6). At this and the next session, they discuss ways to make decisions as a couple (chapter 7). They focus on the pros and cons of moving to different plant sites (where Akisha will be temporarily unemployed) or remaining at their present location (where Jonathan will be unemployed). The counselor reviews for the couple how specific decisions can benefit a single partner, both partners, or neither partner. Additionally, the counselor offers some pointers for effective skills in negotiation (chapter 7), communication (chapter 7), and conflict resolution (chapter 8).

At the initial sessions, the counselor feels that both Akisha and Jonathan are assuming that Jonathan's career takes priority because he is the man, even though that is not the way that they have chosen to live their lives. Therefore, in a third session, the counselor focuses on gender issues and suggests that Akisha and Jonathan may be reverting to traditional patterns of functioning because of stress, when, in fact, their life and career choices reflect a nontraditional pattern. At this point the counselor also introduces the question of how relocation might change the balance of home-career equity. If Akisha is unemployed in a new location, will she be expected to have primary home responsibilities, and will this diminish her opportunities to look for employment?

In a fourth session, Akisha and Jonathan discuss with the counselor the issue of pension, retirement, and other benefits that Jonathan and Akisha will forego if he leaves the company. The small business where Akisha has been employed has no comparable benefits. A final concern is that Akisha's skills are not up to date. Because she completed only 2 years of college, she is concerned that she will not be able to find a new position comparable to her current work as office manager at a similar level of occupational status or income.

The cost of living at any one of three possible relocations sites would be far lower than in their current locale, reducing the financial pressures necessary to maintain their accustomed lifestyle after relocation. Because Jonathan would retain his current salary, even if Akisha were temporarily unemployed because of the recessionary economy, they could still live comfortably. At the end of the fourth session, Jonathan and Akisha develop a list of expectations for their satisfaction with future relationship functioning:

1. maintaining their standard of living and their lifestyle;
2. planning for retirement;

3. retaining the autonomy that Akisha wants and that is associated with having her own income and occupational status;
4. facilitating Jonathan's need to continue working in a large corporation where he can have opportunities for upward mobility; and
5. understanding each partner's specific success needs:

For Akisha it is to maintain:

    a. a career where she is respected;
    b. autonomy at work and at home;
    c. many friends; and
    d. opportunities for special time with Jonathan.

For Jonathan it is to maintain:

    a. employment with a congenial group of coworkers;
    b. opportunity for exciting work where he can exercise leadership quality; and
    c. a close relationship with Akisha.

They decide to move to a site in the Midwest and to live in a large city about 40 minutes from the company plant. Akisha will try to find a job in the city and also enroll in school to develop some additional high tech skills that will help her reclaim the level of earning and autonomy to which she had been accustomed. They hope that living in a city will offer them opportunities for pursuing the active social life to which they are accustomed.

SIGNIFICANCE OF DUAL CAREER COUPLE EQUITY

The goal of using the integrated approach is to help dual career couples achieve equity so that their partner, family, and career needs can be met. Family and career equity exists when partners feel that their family and career roles and responsibilities are shared fairly. It does not mean that the contributions of each partner to the family are equal or actually balanced at any one point in time. Rather, partners feel that the balance is fair over time and neither partner regularly shoulders the bulk of home or family responsibilities alone.

Why is couple equity important for the dual career couple? Couples have the potential to provide far more to each partner than what is available to either individual alone. Partners in equitable couples can perform more effectively at work and give more freely to their significant other because of their interdependent mutual support. In nonequitable couples, one partner may demand career priority or refuse to participate at home, leading to resentment on the part of the other partner. In some cases, the frustrated partner may change to a less demanding career, move out of the work force, or divorce (cf., Hochschild, 1989; Philliber & Hiller, 1983). Devaluation of career, family, or couple roles may also result from nonequity.

Couple equity is not identical for all couples, nor do equitable couples necessarily seem much different from other couples. For example, Rapoport and Rapoport (1976) described one high-performing couple where the woman did all the cooking and the man was responsible for routine household maintenance because that balance of responsibilities worked for them, not because of any societal rules about which partner should perform specific chores. Each family task, however, was performed with another family member so that time with children or partner always overlapped with time for chores, and no one person felt that he or she worked at home while the rest of the family relaxed.

GUIDELINES FOR ASSISTING DUAL CAREER COUPLES IN ACHIEVING EQUITY

Five principles have been addressed in this book that are critical for counselors in helping couples achieve equity. First, addressing the needs of dual career couples requires attending to their couple relationship as well as their career development. It is assumed that couples are concerned with continuing their relationships throughout their life spans and also attribute high priority to their relationship. Therefore, long-lasting decisions can be made only when the needs and concerns of both partners are articulated and addressed through effective communication concerning their careers and their couple, family, and career goals. In addition, all couples face a variety of problems and conflicts throughout their life spans. When these conflicts can be recast as problems to be solved, the couple relationship will grow. Mastering effective conflict resolution techniques will enable couples to resolve many problems creatively. Counselors can assist couples in learning relevant communication, negotiation, and problem-solving skills.

Second, dual career couple achievement is most accurately evaluated within the context of life-span achievements. Just as equity cannot be assessed on a day-to-day basis, success also must be looked at over time. In well-functioning dual career couples, there is respect and support for the careers of both partners so that each partner will make a variety of concessions to facilitate the success of the significant other. This means that each partner may reach career goals at a slower rate than single earner couples or unpartnered singles without children. Nonetheless, lifetime career achievement is possible if both partners carefully plan short-term goals within a life-span plan for long-term success, and are willing to be flexible about achieving these long-term goals. Although success may be achieved at a slower rate, partners will have the satisfaction of knowing that both partners achieved their goals rather than one person succeeded at the expense of the other. Third, patterns of growth and development through the life span vary for couples, families, and partners. Because individual behavior is embedded within a variety of subsystems, choices made about family and career issues affect functioning within all other domains, and individual behaviors affect the opportunities and roles available to the significant other. Interrelations among personal roles or interdependent roles of partners may remain the same over time or change as demands evolve and new roles, like that of parent, are adopted.

At the earliest stages of couple development, partners discuss how they will negotiate their dual career relationship. If children are born, new plans for balancing family and career must be adopted. When children leave home, new opportunities for career pursuits become available, especially for those employees who had changed their work schedules to accommodate to children's needs. Thus, couple development and interactions at different stages are partially dependent on individual stage of development.

Career development also exhibits a progressive development from the early stages of career exploration to later stages of career mastery and eventual retirement. Career success is associated with factors like career maturity and is also related to individual self-esteem. Career demands at different stages create a distinct impact on individuals' and couples' ability to balance family and career needs.

Fourth, gender differences between men and women in dual career couples are associated with different responses to equitable sharing between partners. Gender differences also affect what partners feel they can request of a significant other, what they feel obligated to contribute to the relationship, and how their role performance is manifested. Men and women communicate differently, and knowledge about these distinctions is necessary to avoid misunderstandings.

When men and women consider changing balance within their relationship, discussion of the gains and losses of each partner must be undertaken. Men lose the power associated with their role as primary provider. Women, in contrast, lose the power associated with their role as primary family caretaker. These represent losses for both partners and must be acknowledged. However, changing rules for family functions provides an opportunity for both partners to share provider and caretaker roles, and offers new areas for growth and development.

Individuals may respond in accordance with gender stereotypes of how they think they should behave. For example, a woman who says that she would like to spend more time with her children may be expressing what she thinks she should feel, even if she would not like to spend more time at home. Similarly, a man may say that he wants to reach the pinnacle of success within his chosen career, because he thinks that's what "good" men say, when he would really prefer to admit that he has plateaued and enjoys the level of success he has achieved and appreciates more time with his family without continually having to compete to keep moving up.

Fifth, the corporate response to the concerns of dual career couples affects how the couple can balance family and career concerns. When flexible programs are available in the workplace, parents can plan creatively for a balance of their roles. In contrast, when employers are unsympathetic to the needs of parents or offer no special benefits, families often feel overwhelmed, worker productivity may be diminished, and even conscientious employees may consider working elsewhere or taking a time-out.

TYPES OF EQUITY

Family-career equity consists of five distinct aspects: family equity, couple equity, career equity, home equity, and gender equity. Although couples may be equitable in any one role, family-career equity can exist only when couples are equitable in all roles. Couples may also attempt to balance family and career responsibilities across roles. For example, one partner does the housework, the other performs most of the child care. For some couples, this may work. For other couples, there may be a sense of having to do the boring responsibilities while the partner performs the more interesting roles.

Family Equity

Families have many responsibilities to their children, parents, friends, and neighbors. With respect to children, they have daily responsibilities for food and shelter, and more periodic responsibilities of caring for medical needs or clothing. Child-related responsibilities also include involvement with the children's school, carpooling, and play-time (or communication time for older children). Families also have responsibilities for elderly parents with respect to visiting or arranging medical care or home care. Within their neighborhood, families must maintain their social contacts by visiting, phone calling, and arranging time to get together. Family members must share these various activities and responsibilities to achieve family equity.

Couple Equity

Each partner has a variety of needs that must be met, some of which overlap with family needs. Time must be available for couple growth, and support for independent interests of partners must be arranged. Partners will have different interdependence and autonomy needs, different extracurricular interests, and different needs for intimacy and for being with friends. Partners can achieve couple equity by compromising between their different needs, goals, and expectations.

Career Equity

Each partner has independent needs for career achievement. These may complement or conflict with a partner's career needs. To achieve career equity, each partner's career goals must be favored at different times. Decisions about relocation possibilities, promotions, or new work responsibilities must be discussed and decided upon within a context of the relationship benefits and drawbacks of one partner's career decisions with respect to the other partner's career goals.

Home Equity

A variety of home-related responsibilities must be managed for family well-functioning. These include paying bills, gardening, periodic maintenance chores, shopping, cooking, washing, and picking up. Decisions about who has prime responsibilities for various chores must be made according to interests, capabilities, and inclinations concerning who should do which tasks so that both partners feel that home roles are shared equitably.

Gender Equity

Partners must acknowledge gender as an organizing construct for many other family roles, and consider how gender may be constraining their using a rich behavioral repertoire. Gender equity involves mutual respect for men's and women's different ways of doing things or distinct patterns of choosing roles and responsibilities.

FAMILY AND CAREER EQUITY IS DIFFERENT FOR EACH COUPLE

Family and career equity is a life-span phenomenon achieved when roles and responsibilities balance over the course of time. Among equitable couples there is a willingness to discuss and rediscuss family and career issues as time passes and personal demands change. Throughout the second half of this book, tools for enhancing dual career couple functioning were presented to be used as springboards for stimulating the counselor's creative approach to addressing the equity needs of dual career couples. The various family therapy approaches discussed also offer the counselors ideas for helping clients devise multiple ways of achieving couple equity and balance. Although the pursuit of family and career equity may be similar for many clients, definitions of family and career equity can vary dramatically. Equitable couples, however, must provide rules for expressing emotions, achieving personal goals, meeting family/couple needs, and dealing with crises.

An essential element for achieving equity in dual career couples is developing a relationship where mutual concern and respect can be expressed. This does not signify in any way how that concern should be expressed, nor does it specify how often or in what form it is to be expressed. In one couple, mutual concern might involve routine discussions about individual career challenges. In another couple, it might involve one partner's accommodating to the frequent business-related travel of his or her significant other.

Mutual concern and respect also provide positive feedback to partners regarding their performance in achieving couple goals rather than only individual goals. Positive feedback also promotes couple growth. In couples where this mutuality of concern and respect does not exist, there may instead be resentment and competition that can undermine the well-functioning of the relationship and preclude the possibility of family and career equity.

Partners exhibit commitment to the relationship through mutual support and also expect that personal goals can be satisfied within their relationship. As discussed earlier, these goals are composed of the overt, stated goals as well as a variety of conscious and unconscious covert goals, which must both be addressed within equitable couples. The various activities discussed in earlier chapters as well as a variety of assessment instruments on the market can help identify goals and needs. Within the personal domain, issues related to relationships, work achievement, time with the family, personal success, free time, and so on are all relevant areas to explore and discuss. Questions that individuals should ask themselves should be specific so that both partners are aware of their mutual goals. For example, it is not enough to specify that they want a reasonable work schedule; rather, the question of what constitutes a reasonable work schedule should be addressed. Similarly, saying, ''I want to spend more time with my children'' is not specific enough; rather, ''I would like to spend 1 hour an evening playing with my children'' is more appropriate. The realistic nature of these goals should be evaluated, and if statements represent impossible dreams, then more realistic time frames should be developed.

Besides identifying personal needs and goals, individuals who wish to achieve family and career equity should recognize how they would like to achieve balance. Family and career equity cannot be negotiated unless each partner understands his or her personal ability to give or to demand. Questions partners may ask include: Are personal interests like pleasure reading or spending time with a significant other important? For personal satisfaction, is it more important to work long hours at the expense of family time, or to have more time with partners and family at home, even if it means a lower level of work achievement? How do relationships with friends present themselves within the balance of responsibilities? The more honest clients can be about these issues the more likely that their personal needs can be met. Achieving equity requires the use of the various interpersonal skills discussed in previous chapters, but is additionally dependent on a good deal of self-knowledge. Counselors can use the exercises discussed in chapter 6 to help couples develop greater self-knowledge and a more sophisticated appreciation of the relative values that they place on family and career concerns. A variety of published instruments can also be useful, including The Salience Inventory (Nevill & Super, 1986), The Relationship Discovery Profile (Carlson Learning Company), and Career Values Card Sort (Values Card Sort, 1981).

Once couples have focused on balance within their own lives, they can begin to discuss, communicate, and negotiate for balance between themselves and their significant others. Equity requires direct expression of what each person considers a fair balance and discussion of how each person will achieve his or her personal balance within the couple/family parameters. For example, women or men who want to have a meaningful career and a close relationship with their children may prefer to have prime responsibility for daily child care, whereas the spouse or significant other cares for other periodic child-related tasks. In a couple without children where both members of the couple want to move up the career ladder and are not particularly interested in home responsibilities, discussion may focus on how to perform household chores to maximize the time available for career pursuit. This may involve hiring household help, learning to be neater, or eating meals away from home to minimize the couple's home responsibilities.

Some issues that couples and individuals may want to think about include what constitutes equity, what responsibilities they are willing to take on, and what they do not wish to be responsible for. Does their current employment allow for flexibility for family issues? What are some specific changes they can make in their own schedules to balance responsibilities more equitably?

Equity is a balance achieved at a particular point in time between individual, couple, and family needs and goals. Does role balance mean that it is necessary that, in performing any family action, the woman should do half the work and the man should do the other half? Or is it sufficient that behaviors balance over time? Moreover, what constitutes an equitable balance? Is there some other formula? Or is it the balance of responsibility that feels fair to both partners? True equity means that things feel fair over time. However, descriptive answers to these questions may differ across couples. For example, in a couple where neither person enjoys any aspect of housework, partners may develop a system where they both perform chores at the same time so they can maximize personal free time, which they can spend together, and will not lose sight of the real fairness within their relationship as they watch their partner relax while they perform distasteful household chores. This couple's operative system means that balance is achieved only when each person is doing a fair portion at any point in time. In another couple, balance is achieved by a formula accepted and understood only by both partners. In still other couples, balance is achieved by reducing household work through hiring outside help to perform a variety of household chores.

Family and career equity is also predicated on discussing the relative balance between the career priorities of both partners. The couple must address questions concerning whose career comes first or the relative priority of each partner's career over time. Moreover, personal and partner perspectives must be discussed prior to the time when stress decisions about transitions, relocations, promotions, or offers of new jobs are made. Couples may decide that one person's career takes priority because of income earned, productivity, ability to make a contribution to society, or personal need for success. Or they may decide that both careers have equal priority and no decision can be made unless it represents positive growth for both partners. Contemporary perspectives in adult development view workers within the context of other activities they pursue. Therefore, the goal is for the worker to find balance between various roles as employee, partner, family member, leisurite, and parent (e.g., Super, 1986). Although counselors may be able to help the couple to identify their ideal balance, actually implementing career and family priorities may be a difficult task. Perhaps a woman would like to spend a significant amount of time with her family, but her high-paying profession demands long hours of work every week, and both she and her family have become accustomed to the lifestyle achieved through her high-paying career. Or perhaps a man would like to work part-time while his children are preschoolers, but his company does not offer any part-time or flexible work scheduling, and he is not willing to relinquish his tenure and employment benefits within the company.

POSITIVE IMPACT OF EQUITY ON MEN'S CAREERS

Much has been said about the socialization of women for nurturant roles and how this affects their ability to perform in the work force. Little, however, has been written about the limiting effects of men's socialization experiences. Over the last two decades, vast numbers of women have capably added the role of career-committed employee to their many other roles, yet far fewer men have capably added the role of household participant or equitable parent. Men's early constricting socialization is a major obstacle to equity among dual career couples.

If trends continue, gender role norms for men can be expected to become more flexible so that men will more easily adopt gender-sensitive roles as they share responsibilities with their female significant others. Moreover, younger men will be encouraged to develop their own nurturant styles as they mature, and to learn to express themselves through concern and caring for others.

THE ROLE OF THE COUNSELOR

Career theories were presented in the first part of the book so that counselors could develop new conceptual frameworks for working with dual career couples. By assimilating information from gender psychology, career counseling, couple/family systems theory, and life-span development theory, and integrating these theoretical approaches, counselors can successfully develop a new framework for the concerns of dual career couples. A critical aspect of working with dual career couples is to try to see both partners conjointly at least during some counseling sessions. As the section on family systems underscored, change not supported by the couple/family system is ultimately not successful. For example, a career counselor may discuss a particular career change with a woman client that will require longer work hours and more active participation of her husband in routine child care. Without preparing the husband for this change by exploring his ability to change his career and family priorities, his personal needs and goals, or his gender perspectives, it is difficult to imagine the partners' equitably pursuing the new couple balance.

Another critical aspect of the dual carer relationship where counselors can have major impact is to encourage partners to express their positive support for one another. Because of the constraints on their discretionary time, couples may only rarely see anyone who is not a coworker or a member of their nuclear families. Thus, partners provide the most important resource for encouraging the career pursuits of their significant other. Much time together may be spent in reporting the day's events or planning for family needs. It may be difficult for the couple to set aside time for nurturing their relationship. Counselors can help couples distinguish between "report" talk and "family" talk and other nonproblem-oriented conversations that continually lead the couple to develop and grow. Also, couples may need assistance in developing a plan for spending periodic time alone as a couple. Within the integrated approach to counseling dual career couples, it is assumed that couples are negotiating for a fair balance of responsibilities from a perspective of true concern for the needs of their significant other. Therefore, a pivotal question for each client revolves around the compromises and choices that can be made to maximize opportunities for satisfying both partners' needs and goals.

Counselors may need to help clients focus not only on what they require but also on what they are willing to contribute or to give up. It is much easier to ask someone else to make concessions than to make concessions oneself. Yet equity demands that individuals be able to demand and also to change. Expression of one's commitment to the needs of the significant other will vary from couple to couple, and counselors can support this expression. Before couples can act on their commitments to their partners, they must effectively communicate their own needs, aspirations, and goals by using the techniques of active listening, communication, negotiation, and planning for success.

The importance of direct, clear communication is exemplified in the following statements. A partner can say: "I need you to do more around the house" as compared with "I need to work longer hours if I am going to become a vice president in my company." In the first case, negotiation revolves around partners' commitment to the home and caretaking, whereas the second revolves around partners' commitment to the career achievement of a significant other and the relative balance and priority of the career aspirations of both members of the couple. Counselors can help couples learn to speak clearly and directly.

A CREDO OF EQUITY

Companies typically have a credo that defines the guiding principles for the functioning of the company and the direction for the company to take in times of crisis. Couples can look at equity decisions as similar kinds of credos involving principles relating to their commitment to the relationship, recognition of individual needs and goals, gender differences, life-span development, family and career equity, and identification of career/family priorities. An important aspect of a credo of equity is that there is no right or wrong way to be equitable. Fairness will vary substantially from couple to couple. In one couple, equity might involve the man's bringing in half of the income and doing half of the household responsibilities, whereas the woman does the other half. In another couple, equity might involve the man's picking up the clothes at the cleaners and the woman's having primary responsibility for cooking. The actual dimensions of equity are not essential as long as **both partners** feel that it is fair.

A credo of equity can be written down or can be achieved through verbal discussion of the six elements essential for equity: (1) personal needs, (2) preferences for balance, (3) gender issues, (4) life-span issues, (5) balance of career concerns, and (6) commitment to redeveloping the credo. This credo will direct individual performance and couple balance, and result in greater satisfaction with the couple relationship. Moreover, it can specify functional ways to deal with the normal stresses and strains of the relationship over time.

The rewards of couple growth associated with negotiated equity will enhance both individual and family functioning and lead to richer dimensions in the couple relationship. Moreover, equitable couples will be able to pursue a greater variety of challenging business and personal roles. This balance will be attained through discussion of, commitment to, and concern with family and career achievements. Family and career equity may be quite difficult to negotiate, but when it exists, it represents life-span success.

References

Ables, B., & Brandsma, J. (1984). *Therapy for couples: A clinician's guide for effective treatment.* San Francisco, CA: Jossey-Bass.

Ace, M. E., Graen, G. B., & Dawis, R. V. (1972). Biographic correlates of work attitudes. *Journal of Vocational Behavior, 2,* 191–199.

Ackerman, N. W. (1938). The unity of the family. *Archives of Pediatrics, 55,* 51–61.

Ackerman, N. W. (1954). Interpersonal disturbances in the family: Some unresolved problems in psychotherapy. *Psychiatry: Journal for the Study of Interpersonal Processes, 17,* 359–368.

Ackerman, N. W. (1956). Interlocking pathology in family relationships. In S. Redo & G. Daniels (Eds.), *Changing concepts of psychoanalytic medicine.* New York: Grune & Stratton.

Ackerman, N. W. (1958). *The psychodynamics of family life.* New York: Basic Books.

Ackerman, N. W. (1960). Theory of family dynamics. *Psychoanalysis and the Psychoanalytic Review, 46,* 33–49.

Ackerman, N. W. (1965). The family approach to marital disorders. In B. Greene (Ed.), *The psychotherapies of marital disharmony.* New York: The Free Press.

Ackerman, N. W. (1968). The family approach and levels of intervention. *American Journal of Psychotherapy, 1,* 5–14.

Ackerman, N. W. (1970a). Family psychotherapy and psychoanalysis: The implications of difference. In N. W. Ackerman (Ed.), *Family process.* New York: Basic Books.

Ackerman, N. W. (Ed.) (1970b). *Family therapy in transition.* Boston: Little, Brown.

Ackerman, N. W., & Behrens, M. L. (1974). Family diagnosis and clinical process. In S. Arieti & G. Caplan (Eds.), *American handbook of psychiatry II. Child and adolescent psychiatry, sociocultural and community psychiatry* (2nd ed.). New York: Basic Books.

Adelmann, P. K. (1987). Occupational complexity, control and personal income: Their relation to psychological well-being in men and women. *Journal of Applied Psychology, 72,* 529–537.

Adler, A. (1964). *Social interest: A challenge to mankind.* New York: Capricorn Books.

Adler, S., & Aranya, N. (1984). A comparison of the work needs, attitudes, and preferences of professional accountants at different career stages. *Journal of Vocational Behavior, 25,* 45–57.

Ainsworth, M., Blehar, M., Waters, E., & Wall, S. (1978). *Patterns of attachment.* Hillsdale, NJ: Lawrence Erlbaum Associates.

Allen, L., & Britt, D. W. (1983). Black women in American society: A resource developmental perspective. *Issues in Mental Health Nursing, 5,* 61–79.

Anderson, N. S. (1987). Cognition, learning, and memory. In M. A. Baker (Ed.), *Sex differences in human performance* (pp. 37–54). New York: Wiley.

Aneshensel, C. S., & Rosen, B. C. (1980). Domestic roles and sex differences in occupational expectations. *Journal of Marriage and the Family, 42,* 121–131.

Apostal, R. A. (1988). Status of career development and personality. *Psychological Reports, 66,* 811–816.

Archer, J. (1984). Gender roles as developmental pathways. *British Journal of Social Psychology, 23,* 245–256.

Archer, J., & Lloyd, B. B. (1980). Problems and issues in research on sex differences. In J. Sants (Ed.), *Developmental psychology and society.* London: Macmillan.

Armstrong, J. M. (1979). *A national assessment of achievement and participation of women in mathematics.* Denver: Education Commission of the States (ERIC Document Reproduction Service No. ED 187562).

Arvey, R. D. (1979). Unfair discrimination in the employment interview: Legal and psychological aspects. *Psychological Bulletin, 86,* 736–765.

Austin, A. M. B., Salehi, M., & Leffler, A. (1987). Gender and developmental differences in children's conversations. *Sex Roles, 16,* 497–510.

Avioli, P. S. (1985). The labor-force participation of married mothers of infants. *Journal of Marriage and the Family, 47,* 739–745.

Baber, K. M., & Monaghan, P. (1988). College women's career and motherhood expectations: New options, old dilemmas. *Sex Roles, 19,* 189–203.

Baker, M. A. (1987a). Sensory functioning. In M. A. Baker (Ed.), *Sex differences in human performance* (pp. 5–36). New York: Wiley.

Baker, M. A. (Ed.) (1987b). *Sex differences in human performance.* New York: Wiley.

Bandura, A. (1977). Self-efficacy: Toward a unifying theory of behavioral change. *Psychological Review, 84,* 191–215.

Barglow, P., Vaughn, B., & Molitor, N. (1987). Effects of maternal absence due to employment on the quality of infant-mother attachment in a low-risk sample. *Child Development, 58,* 945–954.

Barkley, R. A., Ullman, D. G., Otto, L., & Brecht, J. M. (1977). The effects of sex-typing and sex appropriateness of modelled behavior on children's imitation. *Child Development, 48,* 721–725.

Barnett, R., & Baruch, G. (1978a). Women in the middle years: A critique of research and theory. *Psychology of Women Quarterly, 3,* 187–197.

Barnett, R. C., & Baruch, G. K. (1978b). *The competent woman: Perspectives on development.* New York: Irvington.

Barnett, R. C., & Baruch, G. K. (1987). Determinants of father's participation in family work. *Journal of Marriage and the Family, 49,* 29–40.

Barrett, N. (1979). Women in the job market: Unemployment and work schedules. In R. Smith (Ed.), *The subtle revolution: Women at work*. Washington, DC: Urban Institute.

Baumrind, D. (1982). Are androgynous individuals more effective persons and parents? *Child Development, 53*, 44–75.

Becker, B. J. (1986). Influence again: An examination of reviews and studies of gender differences in social influence. In J. S. Hyde & M. C. Linn, *The psychology of gender: Advances through meta-analysis*. Baltimore, MD: Johns Hopkins University Press.

Beilin, H. (1955). The application of general developmental principles to the vocational area. *Journal of Counseling Psychology, 2*, 53–57.

Belsky, J. (1988). The "effects" of infant day care reconsidered. *Early Childhood Research Quarterly, 3*, 235–272.

Belsky, J., & Rovine, M. (1988). Nonmaternal care in the first year of life and infant-parent attachment security. *Child Development, 59*, 157–167.

Bem, D. J. (1972). Self-perception theory. In L. Berkowitz (Ed.), *Advances in experimental social psychology*. New York: Academic Press.

Bem, S. L. (1974). The measurement of psychological androgyny. *Journal of Consulting and Clinical Psychology, 42*, 155–162.

Bem, S. L. (1979). Theory and measurement of androgyny: A reply to the Pedhazur-Tetenbaum and Locksley-Colten critiques. *Journal of Personality and Social Psychology, 88*, 354–364.

Bem, S. L. (1980). Beyond androgyny: Some presumptuous prescriptions for a liberated sexual identity. In J. Sherman & F. Denmark (Eds.), *Psychology of women: Future directions of research, psychological dimensions*. New York: Psychological Dimensions.

Bem, S. L. (1981). Gender schema theory: A cognitive account of sex typing. *Psychological Review, 88*, 369–371.

Benin, M. H., & Agostinelli, J. (1988). Husbands' and wives' satisfaction with the division of labor. *Journal of Marriage and the Family, 50*, 349–361.

Benin, M. H., & Nienstedt, B. C. (1985). Happiness in single and dual-earner families: The effects of marital happiness, job satisfaction and life cycle. *Journal of Marriage and the Family, 47*, 975–984.

Benn, R. (1986). Factors promoting secure attachment relationships between employed mothers and their sons. *Child Development, 57*, 1224–1231.

Berardo, D. H., Shehan, C. L., & Leslie, G. R. (1987). A residue of tradition: Jobs, careers, and spouses' time in housework. *Journal of Marriage and the Family, 49*, 381–390.

Berk, S. F. (1985). *The gender factory: The apportionment of work in American households*. New York: Plenum Press.

Berman, E., Sacks, S., & Lief, H. (1975). The two-professional marriage: A new conflict syndrome. *Journal of Sex and Marital Therapy, 1*, 242–253.

Bernard, J. (1966). *Academic women*. Cleveland, OH: World.

Bernard, J. (1988). The inferiority curriculum. *Psychology of Women Quarterly, 12*, 261–268.

Betz, N. E., & Fitzgerald, L. F. (1987). *The career psychology of women*. Boston, MA: Academic Press.

Betz, N. E., & Hackett, G. (1981). The relationship of career-related self-efficacy expectations to perceived career options in college women and men. *Journal of Counseling Psychology, 28,* 399–410.

Betz, N. E., Heesacker, R. S., & Shuttleworth, C. (1990). Moderators of the congruence and realism of major and occupational plans in college students: A replication and extension. *Journal of Counseling Psychology, 37,* 269–276.

Beutell, N. J., & Brenner, O. C. (1986). Sex differences in work values. *Journal of Vocational Behavior, 28,* 29–41.

Bianchi, S. M., & Spain, D. (1986). *American women in transition.* New York: Russell Sage Foundation.

Bird, G. W., & Bird, G. A. (1986). Strategies for reducing role strain among dual-career couples. *International Journal of the Sociology of the Family, 16,* 83–94.

Bird, G. W., Bird, G. A., & Scruggs, M. (1984). Determinants of family task sharing: A study of husbands and wives. *Journal of Marriage and the Family, 46,* 345–355.

Bird, G. W., & Ford, R. (1985). A source of role strain among dual-career couples. *Home Economics Research Journal, 14,* 187–194.

Birnbaum, D. W., & Croll, W. L. (1984). The etiology of children's stereotypes about sex differences in emotionality. *Sex Roles, 10,* 677–691.

Birnbaum, D. W., Nosanchuk, T. A., & Croll, W. L. (1980). Children's stereotypes about sex differences in emotionality. *Sex Roles, 6,* 435–443.

Black, B., & Hazen, N. L. (1990). Social status and patterns of communication in acquainted and unacquainted preschool children. *Developmental Psychology, 26,* 379–387.

Bloch, D., & Simon, R. (Eds.) (1982). *The strength of family therapy: Selected papers of Nathan W. Ackerman.* New York: Brunner/Mazel.

Block, J. H. (1973). Conceptions of sex role. Some cross-cultural and longitudinal perspectives. *American Psychologist, 28,* 512–526.

Block, J. H. (1984). *Sex-role identity and ego development.* San Francisco: Jossey-Bass.

Bloom-Feshbach, S., Bloom-Feshbach, J., & Heller, K. A. (1982). Work, family and children's perceptions of the world. In S. B. Kamerman & C. S. Hayes (Eds.), *Families that work: Children in a changing world.* Washington, DC: National Academy Press.

Blustein, D. L., & Phillips, S. D. (1990). Relations between ego identity statuses and decision making styles. *Journal of Counseling Psychology, 37,* 160–168.

BNA: The Bureau of National Affairs. (1989a). Corporate work and family programs: A step-by-step corporate guide. *The BNA Special Report Series on Work and Family,* Special Report #19.

BNA: The Bureau of National Affairs. (1989b). Corporate work and family programs for the 1990s: Five case studies. *The BNA Special Report Series on Work and Family,* Special Report #13.

Booth, A. (1979). Does wives' employment cause stress for husbands? *Family Coordinator, 28,* 445–450.

Borman, K. M. (1988a). Policy endnote. In J. T. Mortimer & K. M. Borman (Eds.), *Work experience and psychological development through the life span* (pp. 233–280). American Association for the Advancement of Science Selected Symposia Series. Boulder, CO: Westview Press.

Borman, K. M. (1988b). The process of becoming a worker. In J. T. Mortimer & K. M. Borman (Eds.), *Work experience and psychological development through the life span* (pp. 51–78). American Association for the Advancement of Science Selected Symposia Series. Boulder, CO: Westview Press.

Bowlby, J. (1969). *Attachment.* New York: Basic Books.

Braverman, L. (1989). Beyond the myth of motherhood. In M. McGoldrick, C. Anderson, & F. Walsh (Eds.), *Women in families: A framework for family therapy.* New York: Norton.

Bridges, J. S. (1987). College females' perceptions of adult roles and occupational fields for women. *Sex Roles, 16,* 591–604.

Bridges, J. S. (1988). Sex differences in occupational performance expectations. *Psychology of Women Quarterly, 12,* 75–90.

Brody, L. (1985). Gender differences in emotional development: A review of theories and research. In A. J. Stewart & M. B. Lykes (Eds.), *Gender and personality: Current perspectives on theory and research.* Durham, NC: Duke University Press.

Bronfenbrenner, U. (1979). *The ecology of human development.* Cambridge, MA: Harvard University Press.

Bronfenbrenner, U., & Crouter, A. C. (1982). Work and family through time and space. In S. B. Kamerman & S. D. Hayes (Eds.), *Families that work.* Washington, DC: National Academy Press.

Brown, L. S. (1991). Ethical issues in feminist therapy: Selected topics. *Psychology of Women Quarterly, 15,* 323–326.

Callanan, M. A. (1989). Development of object categories and inclusion relations: Preschooler's hypotheses about word meaning. *Developmental Psychology, 25,* 207–216.

Campbell, A., Converse, P., & Rodgers, W. (1976). *The quality of American life.* New York: Sage.

Capps, R., Dodd, C. H., & Winn, L. J. (1981). *Communication for the business and professional speaker.* New York: Macmillan.

Card, J. J., Steel, L., & Abeles, R. P. (1980). Sex differences in realization of individual potential for achievement. *Journal of Vocational Behavior, 17,* 1–21.

Carden, A. D. (1990). Mentoring and adult career development: The evolution of a theory. *The Counseling Psychologist, 18,* 275–299.

Career Values Card Sort. (1981). San Jose, CA: Career Research & Testing.

Carlsson, M., & Jaderquist, P. (1983). Note on sex-role opinions as conceptual schemata. *British Journal of Social Psychology, 22,* 65–68.

Carter, D. B. (1987). The roles of peers in sex role socialization. In D. B. Carter (Ed.), *Current conceptions of sex roles and sex typing: Theory and research.* New York: Praeger.

Catalyst. (1983). Why should companies think about women? *Catalyst Perspective, 2.* (Available from Catalyst, 250 Park Avenue South, New York, NY 10003, RR #2.)

Chartrand, J. M., & Camp, C. C. (1991). Invited contribution: Advances in the measurement of career development constructs: A 20-year review. *Journal of Vocational Behavior, 39,* 1–39.

Chase-Lansdale, L., & Owen, M. (1987). Maternal employment in a family context: Effects on infant-mother and infant-father attachments. *Child Development, 58,* 1505–1512.

Chester, N. L. (1990). Achievement motivation and employment decisions: Portraits of women with young children. In H. Y. Grossman & N. L. Chester (Eds.), *The experience and meaning of work in women's lives.* Hillsdale, NJ: Lawrence Erlbaum Associates.

Chester, N. L., & Grossman, H. Y. (1990). Introduction: Learning about women and their work through their own accounts. In H. Y. Grossman & N. L. Chester (Eds.), *The experience and meaning of work in women's lives.* Hillsdale, NJ: Lawrence Erlbaum Associates.

Chipman, S. F., Brush, L., & Wilson, D. (Eds.) (1985). *Women and mathematics: Balancing the equation.* Hillsdale, NJ: Lawrence Erlbaum Associates.

Chodorow, N. (1978). *The reproduction of mothering: Psychoanalysis and the sociology of gender.* Berkeley: University of California Press.

Clarke-Stewart, K. A. (1988). "The 'effects' of infant day care reconsidered" reconsidered: Risks for parents, children, and researchers. *Early Childhood Research Quarterly, 3,* 293–318.

Clarke-Stewart, K. A. (1991). A home is not a school: The effects of child care on children's development. *Journal of Social Issues, 47,* 105–123.

Coltrane, S. (1990). Birth timing and the division of labor in dual-earner families. *Journal of Family Issues, 11,* 157–181.

Cook, E. P. (1990). Gender and psychological distress. *Journal of Counseling & Development, 68,* 371–375.

Cotton, S., Antill, J. K., & Cunningham, J. D. (1990). The work attachment of mothers with preschool children. *Psychology of Women Quarterly, 14,* 255–270.

Coverman, S., & Sheley, J. F. (1986). Changes in men's housework and child-care time, 1965–1975. *Journal of Marriage and the Family, 48,* 413–422.

Covin, T. J., & Brush, C. C. (1991). An examination of male and female attitudes toward career and family issues. *Sex Roles, 25,* 393–415.

Crites, J. O. (1973). *Career Maturity Inventory.* Monterey, CA: California Testing Bureau/McGraw-Hill.

Crites, J. O. (1975). *The Career Adjustment and Development Inventory.* College Park, MD: Gumpert.

Crites, J. O. (1978). *The Career Maturity Inventory.* Monterey, CA: CTB/McGraw-Hill.

Crites, J. O. (1982). Testing for career adjustment and development. *Training & Development Journal, 36,* 20–24.

Crohan, S. E., Antonucci, T. C., Adelmann, P. K., & Coleman, L. M. (1989). Job characteristics and well-being at midlife: Ethnic and gender comparisons. *Psychology of Women Quarterly, 13,* 223–235.

Culp, R. E., Cook, A. S., & Housley, P. C. (1983). A comparison of observed and reported adult-infant interactions: Effects of perceived sex. *Sex Roles, 9,* 475–479.

D'Amico, R. (1983). Status maintenance or status competition: Wife's relative wages as a determinate of labor supply and marital instability. *Social Forces, 61,* 1186–1205.

Deaux, K. (1976a). *The behavior of women and men.* Monterey, CA: Brooks-Cole.

Deaux, K. (1976b). Sex: A perspective on the attribution process. In J. H. Harvey, W. J. Ickes, & R. F. Kidd (Eds.), *New directions in attribution research* (vol. 1). New York: Wiley.

Deaux, K., & Kite, M. E. (in press). Gender stereotypes. In F. Denmark & M. Paludi (Eds.), *Handbook on the psychology of women.* Westport, CT: Greenwood Press.

DeMeis, D. K., Hock, E. E., & McBride, S. L. (1986). The balance of employment and motherhood: Longitudinal study of mothers' feelings about separation from their first-born infants. *Developmental Psychology, 22,* 627–632.

Diamond, E. E. (1971). Occupational interests: Male-female or high level-low level dichotomy. *Journal of Vocational Behavior, 1,* 305–315.

Dilley, J. S. (1965). Decision making ability and vocational maturity. *Personnel & Guidance Journal, 44,* 423–427.

Dinklage, L. B. (1968). *Decision strategies of adolescents.* Unpublished doctoral dissertation, Harvard University, Cambridge, MA.

Dorn, F. J. (1990). Career counseling: A social psychological perspective. In W. B. Walsh & S. H. Osipow (Eds.), *Career counseling: Contemporary topics in vocational psychology.* Hillsdale, NJ: Lawrence Erlbaum Associates.

Dudley, G. A., & Tiedeman, D. V. (1977). *Career development: Exploration and commitment.* Muncie, IN: Accelerated Development.

Durkin, K. (1987). Social cognition and social context in the construction of sex differences. In M. A. Baker (Ed.), *Sex differences in human performance* (pp. 141–170). New York: Wiley.

Eagly, A. H. (1986). Some meta-analytic approaches to examining the validity of gender-difference research. In J. S. Hyde & M. C. Linn, *The psychology of gender: Advances through meta-analysis.* Baltimore, MD: Johns Hopkins University Press.

Eagly, A. H., & Carli, L. L. (1981). Sex of researchers and sex-typed communications as determinants of sex differences in infuenceability: A meta-analysis of social influence studies. *Psychological Bulletin, 90,* 1–20.

Eagly, A. H., & Mladinic, A. (1989). Gender stereotypes and attitudes toward women and men. *Personality and Social Psychology Bulletin, 15,* 543–558.

Eagly, A. H., Mladinic, A., & Otto, S. (1991). Are women evaluated more favorably than men? An analysis of attitudes, beliefs, and emotions. *Psychology of Women Quarterly, 15,* 203–216.

Eagly, A. H., & Steffen, V. J. (1984). Gender stereotypes stem from the distribution of women and men into social roles. *Journal of Personality and Social Psychology, 46,* 735–754.

Eagly, A. H., & Wood, W. (1982). Inferred sex differences in status as a determinant of gender stereotypes about social influence. *Journal of Personality and Social Psychology, 43,* 915–928.

Easterbrooks, M., & Goldberg, W. (1985). Effects of early maternal employment on toddlers, mothers and fathers. *Developmental Psychology, 21,* 774–783.

Eccles, J. (1987). Gender roles and women's achievement-related decisions. *Psychology of Women Quarterly, 11,* 135–172.

Eccles, J., Adler, T., & Meece, J. L. (1984). Sex differences in achievement: A test of alternate theories. *Journal of Personality and Social Psychology, 46,* 26–43.

Eckerman, C. C., & Didow, S. M. (1989). Toddlers' social coordinations: Changing responses to another's invitation to play. *Developmental Psychology, 25,* 794–805.

Eisenberg, N., Murray, E., & Hite, T. (1982). Children's reasoning regarding sex-typed toy choices. *Child Development 53,* 81–86.

Eldridge, N. S., & Gilbert, L. A. (1990). Correlates of relationship satisfaction in lesbian couples. *Psychology of Women Quarterly, 24,* 43–62.

Elman, M. R., & Gilbert, L. A. (1984). Coping strategies for role conflict in married professional women with children. *Family Relations, 33,* 317–327.

Erez, M. (1988). Woman's choice of innovative-technical fields of studies. *Applied Psychology: An International Review, 37,* 183–200.

Erikson, E. H. (1950). *Childhood and society.* New York: Norton.

Erikson, E. H. (1968a). *Identity: Youth and crisis.* New York: Norton.

Erikson, E. H. (1968b). Life Cycle, *The International Encyclopedia of the Social Sciences,* David L. Sills, (Ed.), *9,* 286–292.

Etaugh, C., Houtler, B. D., & Ptasnik, P. (1988). Evaluating competence of women and men: Effects of experimenter gender and group gender composition. *Psychology of Women Quarterly, 12,* 191–200.

Fagot, B. I., & Hagan, R. (1991). Observations of parent reactions to sex-stereotyped behaviors: Age and sex effect. *Child Development, 62,* 617–628.

Falk, W. W., & Cosby, A. G. (1978). Women's marital-familial statuses and work histories: Some conceptual considerations. *Journal of Vocational Behavior, 13,* 126–140.

Fassinger, R. (1990). Causal models of career choice in two samples of college women. *Journal of Vocational Behavior, 36,* 225–248.

Featherman, D. L., & Hauser, R. M. (1976). Sexual inequalities and socioeconomic achievement in the US, 1962–1973. *American Sociological Review, 41,* 462–483.

Felmlee, D. H. (1984). The dynamics of women's job mobility. *Work and Occupations, 11,* 259–281.

Ferber, M. A. (1982). Labor market participation of young married women: Causes and effects. *Journal of Marriage and the Family, 44,* 457–468.

Ferber, M. A., & Birnbaum, B. (1980). One job or two jobs: The implications for young wives. *Journal of Consumer Research, 7,* 263–271.

Ferber, M., & Kordick, B. (1978). Sex differentials in the earnings of PhD's. *Industrial and Labor Relations Review, 31,* 227–238.

Feree, M. M. (1976). Working class jobs, housework and paid work as sources of satisfaction. *Social Problems, 22,* 431–441.

Field, T., Vega-Lahr, N., Goldstein, S., & Scafidi, F. (1987). Interaction behavior of infants and their dual-career parents. *Infant Behavior and Development, 10,* 371–377.

Finch, M. D., & Mortimer, J. T. (1985). Adolescent work hours and the process of achievement. In A. C. Kerchkoff (Ed.), *Research on Sociology of Education and Socialization, 5,* 171–196.

Fischer, J. L., & Narus, L. R. (1981). Sex-role development in late adolescence and adulthood. *Sex Roles, 7,* 97–106.

Fitzgerald, L. S., & Crites, J. O. (1980). Toward a career psychology of women: What do we know? What do we need to know? *Journal of Counseling Psychology, 27*, 44–62.

Frank, E. J. (1988). Business students' perceptions of women in management. *Sex Roles, 19*, 107–118.

Freud, S. (1931). Libidinal types. In J. Strachey (Ed.) (1959). *Sigmund Freud: Collected papers* (vol. 5). New York: Basic Books.

Freud, S. (1940). *Outlines of psychoanalysis.* New York: Norton.

Freud, S. (1951). Libidinal types. In J. Strachey (Ed.), *Sigmund Freud: Collected papers* (vol. 5). New York: Basic Books.

Friedman, D. E. (1991). Linking work-family issues to the bottom line. *The Conference Board*, Report Number 962.

Friedman, D. E., & Johnson, A. A. (1991). Strategies for promoting a work-family agenda. *The Conference Board*, Report Number 973.

Frieze, I. H. (1980). Beliefs about success and failure in the classroom. In J. McMillan (Ed.), *The social psychology of school learning*. New York: Academic Press.

Frieze, I. H., Fisher, J., Hanusa, B. H., McHugh, M. C., & Valle, V. A. (1978). Attributions of the causes of success and failure as internal and external barriers to achievement in women. In J. Sherman & F. Denmark (Eds.), *Psychology of women: Future directions of research*. New York: Psychological Dimensions.

Frieze, I. H., Whitley, B. E., Hanusa, B. H., & McHugh, M. C. (1982). Assessing the theoretical models for sex differences in causal attributions for success and failure. *Sex Roles, 8*, 333–343.

Gaddy, C. D., Glass, C. R., & Arnkoff, D. B. (1983). Career involvement of women in dual-career families: The influence of sex-role identity. *Journal of Counseling Psychology, 30*, 388–394.

Garland, T. N. (1972). The better half: The male in the dual-career professional family. In C. Safilios-Rothschild (Ed.), *Toward a sociology of women*. Lexington, MA: Xerox College Publishing.

Garvey, C. (1977). *Play.* Cambridge, MA: Harvard University Press.

Gavin, L., & Furman, W. (1989). Age differences in adolescents' perceptions of their peer group. *Developmental Psychology, 25*, 827–834.

Geerken, M., & Gove, W. (1983). *At home and at work: The family's allocation of labor.* Beverly Hills, CA: Sage.

George, J. M., & Brief, A. P. (1990). The economic instrumentality of work: An examination of the moderating effects of financial requirements and sex on the pay-life satisfaction relationship. *Journal of Vocational Behavior, 37*, 357–368.

Gerdes, E. P., & Garber, D. M. (1983). Sex bias in hiring: Effects of job demands and applicant competence. *Sex Roles, 9*, 307–319.

Gergen, M. M. (1990). Finished at 40: Women's development within the patriarchy. *Psychology of Women Quarterly, 14*, 471–493.

Gerstel, N. R. (1977). The feasibility of commuter marriage. In P. Stein, J. Richman, & N. Hannon (Eds.), *The family: Functions and conflicts and symbols*. Reading, MA: Addison-Wesley.

Gilbert, L. (1985). *Men in dual-career families: Current realities and future prospects.* Hillsdale, NJ: Lawrence Erlbaum Associates.

Gilbert, L. (1988). *Sharing it all: The rewards and struggles of two-career families.* New York: Plenum Press.

Gilbert, L., Dancer, L. S., Rossman, K. M., & Thorn, B. L. (1991). Assessing perceptions of occupational-family integration. *Sex Roles, 24,* 107–119.

Gilligan, C. (1982). *In a different voice.* Cambridge, MA: Harvard University Press.

Gilligan, C. (1988). Remapping the moral domain: New images of self in relationship. In C. Gilligan, J. V. Ward, & J. M. Taylor (Eds.), *Mapping the moral domain: A contribution of women's thinking to psychological theory and education.* Cambridge, MA: Harvard University Press.

Ginzberg, E. (1972). Toward a theory of occupational choice: A restatement. *Vocational Guidance Quarterly, 20,* 169–176.

Ginzberg, E. (1984). Career development. In D. Brown & L. Brooks (Eds.), *Career choice and development* (pp. 169–191). San Francisco, CA: Jossey-Bass.

Ginzberg, E., Ginsburg, S. W., Axelrad, S., & Herma, J. L. (1951). *Occupational choice: An approach to a general theory.* New York: Columbia University Press.

Gleitman, L. R., Newport, E. L., & Gleitman, H. (1984). The current status of the Motherese hypothesis. *Journal of Child Language, 11,* 43–79.

Glenn, N. D., & Weaver, C. N. (1978). A multivariate multisurvey study of marital happiness. *Journal of Marriage and the Family, 40,* 269–282.

Glisson, C., & Durrick, M. (1988). Predictors of job satisfaction and organizations. *Administrative Science Quarterly, 33,* 61–81.

Goffman, E. (1981). *Forms of talk.* Philadelphia: University of Pennsylvania Press.

Goh, S. C. (1991). Sex differences in perceptions of interpersonal work style, career emphasis, supervisory mentoring behavior, and job satisfaction. *Sex Roles, 24,* 701–710.

Goldenberg, I., & Goldenberg, H. (1980). *Family therapy: An overview.* Belmont, CA: Wadsworth.

Goodrich, T. J., Rampage, C., Ellman, B., & Halstead, K. (1988). *Feminist family therapy: A case book.* New York: Norton.

Gould, S., & Werbel, D. (1983). Work involvement: A comparison of dual wage earner and single wage earner families. *Journal of Applied Psychology, 68,* 313–319.

Gove, W. R., & Geerken, M. (1977). The effect of children and employment on the mental health of married men and women. *Social Forces, 56,* 66–76.

Gove, W. R., & Tudor, J. F. (1973). Adult sex roles and mental illness. *American Journal of Sociology, 78,* 812–835.

Graddol, D., & Swann, J. (1989). *Gender voices.* Oxford: Basil Blackwell.

Gray, J. D. (1983). The married professional woman: An examination of her role conflicts and coping strategies. *Psychology of Women Quarterly, 7,* 235–243.

Greenberger, D. B., Strasser, S., Cummings, L. L., & Dunham, R. B. (1989). The impact of personal control on performance and satisfaction. *Organizational Behavior and Human Decision Process, 43,* 29–51.

Greenberger, E., Goldberg, W. A., Crawford, T. J., & Granger, J. (1988). Beliefs about the consequences of maternal employment for children. *Psychology of Women Quarterly, 12*, 35–59.

Greene, T. C., & Peell, P. A. (1987). Environmental stress. In M. A. Baker (Ed.), *Sex differences in human performance* (pp. 81–106). New York: Wiley.

Greenhaus, J. H. (1971). An investigation of the role of career salience in vocational behavior. *Journal of Vocational Behavior, 1*, 209–216.

Greenhaus, J. H., Bedeian, A. G., & Mossholder, K. W. (1987). Work experiences, job performance, and feelings of personal and family well-being. *Journal of Vocational Behavior, 31*, 200–215.

Greenhaus, J. H., & Beutell, N. J. (1985). Sources of conflict between work and family roles. *Academy of Management Review, 10*, 76–88.

Greenhaus, J. H., Parasuraman, S., Granrose, C. S., Rabinowitz, S., & Beutell, N. J. (1989). Sources of work-family conflict among two-career couples. *Journal of Vocational Behavior, 34*, 133–153.

Gribbons, W. D., & Lohnes, P. R. (1968). *Emerging careers.* New York: Columbia University, Teachers College Press.

Gribbons, W. D., & Lohnes, P. R. (1982). *Careers in theory and experience.* Albany: State University of New York Press.

Gross, R. H., & Arvey, R. D. (1977). Marital satisfaction, job satisfaction, and task distribution in the homemaker job. *Journal of Vocational Behavior, 11*, 1–13.

Grossman, H. Y., & Chester, N. L. (1990). *The experience and meaning of work in women's lives.* Hillsdale, NJ: Lawrence Erlbaum Associates.

Grossman, H. Y., & Stewart, A. J. (1990). Women's experience of power over others: Case studies of psychotherapists and professors. In H. Y. Grossman & N. L. Chester (Eds.), *The experience and meaning of work in women's lives.* Hillsdale, NJ: Lawrence Erlbaum Associates.

Guelzow, M. G., Bird, G. W., & Koball, E. H. (1991). An exploratory path analysis of the stress process for dual-career men and women. *Journal of Marriage and the Family, 53*, 151–164.

Gunter, N. C., & Gunter, B. G. (1990). Domestic division of labor among working couples. Does androgyny make a difference? *Psychology of Women Quarterly*, 355–370.

Gysbers, N., & Moore, E. (1987). *Career-counseling: Skills and techniques for practitioners.* Englewood Cliffs, NJ: Prentice-Hall.

Hackett, G. (1985). Role of mathematics self-efficacy in the choice of math-related majors of college women and men: A path analysis. *Journal of Counseling Psychology, 32*, 47–56.

Haley, J. (1970). Family therapy. *International Journal of Psychiatry, 9*, 233–242.

Haley, J. (1976). *Problem-solving therapy.* San Francisco: Jossey-Bass.

Hall, D. T. (1972). A model of coping with role conflict. *Administrative Science Quarterly, 4*, 471–486.

Hall, D. T. (1987). *Career development in organizations.* New York: Jossey-Bass.

Hall, J. A. (1984). *Nonverbal sex differences: Communication accuracy and expressive style.* Baltimore, Johns Hopkins University Press.

Hardesty, C., & Betz, N. (1980). The relationships of career salience, attitudes toward women, and demographic and family characteristics to marital adjustment in dual-career couples. *Journal of Vocational Behavior, 17,* 242–250.

Hardesty, C., & Bokemeier, J. (1989). Finding time and making do: Distribution of household labor in nonmetropolitan marriages. *Journal of Marriage and the Family, 51,* 253–267.

Hargreaves, D. (1976). What are little boys and girls made of? *New Society, 37,* 542–544.

Harmon, L. (1981). The life and career plans of young adult college women: A follow-up study. *Journal of Counseling Psychology, 28,* 416–427.

Harren, V. A. (1979). A model of career decision making for college students. *Journal of Vocational Behavior, 14,* 271–277.

Harren, V. A. (1980). *Assessment of Career Decision Making (ACDM) preliminary manual.* Carbondale, IL: Author.

Harren, V. A. (1984). *Assessment of Career Decision Making.* Los Angeles, CA: Western Psychological Services.

Hartnett, O. (1978). Sex-role stereotyping at work. In J. Chetwynd & O. Hartnett (Eds.), *The sex-role system.* London: Routledge & Kegan Paul.

Hatcher, M. A. (1991). The corporate woman of the 1990s: Maverick or innovator. *Psychology of Women Quarterly, 15,* 251–259.

Hays, C. D., & Kamerman, S. B. (Eds.) (1983). *Children of working parents: Experiences and outcomes.* Washington, DC: National Academy Press.

Hazard, L. B., & Koslow, D. (1986). Conjoint career counseling: Counseling dual-career couples. In Z. Leibowitz & D. Lea (Eds.), *Adult career development: Concepts, issues, and practices* (pp. 171–186). Alexandria, VA: National Career Development Association.

Heaston, P. Y. (1976). An analysis of selected role perceptions among successful Black women in the professions. *Psychology of Women Quarterly, 6,* 261–289.

Heckman, N. A., Bryson, R., & Bryson, J. B. (1977). Problems of professional couples: A content analysis. *Journal of Marriage and the Family, 39,* 323–330.

Hefner, R., Rebecca, M., & Oleshansky, B. (1975). Development of sex-role transcendence. *Human Development, 18,* 143–158.

Helmreich, R. L., & Spence, J. T. (1978). The Work and Family Orientation Questionnaire: An objective instrument to assess components of achievement motivation and attitudes toward family and career. *JSAS Catalog of Selected Documents in Psychology, 8,* 35. (cited in Betz & Fitzgerald, 1987).

Hesse-Biber, S. (1985). Male and female students' perceptions of their academic environment and future career plans. *Human Relations, 38,* 91–105.

Hill, C. R., & Stafford, F. (1980). Parental care of children: Time diary estimates of quantity, predictability and variety. *Journal of Human Resources, 15,* 219–239.

Hiller, D. V., & Dyehouse, J. (1987). A case for banishing "dual-career" marriages from the research literature. *Journal of Marriage and the Family, 49,* 787–795.

Hiller, D. V., & Philliber, W. W. (1978). The derivation of status benefits from occupational attainments of working wives. *Journal of Marriage and the Family, 40,* 63–69.

Hiller, D. V., & Philliber, W. W. (1980). Necessity, compatibility and status attainment as factors in the labor-force participation of married women. *Journal of Marriage and the Family, 42*, 347–354.

Hiller, D. V., & Philliber, W. W. (1986). Determinants of social class identification for dual-earner couples. *Journal of Marriage and the Family, 48*, 583–587. See also Vannoy-Hiller, D. V.

Hochschild, A., with Machung, A. (1989). *The second shift: Working parents and the revolution at home.* New York: Viking.

Hock, E. (1980). Working and nonworking mothers and their infants: A comparison study of maternal caregiving characteristics and infant social behavior. *Merrill-Palmer Quarterly, 26*, 79–101.

Hock, E., Gnezda, M. T., & McBride, S. L. (1984). Mothers of infants: Attitudes toward employment and motherhood following birth of the first child. *Journal of Marriage and the Family, 46*, 425–431.

Hoffman, L. W. (1960). Effects of the employment of mothers on parental power relations and the division of household tasks. *Journal of Marriage and Family Living, 22*, 27–35.

Hoffman, L. W. (1974). The effects of maternal employment on the child: A review of the research. *Developmental Psychology, 10*, 204–228.

Hoffman, L. W. (1979). Maternal employment: 1979. *American Psychologist, 34*, 859–865.

Hoffman, L. (1984). Maternal employment and the young child. In M. Perlmutter (Ed.), *Parent-child interactions and parent-child relations in child development.* Hillsdale, NJ: Lawrence Erlbaum Associates.

Hoffman, L. W. (1989). Effects of maternal employment in the two-parent family. *American Psychologist, 44*, 283–292.

Hoffman, L. W., & Nye, F. I. (1974). *Working mothers.* San Francisco: Jossey-Bass.

Holden, C. (1991). Is "gender gap" narrowing? *Science, 253*, 959–960.

Holder, D., & Anderson, C. (1989). Women, work, and the family. In M. McGoldrick, C. Anderson, & F. Walsh (Eds.), *Women in families: A framework for family therapy.* New York: Norton.

Holmstrom, L. L. (1972). *The two-career family.* Cambridge, MA: Schenkman.

Houseknecht, S. K., & Macke, A. S. (1981). Combining marriage and career: The marital adjustment of professional women. *Journal of Marriage and the Family, 43*, 651–661.

Houseknecht, S. K., & Spanier, G. B. (1980). Marital disruption and higher education among women in the United States. *Sociological Quarterly, 21*, 375–389.

Humphrey, F. G. (1983). *Marital therapy.* Englewood Cliffs, NJ: Prentice-Hall.

Hyde, J. S. (1986). Introduction: Meta-analysis and the psychology of gender. In J. S. Hyde & M. C. Linn, *The psychology of gender: Advances through meta-analysis.* Baltimore, MD: Johns Hopkins University Press.

Hyde, J. S., Fennema, E., Ryan, M., Frost, L. A., & Hopp, C. (1990). Gender comparisons of mathematics attitudes and affect: A meta-analysis. *Psychology of Women Quarterly, 14*, 299–324.

Hyde, J., Krajnik, M., & Skuldt-Niederberger, K. (1991). Androgyny across the lifespan: A replication and longitudinal follow-up. *Developmental Psychology, 27*, 516–519.

Ivey, A. E., & Goncalves, O. F. (1988). Developmental therapy: Integrating developmental processes into clinical practice. *Journal of Counseling and Development, 66,* 406–413.

Jacobs, B. S., & Moss, H. A. (1976). Birth order and sex of sibling as determinants of mother-infant interaction. *Child Development, 47,* 315–322.

Jacobson, M. B., & Effertz, J. (1974). Sex roles and leadership: Perceptions of the leaders and the led. *Organizational Behavior and Human Performance, 12,* 383–396.

James, J. B. (1990). Employment patterns and midlife well-being. In H. Y. Grossman & N. L. Chester (Eds.), *The experience and meaning of work in women's lives.* Hillsdale, NJ: Lawrence Erlbaum Associates.

Janson, P., & Martin, J. K. (1982). Job satisfaction and age: A test of two views. *Social Forces, 60,* 1089–1102.

Jenkins, S. R. (1989). Longitudinal prediction of women's careers: Psychological, behavioral, and sociostructural influences. *Journal of Vocational Behavior, 34,* 204–235.

Jepsen, D. (1974). The stage construct in career development. *Counseling and Values, 18,* 124–131.

Jepsen, D. (1990). Developmental career counseling. In W. B. Walsh & S. H. Osipow (Eds.), *Career counseling: Contemporary topics in vocational psychology.* Hillsdale, NJ: Lawrence Erlbaum Associates.

Johnson, A. A. (1990). Relocating two-earner couples: What companies are doing. *The Conference Board,* Research Bulletin Number 247.

Johnston, W. B., & Packer, A. H. (1987). *Workforce 2000: Work and workers for the 21st century.* Indianapolis, IN: Hudson Institute.

Kalleberg, A. L. (1977). Work values and job rewards: A theory of job satisfaction. *American Sociological Review, 42,* 124–143.

Kalleberg, A. L., & Loscocco, K. A. (1983). Aging, values, and rewards: Explaining age differences in job satisfaction. *American Sociological Review, 48,* 78–90.

Kamerman, S. B., & Hayes, S. D. (Eds.) (1982). *Families that work.* Washington, DC: National Academy Press.

Kanter, R. M. (1976). The impact of hierarchical structure on the work behavior of women and men. *Social Problems, 23,* 415–430.

Kanter, R. M. (1977). *Men and women of the corporation.* New York: Basic Books.

Kaplan, A., Brooks, B., McComb, A. L., Shapiro, E. R., & Sodano, A. (1983). Women and anger in psychotherapy. *Women and Therapy, 2,* 29–40.

Katz, D. (1987). Sex discrimination in hiring: The influence of organizational climate and need for approval on decision making behavior. *Psychology of Women Quarterly, 11,* 11–20.

Katz, P. A. (1979). The development of female identity. *Sex Roles, 5,* 155–178.

Katz, P. A. (1986). Modification of children's gender-stereotyped behavior: General issues and research considerations. *Sex Roles, 14,* 591–602.

Keefe, W. (1971). *Listen, management: Creative listening for better managing.* New York: McGraw-Hill.

Keller, M., & Wood, P. (1989). Development of friendship reasoning: A study of interindividual differences in intraindividual change. *Developmental Psychology, 25,* 820–826.

Kessler, R. C., & McRae, J. A., Jr. (1982). The effect of wives' employment on the mental health of married men and women. *American Sociological Review, 47*, 216–227.

Kohlberg, L. (1975). Counseling and counselor education: A developmental approach. *Counselor Education and Supervision*, 250–256.

Kohlberg, L. (1976). Moral stages and moral development: The cognitive developmental approach. In T. Lickona (Ed.), *Moral development and behavior: Theory, research, and social issues*. New York: Holt, Rinehart & Winston.

Kopper, B. A., & Epperson, D. L. (1991). Women and anger: Sex and sex-role comparisons in the expression of anger. *Psychology of Women Quarterly, 15*, 7–14.

Kotelchuk, M. (1976). The infant's relationship to the father: Experimental evidence. In M. Lamb (Ed.), *The role of the father in child development*. New York: Wiley.

Kreidler, W. J. (1984). *Creative conflict resolution*. Glenview, IL: Scott, Foresman.

Krumboltz, J. D., & Nichols, C. W. (1990). Integrating the social learning theory of career decision making. In W. B. Walsh & S. Osipow (Eds.), *Career counseling: Contemporary topics in vocational psychology*. Hillsdale, NJ: Lawrence Erlbaum Associates.

Krumboltz, J. D., Scherba, D. S., Hamel, D. A., Mitchell, L., Rude, S., & Kinnier, R. (1979). *The effect of alternate career decision making strategies on the quality of resulting decisions*. First report. Stanford, CA: Stanford University. (ERIC Document Reproductions Service No. 195 824).

Kuhn, D., Nash, S. C., & Brucken, L. (1978). Sex role concepts of two- and three-year-olds. *Child Development, 49*, 445–451.

Ladewig, B. H., & McGee, G. W. (1986). Occupational commitment, a supportive family environment, and marital adjustment: Development and estimation of a model. *Journal of Marriage and the Family, 48*, 821–829.

Ladewig, B. J., & White, P. N. (1984). Dual earner marriage: The family social environment and dyadic adjustment. *Journal of Family Issues, 5*, 193–202.

Lamb, M. E. (1977a). The development of mother-infant and father-infant attachments in the second year of life. *Developmental Psychology, 13*, 637–648.

Lamb, M. E. (1977b). Father-infant and mother-infant interaction in the first year of life. *Child Development, 48*, 167–181.

Laws, J. L. (1976). Work aspiration of women: False leads and new starts. *Signs, 1*, 33–49.

Leaper, C. (1991). Influence and involvement in children's discourse: Age, gender, and partner effects. *Child Development, 62*, 797–811.

Leaper, C., Gleason, J. B., & Hirsch, T. (1990). *Parent-child verbal interaction and the socialization of gender in preschool children*. Unpublished manuscript (cited in Leaper, 1991).

Leaper, C., Hauser, S. T., Kremen, A., Powers, S. I., Jacobson, A. M., Noam, G. G., Weiss-Perry, B., & Follansbee, D. (1989). Adolescent-parent interactions in relation to adolescents' gender and ego development pathway: A longitudinal study. *Journal of Early Adolescence, 9*, 335–361.

Leibowitz, Z., & Schlossberg, N. (1981, July). Training managers for their role in a career development system. *Training and Development Journal*, 72–79.

Lemkau, J. P. (1979). Personality and background characteristics of women in male-dominated occupations: A review. *Psychology of Women Quarterly, 4,* 221–240.

Lemkau, J. P. (1983). Women in male-dominated professions: Distinguishing personality and background characteristics. *Psychology of Women Quarterly, 8,* 144–165.

Lemkau, J. P., & Landau, C. (1986). The "selfless syndrome": Assessment and treatment considerations. *Psychotherapy, 23,* 226–233.

Lenney, E. (1977). Women's self-confidence in achievement settings. *Psychological Bulletin, 84,* 1–13.

Lerner, H. G. (1985). *The dance of anger.* New York: Harper & Row.

Lewis, M., Stranger, C., & Sullivan, M. W. (1989). Deception in 3-year-olds. *Developmental Psychology, 25,* 439–443.

Levinson, D. J. (1986). A conception of adult development. *American Psychologist, 41,* 3–13.

Levinson, D. J., Darrow, C. N., Klein, E. B., Levinson, M. H., & McKee, B. (1978). *The seasons of a man's life.* New York: Knopf.

Levinson, D. J., & Gooden, W. E. (1985). The life cycle. In H. I. Kaplan & B. J. Sadock (Eds.), *Comprehensive textbook of psychiatry* (4th ed.) (pp. 1–12). Baltimore, MD: Williams & Wilkins.

Lewis, J. M., Beavers, W. R., Gossett, J. T., & Phillips, V. A. (1976). *No single thread: Psychological health in family systems.* New York: Brunner/Mazel.

Liben, L. S., & Signorella, M. L. (1980). Gender-related schemata and constructive memory in children. *Child Development, 51,* 11–18.

Lincoln, J. R., & Kalleberg, A. L. (1985). Work organization and workforce commitment: A study of plants and employees in the U.S. and Japan. *American Sociological Review, 50,* F38–F60.

Linn, M. C., & Petersen, A. C. (1986). A meta-analysis of gender differences in spatial ability: Implications for mathematics and science achievement. In J. S. Hyde & M. C. Linn, *The psychology of gender: Advances through meta-analysis.* Baltimore, MD: Johns Hopkins University Press.

Locksley, A. (1980). On the effects of wives' employment on marital adjustment and companionship. *Journal of Marriage and the Family, 42,* 337–346.

Locksley, A., & Colten, M. E. (1979). Psychological androgyny: A case of mistaken identity? *Journal of Personality and Social Psychology, 37,* 1017–1031.

Loerch, K. J., Russell, J. E., & Rush, M. C. (1989). The relationship among family domain variables and work-family conflict for men and women. *Journal of Vocational Behavior, 35,* 288–308.

Long, B. C. (1989). Sex-role orientation, coping strategies, and self-efficacy of women in traditional and nontraditional occupations. *Psychology of Women Quarterly, 13,* 307–324.

Lorence, J., & Mortimer, J. T. (1985). Work involvement through the life course: A panel study of three age groups. *American Sociological Review, 50,* 618–638.

Loscocco, K. A. (1990). Career structures and employee commitment. *Social Science Quarterly, 71,* 53–68.

Loscocco, K. A., & Roschelle, A. R. (1991). Invited contribution: Influences on the quality of work and nonwork life: Two decades in review. *Journal of Vocational Behavior, 39*, 185–225.

Loscocco, K. A., & Spitze, G. (1990). Working conditions, social support and the well-being of female and male factory workers. *Journal of Health and Social Behavior, 31*, 313–327.

Lott, B. (1987). Sexist discrimination as distancing behavior: I. A laboratory demonstration. *Psychology of Women Quarterly, 11*, 47–58.

Lowe, G. S., & Northcott, H. C. (1988). The impact of working conditions, social roles and personal characteristics on gender differences in distress. *Work and Occupations, 15*, 55–77.

Maccoby, E. E. (1990). Gender and relationships: A developmental account. *American Psychologist, 45*, 513–520.

Maccoby, E. E., & Jacklin, C. N. (1974). The psychology of sex differences (summary and commentary). Palo Alto, CA: Stanford University Press.

Maccoby, E. E., & Jacklin, C. N. (1987). Gender segregation in childhood. In E. H. Reese (Ed.), *Advances in child development and behavior* (vol. 20). New York: Academic Press.

Maccoby, E. E., & Martin, J. A. (1983). Socialization in the context of the family: Parent-child interaction. In P. H. Mussen (Series Ed.) & E. M. Hetherington (Vol. Ed.) *Handbook of child psychology: Vol. 4: Socialization, personality and social development.* New York: Wiley.

MacEwen, K. E., & Barling, J. (1991). Effects of maternal employment experiences on children's behavior via mood, cognitive difficulties, and parenting behavior. *Journal of Marriage and the Family, 53*, 635–644.

Malatesta, C. Z., & Haviland, J. M. (1982). Learning display rules: The socialization of emotion expression in infancy. *Child Development, 53*, 991–1003.

Maltz, D. N., & Borker, R. A. (1982). A cultural approach to male-female miscommunication. In J. Gumperz (Ed.), *Language and social identity.* Cambridge, England: Cambridge University Press.

Marcia, J. E. (1966). Development and validation of ego-identity status. *Journal of Personality and Social Psychology, 3*, 551–558.

Maret, E., & Finlay, B. (1984). The distribution of household labor among women in dual-earner families. *Journal of Marriage and the Family, 46*, 357–364.

Martin, C. L., & Halverson, C. F., Jr. (1981). A schematic processing model of sex-typing and stereotyping in children. *Child Development, 52*, 1119–1134.

Martin, C. L., & Halverson, C. F., Jr. (1983). The effects of sex-typing schemes on young children's memory. *Child Development, 54*, 563–574.

Masih, L. K. (1967). Career saliency and its relation to certain needs, interests and job values. *Personnel and Guidance Journal, 45*, 653–658.

Matas, L., Arend, R. A., & Sroufe, L. A. (1978). Continuity of adaptation in the second year: The relationship between quality of attachment and later competence. *Child Development, 49*, 547–556.

Mazen, A. M., & Lemkau, J. P. (1990). Personality profiles of women in traditional and nontraditional occupations. *Journal of Vocational Behavior, 37*, 46–59.

McClelland, D. C. (1985). How motives, skills, and values determine what people do. *American Psychologist, 40*, 812–825.

McClelland, D. C., Koestner, R., & Weinberger, J. (1989). How do self-attributed and implicit motives differ? *Psychological Review, 96*, 690–702.

McCloskey, L. A. (1987). Gender and conversation: Mixing and matching styles. In D. B. Carter (Ed.), *Current conceptions of sex roles and sex typing: Theory and research.* New York: Praeger.

McCook, L. I., Folzer, S. M., Charlesworth, D., & Scholl, J. N. (1991). Dueling careers. *Training and Development, 45*, 40–44.

McGoldrick, M. (1989). Women through the family life cycle. In M. McGoldrick, C. Anderson, & F. Walsh (Eds.), *Women in families: A framework for family therapy.* New York: Norton.

McHugh, M. C. (1975, April). *Sex differences in causal attributions: A critical review.* Paper presented at the annual meeting of the Eastern Psychological Association, New York, NY.

McHugh, M. C., Fisher, J. E., & Frieze, I. H. (1982). Effects of situational factors on the self-attributions of females and males. *Sex Roles, 8*, 389–394.

McHugh, M. C., Frieze, I. H., & Hanusa, B. H. (1982). Attributions and sex differences in achievement: Problems and new perspectives. *Sex Roles, 8*, 467–479.

Megargee, G. (1969). Influence of sex roles on the manifestation of leadership. *Journal of Applied Psychology, 53*, 377–382.

Meglino, B. M., Ravlin, E. C., & Adkins, C. L. (1989). A work values approach to corporate culture: A field test of the value congruence process and its relationship to individual outcomes. *Journal of Applied Psychology, 74*, 424–432.

Meier, S. T. (1991). Review: Vocational behavior, 1988–1990: Vocational choice, decision-making, career development interventions, and assessment. *Journal of Vocational Behavior, 39*, 131–181.

Menaghan, E. G., & Parcel, T. L. (1991). Determining children's home environments: The impact of maternal characteristics and current occupational and family conditions. *Journal of Marriage and the Family, 53*, 417–431.

Miller, J. (1980). Individual and occupational determinants of job satisfaction: A focus on gender differences. *Sociology of Work and Occupations, 7*, 337–366.

Miller, J., Schooler, C., Kohn, M. L., & Miller, K. A. (1979). Women and work: The psychological effects of occupational conditions. *American Journal of Sociology, 85*, 66–94.

Miller, J., Slomczynski, K. M., & Kohn, M. L. (1988). Continuity of learning-generalization: The effect of job on men's intellective process in the United States and Poland. In J. T. Mortimer & K. M. Borman (Eds.), *Work experience and psychological development through the life span* (pp. 79–108). American Association for the Advancement of Science Selected Symposia Series. Boulder, CO: Westview Press.

Miller, J. B. (Ed.) (1973). *Psychoanalysis and women: Eminent psychoanalysts dispel myths and explore realities.* Baltimore, MD: Penguin Books.

Miller, J. B. (1976). *Toward a new psychology of women.* Boston: Beacon Press.

Miller, P. M., Danaher, D. L., & Forbes, D. (1986). Sex-related strategies for coping with interpersonal conflict in children aged five and seven. *Developmental Psychology, 22*, 543–548.

Minuchin, S. (1974). *Families and family therapy*. Cambridge, MA: Harvard University Press.

Minuchin, S., & Fishman, H. C. (1981). *Family therapy techniques*. Cambridge, MA: Harvard University Press.

Mischel, W. (1966). A social learning view of sex differences. In E. E. Maccoby (Ed.), *The development of sex differences*. Stanford, CA: Stanford University Press.

Mischel, W. (1970). Sex-typing and socialization. In P. H. Mussen (Ed.), *Carmichael's manual of child psychology*, vol. 2 (3rd ed.) New York: Wiley.

Moen, P. (1985). Continuities and discontinuities in women's labor force participation. In G. H. Elder, Jr. (Ed.), *Life course dynamics: 1960s to 1980s*. Ithaca, NY: Cornell University Press.

Moore, E., Spain, S., & Bianchi, S. M. (1984). The working wife and mother. *Marriage and Family Review, 7*, 79–98.

Moore, K. A., & Hoffreth, S. L. (1979). Effects of women's employment on marriage: Formation, stability and roles. *Marriage and Family Review, 2*, 27–36.

Moore, K. A., & Sawhill, I. V. (1984). Implications of women's employment for home and family life. In P. Voydanoff (Ed.), *Work and family: Changing roles of men and women*. Palo Alto, CA: Mayfield.

Moorehouse, M. J. (1991). Linking maternal employment patterns to mother-child activities and children's school competence. *Developmental Psychology, 27*, 295–303.

Morgan, K. C., & Hock, E. (1984). A longitudinal study of psychosocial variables affecting the career patterns of women with young children. *Journal of Marriage and the Family, 46*, 383–390.

Mortimer, J. T. (1988). Introduction. In J. T. Mortimer & K. M. Borman (Eds.), *Work experience and psychological development through the life span* (pp. 1–20). American Association for the Advancement of Science Selected Symposia Series. Boulder, CO: Westview Press.

Mortimer, J. T., & Borman, K. M. (Eds.) (1988). *Work experience and psychological development through the life span*. American Association for the Advancement of Science Selected Symposia Series. Boulder, CO: Westview Press.

Mortimer, J. T., & Finch, M. D. (1986). The development of self-esteem in the early work career. *Work and Occupations, 13*, 217–239.

Mortimer, J. T., Finch, M. D., & Maruyama, G. (1988). Implications of the dual roles of adult women for their health. In J. T. Mortimer & K. M. Borman (Eds.), *Work experience and psychological development through the life span* (pp. 109–156). American Association for the Advancement of Science Selected Symposia Series. Boulder, CO: Westview Press.

Mortimer, J. T., & Lorence, J. (1979a). Occupational experience and the self-concept: A longitudinal study. *Social Psychology Quarterly, 42*, 307–323.

Mortimer, J. T., & Lorence, J. (1979b). Work experience and occupational value socialization: A longitudinal study. *American Journal of Sociology, 84*, 1361–1385.

Moss, K. A. (1967). Sex, age and state as determinants of mother-infant interactions. *Merrill-Palmer Quarterly, 13*, 19–36.

Murphy, P. P., & Burck, H. D. (1976). Career development of men at midlife. *Journal of Vocational Behavior, 9*, 337–343.

Murrell, A. J., Frieze, I. H., & Frost, J. L. (1991). Aspiring to careers in male- and female-dominated professions: A study of black and white college women. *Psychology of Women Quarterly, 15*, 103–126.

Nelson, E. N. (1976). *Role conflict and ambivalence in housework.* Paper presented at Pacific Sociological Association Meetings.

Nelson, E. N. (1977). Women's work-housework alienation. *Humboldt Journal of Social Relations, 5*, 91–117.

Nelson, K. E., Denninger, M. M., Bonvillian, J. D., Kaplan, B. J., & Bakes, N. (1983). Maternal input adjustments and non-adjustments as related to children's linguistic advances and to language acquisition theories. In A. D. Pellegrini & T. D. Yawkey (Eds.), *The development of oral and written languages: Readings in developmental and applied linguistics.* Norwood, NJ: Ablex.

Nevill, D., & Super, D. (1986). *The Salience Inventory: Theory, application and research: Manual.* Palo Alto, CA: Consulting Psychologists Press.

Nevill, D., & Super, D. (1989). *The Values Scale: Theory, application, and research: Manual.* Palo Alto, CA: Consulting Psychologists Press.

Noe, R. A. (1988). Women and mentoring: A review and research agenda. *Academy of Management Review, 13*, 65–78.

Noe, R. A., Noe, A. W., & Bachhuber, J. A. (1990). An investigation of the correlates of career motivation. *Journal of Vocational Behavior, 37*, 340–356.

Nyquist, L., Slivken, K., Spence, J. T., & Helmreich, R. L. (1985). Household responsibilities in middle-class couples: The contribution of demographic and personality variables. *Sex Roles, 12*, 15–34.

Nyquist, L. V., & Spence, J. T. (1986). Effects of dispositional dominance and sex role expectations on leadership behaviors. *Journal of Personality and Social Psychology, 50*, 87–93.

O'Connell, L., Betz, M., & Kurth, S. (1989). Plans for balancing work and family life: Do women pursuing nontraditional and traditional occupations differ? *Sex Roles, 20*, 35–45.

O'Connell, L., & Bloom, D. E. (1987). Juggling jobs and babies: America's child care challenge. Washington, DC: *Population Reference Bureau*, No. 12.

Olson, J. E., Frieze, I. H., & Detlefson, E. G. (1990). Having it all? Combining work and family in a male and a female profession. *Sex Roles, 23*, 515–533.

Oppenheimer, V. K. (1977). The sociology of women's economic role in the family. *American Sociological Review, 42*, 387–405.

Ornstein, S., Crohn, W. L., & Slocum, J. W., Jr. (1989). Life stage versus career stage: A comparative test of the theories of Levinson and Super. *Journal of Organizational Behavior, 10*, 117–133.

Ornstein, S., & Isabella, L. (1990). Age vs. stage models of career attitudes of women: A partial replication and extension. *Journal of Vocational Behavior, 36*, 1–19.

Osipow, S. H. (1975). The relevance of theories of career development to special groups: Problems, needed data, and implications. In J. S. Picou & R. E. Campbell (Eds.), *Career behavior of special groups.* Columbus, OH: Merrill.

Osipow, S. H. (1983). *Theories of career development.* (3rd ed.). Englewood Cliffs, NJ: Prentice-Hall.

Osipow, S. (1991). Invited contribution: Observations about career psychology. *Journal of Vocational Behavior, 39,* 291–296.

Osipow, S. H., & Gold, J. A. (1968). Personal adjustment and career development. *Journal of Counseling Psychology, 15,* 439–443.

Papp, P. (1983). *The process of change.* New York: Guilford Press.

Parke, R. D. (1979). Perspectives on father-infant interaction. In J. D. Osofsky (Ed.), *Handbook of infancy.* New York: Wiley.

Parke, R. D., & Sawin, D. B. (1979). *The family in early infancy: Social interactional and attitudinal analysis.* Paper presented at the Society for Research in Child Development meeting, New Orleans. Reported in Parke, 1979.

Parsons, J. E., Adler, T. F., & Kaczala, C. (1982). Socialization of achievement attitudes and beliefs: Parental influences. *Child Development, 53,* 310–321.

Parsons, J. E., Kaczala, C., & Meece, J. (1982). Socialization of achievement attitudes and beliefs: Classroom influences. *Child Development, 53,* 322–339.

Parsons, T. (1942). Age and sex in the social structure of the United States. *American Sociological Review, 7,* 604–616.

Pedhazur, E. J., & Tetenbaum, T. J. (1979). Bem sex role inventory: A theoretical and methodological critique. *Journal of Personality and Social Psychology, 37,* 996–1016.

Pendleton, B. F., Poloma, M. M., & Garland, T. N. (1980). Scales for investigation of the dual career family. *Journal of Marriage and the Family, 42,* 269–276.

Perls, F. (1969). *Gestalt therapy verbatim.* Moab, UT: Real People Press.

Perry, D. G., & Bussey, K. (1979). The social learning theory of sex differences: Imitation is alive and well. *Journal of Personality and Social Psychology, 37,* 1699–1712.

Philliber, W. W., & Hiller, D. V. (1978). The implications of wife's occupational attainment for husband's class identification. *The Sociological Quarterly, 19,* 450–458.

Philliber, W. W., & Hiller, D. V. (1979). A research note: Occupational attainments and perceptions of status among working wives. *Journal of Marriage and the Family, 41,* 59–62.

Philliber, W. W., & Hiller, D. V. (1983). Relative occupational attainments of spouses and later changes in marriage and wife's work experience. *Journal of Marriage and the Family, 45,* 161–170.

Phillips, S. D., & Pazienza, N. J. (1988). History and theory of the assessment of career development and decision making. In W. B. Walsh & S. H. Osipow (Eds.), *Career decision making.* Hillsdale, NJ: Lawrence Erlbaum Associates.

Piaget, J. (1950). *The psychology of intelligence.* New York: Harcourt Brace.

Piaget, J. (1954). *The construction of reality in the child.* New York: Ballantine Books.

Piaget, J. (1962). *Play, dreams and imitation in childhood.* New York: Norton.

Piaget, J. (1969). *The child's conception of the world.* Totowa, NJ: Littlefield, Adam.

Piaget, J. (1970). Piaget's theory. In P. H. Mussen (Ed.), *Carmichael's manual of child psychology* (3rd ed.) (pp. 703–732). Vol. 1. New York: Wiley.

Pistrang, N. (1984). Women's work involvement and experience of new mother-hood. *Journal of Marriage and the Family, 46*, 433–448.

Plake, B. S., Murphy-Berman, V., Derscheid, L. E., Gerber, R. W., Miller, S. K., Speth, C. A., & Tomes, R. E. (1987). Access decisions by personnel directors: Subtle forms of sex bias in hiring. *Psychology of Women Quarterly, 11*, 255–264.

Pleck, J., & Staines, G. (1985). Work schedules and family life in two-earner couples. *Journal of Family Issues, 6*, 61–82.

Poloma, M. M., Pendleton, B. F., & Garland, T. N. (1981). Reconsidering the dual-career marriage: A longitudinal approach. *Journal of Family Issues, 2*, 205–224.

Poole, M. E., & Clooney, G. H. (1985). The relationship between interest-occupation congruence and job satisfaction. *Journal of Vocational Behavior, 26*, 251–263.

Powers, M. G., & Salvo, J. J. (1982). Fertility and child care arrangements as mechanisms of status articulation. *Journal of Marriage and the Family, 44*, 21–34.

Psathas, G. (1968). Toward a theory of occupational choice for women. *Sociology and Social Research, 52*, 253–268.

Quinn, R. P., Staines, G. L., & McCullough, M. R. (1974). Job satisfaction: Is there a trend? *Manpower Research Monograph, 30*. Washington, DC: U.S. Department of Labor, Manpower Administration.

Rabinovich, B., Suwalsky, J., & Pedersen, F. (1984, April). *An observational study of the transition to maternal employment.* Paper presented at the Bi-ennial Meetings of the International Conference of Infancy Studies. New York.

Ragins, B. R., & Sundstrom, E. (1989). Gender and power in organizations: A longitudinal perspective. *Psychological Bulletin, 105*, 51–88.

Rapoport, R., & Rapoport, R. N. (1971). *Dual-career families.* London: Penguin Books.

Rapoport, R., & Rapoport, R. N. (1975). Men, women, and equity. *The Family Coordinator, 24*, 421–432.

Rapoport, R., & Rapoport, R. N. (1976). *Dual-career families re-examined: New integrations of work and family.* London: Martin Robertson.

Reck, R. R., & Long, B. G. (1987). *The win-win negotiator: How to negotiate favorable agreements that last.* Sparten.

Reckers, G. A., & Yates, C. E. (1976). Sex-typed play in feminoid boys versus normal boys and girls. *Journal of Abnormal Child Psychology, 4*, 41–48.

Redgrove, J. (1987). Applied settings. In M. A. Baker (Ed.), *Sex differences in human performance* (pp. 171–185). New York: Wiley.

Reese, H. W., & Overton, W. F. (1970). Models of development and theories of development. In L. R. Goulet & P. B. Baltes (Eds.), *Life-span developmental psychology: Research and theory* (pp. 116–145). New York: Academic Press.

Regan, M. C., & Roland, H. E. (1982). University students: A change in expec-tations and aspirations over the decade. *Sociology of Education, 55*, 223–228.

Rendina, I., & Dickersheid, J. D. (1976). Father involvement with first-born infants. *Family Coordinator, 25*, 373–379.

Rheingold, H., & Cook, K. (1975). The contents of boys' and girls' rooms as an index of parents' behavior. *Child Development, 46*, 459–463.

Rhodes, S. R. (1983). Age-related differences in work attitudes and behavior: A review and conceptual analysis. *Psychological Bulletin, 93*, 328–367.

Rice, D. (1979). *Dual-career marriage: Conflict and treatment.* New York: Free Press.

Richardson, J. G. (1979). Wife occupational superiority and marital troubles: An examination of the hypothesis. *Journal of Marriage and the Family, 41*, 63–72.

Rix, S. E. (Ed.) (1987). *The American woman: 1987–88: A report in depth.* New York: Norton.

Roe, A., & Siegelman, M. (1964). *The origin of interests.* APGA Inquiry Series No. 1. Washington, DC: American Personnel and Guidance Association.

Roos, P. E., & Cohen, L. H. (1987). Sex roles and social support as moderators of life stress adjustment. *Journal of Personality and Social Psychology, 52*, 576–585.

Rose, S. A., Feldman, J. F., Wallace, I. F., & McCarton, C. (1989). Infant visual attention: Relation to birth status and developmental outcomes during the first 5 years. *Developmental Psychology, 25*, 560–576.

Rosen, M. D. (1985, June). Marriage is back in style . . . with a difference. *Ladies Home Journal*, pp. C11, 6, 98–102, 159, 161.

Rosenwasser, S. M., & Dean, N. G. (1989). Gender role and political office: Effects of perceived masculinity/femininity of candidate and political office. *Psychology of Women Quarterly, 13*, 77–85.

Ross, C. (1987). The division of labor at home. *Social Factors, 65*, 816–833.

Sachs, J. (1987). Preschool boys' and girls' language use in pretend play. In S. U. Philips, S. Steele, & C. Tanz (Eds.), *Language, gender, and sex in comparative perspectives.* Cambridge, England: Cambridge University Press.

Safilios-Rothschild, C. (1975). Family and stratification: Some macrosociological observations and hypotheses. *Journal of Marriage and the Family, 37*, 855–860.

Sager, C. J. (1976). *Marriage contracts and couple therapy: Hidden forces in intimate relationship.* New York: Brunner/Mazel.

Sameroff, A. J. (1975). Early influences on development: Fact or fancy? *Merrill-Palmer Quarterly, 21*, 267–294.

Sarason, S. B. (1977). *Work, aging, and social change: Professionals and the one life-one career imperative.* New York: Free Press.

Satir, V. (1967a). *Conjoint family therapy: A guide to theory and techniques.* Palo Alto, CA: Science and Behavior Books.

Satir, V. (1967b). A family of angels. In J. Haley & L. Hoffman (Eds.), *Techniques of family therapy.* New York: Basic Books.

Satir, V. (1972). *Peoplemaking.* Palo Alto, CA: Science and Behavior Books.

Satir, V. (1975a). Intervention for congruence. In V. Satir, J. Stachowiak, & H. A. Taschman, (Eds.), *Helping families to change.* New York: Aronson.

Satir, V. (1975b). Problems and pitfalls in working with families. In V. Satir, J. Stachowiak, & H. A. Taschman, (Eds.), *Helping families to change.* New York: Aronson.

Satir, V. (1975c). You as a change agent. In V. Satir, J. Stachowiak, & H. A. Taschman, (Eds.), *Helping families to change*. New York: Aronson.

Satir, V., Stachowiak, J., & Taschman, H. A. (1975). *Helping families to change*. New York: Aronson.

Savickas, M. L. (1990). The use of career measures in counseling practice. In E. Watkins & V. Campbell (Eds.), *Testing in counseling practice* (pp. 373–417). Hillsdale, NJ: Lawrence Erlbaum Associates.

Schein, V. E., Mueller, R., & Jacobson, C. (1989). The relationship between sex role stereotypes and required management characteristics among college students. *Sex Roles, 20*, 103–110.

Schele, A. (1991, December). Career strategies: The mommy-track trap. *Working Woman*, pp. 28–31.

Schoen, R., & Urton, W. L. (1979). A theoretical perspective on cohort marriage and divorce in twentieth century Sweden. *Journal of Marriage and the Family, 41*, 409–416.

Schwab, D. P., & Heneman, H. G., III. (1977). Age and satisfaction with dimensions of work. *Journal of Vocational Behavior, 10*, 212–220.

Schwartz, F. N. (1989, Jan.–Feb.). Management women and the new facts of life. *Harvard Business Review*, pp. 65–76.

Scott, G. G. (1990). *Resolving conflict: With others and within yourself*. Oakland, CA: New Harbinger Publications.

Sedney, M. A. (1986). Growing more complex: Conceptions of sex roles across adulthood. *International Journal of Aging and Human Development, 22*, 15–29.

Sedney, M. A. (1987). Development of androgyny: Parental influences. *Psychology of Women Quarterly, 11*, 311–326.

Sekaran, U. (1982). An investigation of the career salience of men and women in dual-career families. *Journal of Vocational Behavior, 20*, 111–119.

Sekaran, U. (1986). *Dual-career families*. San Francisco, CA: Jossey-Bass.

Sekaran, U. (1989). Understanding the dynamics of self-concept of members in dual-career families. *Human Relations, 42*, 97–116.

Seliger, S. (1991, June). Champions of childcare. *Working Mother*, pp. 54–68.

Sells, L. (1973). High school mathematics as the critical filter in the job market. In *Developing opportunities for minorities in graduate education*. Proceedings of the Conference on Minority Graduate Education, University of California, Berkeley.

Sewell, W. H., Hauser, R. M., & Wolf, W. (1980). Sex, schooling and occupational status. *American Journal of Sociology, 86*, 551–583.

Shatz, M. (1984). Contributions of mother and mind to the development of communicative competence: A status report. In M. Perlmutter (Ed.), *Parent-child interaction and parent-child relations in child development*. Hillsdale, NJ: Lawrence Erlbaum Associates.

Sheldon, A. (1990). Pickle fights: Gendered talk in preschool disputes. *Discourse Processes, 13*, 5–31.

Shreve, A. (1984, Sept. 9). *The working mother as role model*. New York Times Magazine.

Simon, J. G., & Feather, N. T. (1973). Causal attributions for success and failure at university examinations. *Journal of Educational Psychology, 64*, 46–56.

Simpson, I. H., & England, P. (1981). Conjugal work roles and marital solidarity. *Journal of Family Issues, 2,* 180–204.

Smetna, J. G. (1989). Toddler's social interactions in the context of moral and conventional transgressions in the home. *Developmental Psychology, 25,* 499–508.

Smith, C., & Lloyd, B. B. (1978). Maternal behavior and perceived sex of infant. *Child Development, 49,* 1263–1265.

Sorensen, G., & Mortimer, J. T. (1988). Implications of the dual roles of adult women for their health. In J. T. Mortimer & K. M. Borman (Eds.), *Work experience and psychological development through the life span.* American Association for the Advancement of Science Selected Symposia Series (pp. 157–200). Boulder, CO: Westview Press.

Spade, J. Z., & Reese, C. A. (1991). We've come a long way, maybe: College students' plan for work and family. *Sex Roles, 24,* 309–321.

Spence, J. T. (1991). Do the BSRI and PAQ measure the same or different concepts? *Psychology of Women Quarterly, 15,* 141–165.

Spence, J. T., & Helmreich, R. (1979). The many faces of androgyny: A reply to Locksley and Colten. *Journal of Personality and Social Psychology, 37,* 1032–1046.

Spence, J. T., & Helmreich, R. (1981). Androgyny vs. gender schema: A comment on Bem's gender theory. *Psychology Review, 88,* 365–368.

Spence, J. T., Helmreich, R., & Stapp, J. (1975). Ratings of self and peers on sex role attributes and their relation to self-esteem and conceptions of masculinity and femininity. *Journal of Personality and Social Psychology, 32,* 29–39.

Spitze, G. (1988). Women's employment and family relations: A review. *Journal of Marriage and the Family, 50,* 595–618.

Stachowiak, J. (1975a). Family structure and intervention techniques. In V. Satir, J. Stachowiak, & H. A. Taschman, (Eds.), *Helping families to change.* New York: Aronson.

Stachowiak, J. (1975b). Family therapy in action. In V. Satir, J. Stachowiak, & H. A. Taschman, (Eds.), *Helping families to change.* New York: Aronson.

Stachowiak, J. (1975c). Functional and dysfunctional families. In V. Satir. J. Stachowiak, & H. A. Taschman, (Eds.), *Helping families to change.* New York: Aronson.

Stage, E. K., Kreinberg, N., Eccles, J., & Becker, J. R. (1984). Increasing the participation and achievement of girls and women in mathematics, science, and engineering. In S. S. Klein (Ed.), *Achieving sex equity through education.* Baltimore, MD: Johns Hopkins University Press.

Stake, J. E. (1979). Women's self-estimates of competence and the resolution of the career/home conflict. *Journal of Vocational Behavior, 14,* 33–42.

Stake, J. E., & Rogers, L. L. (1989). Job and home attitudes of undergraduate women and their mothers. *Sex Roles, 20,* 445–463.

Stanley, A. (1991, April 3). Romance novels discover a baby boom. *New York Times,* pp. A1, C18.

Stoltz-Loike, M. (1990, March). *The working family.* Paper presented at the annual conference of the American Association for Counseling and Development, Cincinnati, OH.

Stoltz-Loike, M. (1991, April). *An integrated approach to counseling dual career couples.* Paper presented at the annual conference of the American Association for Counseling and Development, Reno, NV.

Stoltz-Loike, M. (1992a, in press). The working family: Helping women balance the roles of wife, mother, and career woman. *The Career Development Quarterly.*

Stoltz-Loike, M. (1992b, in press). Working family issues. In L. Jones (Ed.), *Encyclopedia of career decisions and social issues.* Phoenix, AZ: Oryx Press.

Stolzenberg, R. M., & Waite, L. J. (1984). Local labor markets, children, and labor force participation of wives. *Demography, 21,* 157–170.

Strange, C. C., & Rea, J. S. (1983). Career choice considerations and sex role self-concept of male and female undergraduates in nontraditional majors. *Journal of Vocational Behavior, 23,* 219–226.

Super, D. E. (1951). Vocational adjustment: Implementing a self-concept. *Occupations, 30,* 88–92.

Super, D. E. (1953). A theory of vocational development. *American Psychologist, 8,* 185–190.

Super, D. E. (1964). A developmental approach to vocational guidance. *Vocational Guidance Quarterly, 13,* 1–10.

Super, D. E. (1980). A life-span, life space approach to career development. *Journal of Vocational Behavior, 16,* 282–298.

Super, D. E. (1983). Assessment in career guidance: Toward truly developmental counseling. *Personnel and Guidance Journal, 63,* 555–562.

Super, D. (1986). Future trends in adult career development. In Z. Leibowitz & D. Lea (Eds.), *Adult career development: Concepts, issues, and practices.* Alexandria, VA: National Career Development Association.

Super, D. E., & Nevill, D. D. (1984). Work role salience as a determinant of career maturity in high school students. *Journal of Vocational Behavior, 25,* 30–44.

Super, D. E., Thompson, A. S., & Lindeman, R. H. (1984). *The Adult Career Concerns Inventory.* Palo Alto, CA: Consulting Psychologists Press.

Super, D. E., Thompson, A. S., Lindeman, R. H., Jordaan, J. P., & Myers, R. A. (1981). *The Career Development Inventory.* Palo Alto, CA: Consulting Psychologist Press.

Swaney, K., & Predeger, D. (1985). The relationship between interest-occupation congruence and job satisfaction. *Journal of Vocational Behavior, 26,* 13–24.

Tannen, D. (1986). *That's not what I meant! How conversational style makes or breaks your relations with others.* New York: Morrow.

Tannen, D. (1990). *You just don't understand: Women and men in conversation.* New York: Ballantine Books.

Taschman, H. A. (1975). Developing in family therapy. In V. Satir, J. Stachowiak, & H. A. Taschman, (Eds.), *Helping families to change.* New York: Aronson.

Terborg, J. R. (1977). Women in management: A research review. *Journal of Applied Psychology, 6,* 647–664.

Thomas, A., Chess, S., & Birch, H. (1970). The origins of personality. *Scientific American, 223,* 102–109.

Thompson, L., & Walker, A. J. (1989). Gender in families: Women and men in marriage, work and parenthood. *Journal of Marriage and the Family, 51,* 845–871.

Thompson, R. A. (1988). The effects of infant day care through the prism of attachment theory. *Early Childhood Research Quarterly, 3*, 273–282.

Thorne, B. (1986). Girls and boys together, but mostly apart. In W. W. Hartup & Z. Rubin (Eds.), *Relationship and development*. Hillsdale, NJ: Lawrence Erlbaum Associates.

Tiedeman, D. V., & O'Hara, R. P. (1963). *Career development: Changes and adjustment*. New York: College Entrance Examination Board.

Tiedje, L. B., Wortman, C. B., Downey, G., Emmons, C., Biernat, M., & Lang, E. (1990). Women with multiple roles: Role-compatibility perceptions, satisfaction, and mental health. *Journal of Marriage and the Family, 52*, 63–72.

Travis, C. B., Phillippi, R. H., & Henley, T. B. (1991). Gender and causal attributions for mastery, personal, and interpersonal events. *Psychology of Women Quarterly, 15*, 233–249.

Treiman, D. J., & Hartman, H. I. (1981). *Women, work, and wages: Equal pay for jobs of equal value*. Washington, DC: National Academy Press.

Trimberger, R., & MacLean, M. (1982). Maternal employment: The child's perspective. *Journal of Marriage and the Family, 44*, 469–476.

Ulrich, D., & Dunne, H. (1986). *To love and work: A systemic interlocking of family, workplace and career*. New York, Brunner/Mazel.

Vannoy-Hiller, D., & Philliber, W. W. (1989). *Equal partners: Successful women in marriage*. Newbury Park, CA: Sage.

Velsor, E. V., & O'Rand, A. M. (1984). Family life cycle, work career patterns and women's wage at midlife. *Journal of Marriage and the Family, 46*, 365–373.

Vetter, B. M. (1980). Working women scientists and engineers. *Science, 207*, 28–34.

Vieira, K. G., & Miller, W. H. (1978). Avoidance of sex-atypical toys by five- and ten-year-old children. *Psychological Reports, 43*, 543–546.

Vodanovich, S. J., & Kramer, T. J. (1989). An examination of the work values of parents and their children. *Career Development Quarterly, 37*, 365–374.

Volling, B. L., & Belsky, J. (1991). Multiple determinants of father involvement during infancy in dual-earner and single-earner families. *Journal of Marriage and the Family, 53*, 461–474.

Vondracek, F. W., Lerner, R. M., & Schulenberg, J. E. (1986). *Career development: A life-span developmental approach*. Hillsdale, NJ: Lawrence Erlbaum Associates.

Voydanoff, P. (1987). *Work and family life*. Beverly Hills, CA: Sage.

Voydanoff, P. (1988). Work role characteristics, family structure demands and work/family conflict. *Journal of Marriage and the Family, 50*, 749–761.

Waite, L. J., & Stolzenberg, R. M. (1976). Intended childbearing and labor force participation of young women: Insights from nonrecursive models. *American Sociological Review, 41*, 235–252.

Wallston, B. (1973). The effects of maternal employment on children. *Journal of Child Psychology and Psychiatry, 14*, 81–95.

Wallston, B. S., & O'Leary, V. E. (1982). Sex makes a difference: Differential perceptions of women and men. *Review of Personality and Social Psychology, 2*, 9–31.

Walsh, D., & Egdahl, R. (1980). *Women, work, and health: Challenges to corporate policy.* New York: Springer-Verlag.

Walsh, F. (1989). Reconsidering gender in the marital quid pro quo. In M. McGoldrick, C. Anderson, & F. Walsh (Eds.), *Women in families: A framework for family therapy.* New York: Norton.

Walters, M., Carter, B., Papp, P., & Silverstein, O. (1988). *The invisible web: Gender patterns in family relationships.* New York: Guilford Press.

Watkins, C. E., & Savickas, M. L. (1990). Psychodynamic career counseling. In W. B. Walsh & S. H. Osipow (Eds.), *Career counseling: Contemporary topics in vocational psychology.* Hillsdale, NJ: Lawrence Erlbaum Associates.

Weiner, B. Frieze, I., Kukla, A., Reed, L., Rest, S., & Rosenbaum, R. M. (1971). *Perceiving the causes of success and failure.* Morristown, NJ: General Learning Press.

Westbrook, B. W. (1976). The relationship between vocational maturity and appropriateness of vocational choices of ninth-grade pupils. *Measurement and Evaluation in Guidance, 34,* 247–254.

White, D., & Wollett, A. (1981, December). *The family at birth.* Paper presented at British Psychological Society London Conference.

Whitley, B. E., Jr., & Frieze, I. H. (1985). *The effect of question wording style and research context on attributions for success and failure: A meta-analysis.* Paper presented at the annual meeting of the Eastern Psychological Association, Boston.

Whitley, B. E., McHugh, M. C., & Frieze, I. H. (1986). Assessing the theoretical models for sex differences in causal attributions of success and failure. In J. S. Hyde & M. C. Linn, *The Psychology of gender: Advances through meta-analysis.* Baltimore, MD: Johns Hopkins University Press.

Wilk, C. A. (1986). *Career women and childbearing: A psychological analysis of the decision process.* New York: Van Nostrand Reinhold.

Wilkie, J. R. (1987). Marriage, family life, and women's employment. In A. H. Stromberg & S. Harkess (Eds.), *Women working* (2nd ed.) Mountain, CA: Mayfield.

Williams, C. P., & Savickas, M. L. (1990). Developmental tasks of career maintenance. *Journal of Vocational Behavior, 36,* 166–175.

Williams, J. C. (1990). Sameness feminism and the work/family conflict. *New York Law School Law Review, 35,* 347–360.

Wolf, T. M. (1975). Response consequences of televised modeled sex-inappropriate play behavior. *Journal of Genetic Psychology, 127,* 35–44.

Worobey, J., & Blajda, V. (1989). Temperamental ratings at 2 weeks, 2 months, and 1 year: Differential stability of activity and emotionality. *Developmental Psychology, 25,* 257–263.

Wright, J. D. (1978). Are working women really more satisfied? Evidence from several national surveys. *Journal of Marriage and the Family, 40,* 301–313.

Wright, J. D., & Hamilton, R. F. (1978). Work satisfaction and age: Some evidence for the "job change" hypothesis. *Social Forces, 56,* 1140–1158.

Wyer, R. S., & Malinowski, C. (1972). Effects of sex and achievement level upon individualism and competitiveness in social interaction. *Journal of Experimental Social Psychology, 8,* 303–314.

Yogev, S. (1981). Do professional women have egalitarian marital relationships? *Journal of Marriage and the Family, 43*, 865–871.

Yogev, S. (1982). Happiness in dual-career couples: Changing research, changing values. *Sex Roles, 8*, 593–605.

Yogev, S., & Brett, J. (1985). Perceptions of the division of housework and child care and marital satisfaction. *Journal of Marriage and the Family, 47*, 609–618.

Zambara, R., Hurst, M., & Hite, R. (1979). The working mother in contemporary perspective. *Pediatrics, 64*, 862–870.

Zytowski, D. G. (1969). Toward a theory of career development for women. *Personnel and Guidance Journal, 47*, 660–664.

N
DE